Cordless Telecommunications in Europe

Wally H. W. Tuttlebee (Ed.)

Cordless Telecommunications in Europe

The Evolution of Personal Communications

With 82 Figures

Springer-Verlag
London Berlin Heidelberg New York
Paris Tokyo Hong Kong

Wally H. W. Tuttlebee, CEng
Roke Manor Research Ltd., Roke Manor, Romsey, Hampshire
SO51 0ZN, UK

ISBN 3-540-19633-1 Springer-Verlag Berlin Heidelberg New York
ISBN 0-387-19633-1 Springer-Verlag New York Berlin Heidelberg

British Library Cataloguing in Publication Data
Cordless telecommunications in Europe
1. Mobile telecommunication systems
I. Tuttlebee, W. H. W. *1953–*
621.38
ISBN 3–540–19633–1 West Germany

Library of Congress Cataloging-in-Publication Data
Cordless telecommunications in Europe/edited by W. H. W. Tuttlebee
p. cm. Includes index
ISBN 0–387–19633–1.   — ISBN 3–540–19633–1
1. Telephone supplies industry–Europe.   2. Cellular radio equipment
industry–Europe.   3.Radio paging equipment industry – Europe
4. Telecommunication equipment industry–Europe.   5. Market
surveys–Europe.
I. Tuttlebee, W. H. W. (Wally H. W.), 1953–
HD9697.T453E853   1990   90–41806
384.5'35–dc20   CIP

© Springer-Verlag London Limited 1990
Printed in Great Britain

The use of registered names, trademarks etc. in this publication does not
imply, even in the absence of a specific statement, that such names are exempt
from the relevant laws and regulations and therefore free for general use.

Typeset by Photo·graphics, Honiton, Devon
Printed by Page Bros (Norwich) Ltd, Mile Cross Lane, Norwich
2128/3916-543210   Printed on acid-free paper

Foreword

The mobile telecommunications industry is experiencing considerable growth at present and with the increased traffic capacities which these systems provide and falling equipment prices, it is expected to continue to grow throughout the 1990s.

Projections of equipment costs indicate that even portable cellular handsets could come within the reach of many customers well before the end of the century. This will transform mobile communications services from a minority, high cost application into a mainstream telecommunications service. For both market and technical reasons it is likely that the distinction between cellular, Telepoint and paging services will decrease, and the provision of common hardware in the form of a Universal Personal Communicator will become increasingly feasible.

The European Commission's June 1987 Green Paper on Telecommunications included the proposal to create a European Telecommunications Standards Institute (ETSI). This has resulted in a major reform of the European standards-setting process with the establishment of ETSI in March 1988 in Sophia-Antipolis, Nice, France. In the field of cordless telecommunications, ETSI has charged its Technical Sub-Committee RES 3 with producing the Digital European Cordless Telecommunications (DECT) standard by October 1991. In the meantime, the UK CT2 Common Air Interface (CAI) has been agreed by ETSI RES in March 1990 as the basis for an Interim European Telecommunications Standard (I-ETS) for Telepoint applications within Europe.

DECT is a system which will provide a variety of applications for cordless telephones, including residential and business use as well as a Telepoint service. The DECT standard will provide full compatibility and interoperability between systems utilised in the home, the public Telepoint service and a wireless PABX system.

The potential market for cordless telecommunications in Europe is enormous, offering considerable opportunities to equipment

manufacturers, network operators and users. Experience with
paging and cellular telephone developments clearly show that a
market for mobile services takes off once a service becomes
available to a large number of potential users covering a very
wide geographical area. Therefore, the potential can only be
realised and exploited by the timely and coordinated establishment
of a fully harmonised DECT standard in the Community, and
the Commission is proposing a Council Recommendation on the
coordinated introduction of DECT and a Council Directive on
the provision of the appropriate frequency band.

European manufacturers of digital cordless telephones are
currently enjoying a world-wide lead. Europe's industry must
make all endeavours to maintain this advantage.

Cordless Telecommunications in Europe addresses this increasingly complex field and considers future trends. Dr Tuttlebee has
been very successful in securing contributions from many of the
leading experts in this field in Europe. I believe the book has
the potential to become a standard reference on this very
important topic for the future of mobile communications in
Europe, and with the current interest in cordless telecommunications it is well timed.

Herbert Ungerer
DG XIII Telecommunications Directorate,
Commission of the European Communities

Acknowledgements

This book is in many ways a testimony to the spirit of international cooperation and collaboration which is emerging in the telecommunications industry within the European Community and which is present particularly in the field of cordless telecommunications. I wish to acknowledge with grateful thanks the support of all the contributors, who have borne patiently my editorial whims and the, at times demanding, schedule imposed upon them! It has been a privilege to have enjoyed their active support, friendship and contribution to this project over the months in which this book has evolved.

My thanks are offered also to those other colleagues in the industry active within the CT2 and DECT fora who have offered encouragement and support for this project in various ways. In particular, the permission of Chris van Diepenbeek, Chairman of the ETSI RES 3 subcommittee, to include provisional information describing the current status of the Digital European Cordless Telecommunications (DECT) specification is gratefully acknowledged.

I wish to acknowledge the management of Roke Manor Research for their willing agreement to allow me to undertake this project, reflecting as it does a decade of involvement of that organisation in the research and development of cordless telecommunications. The encouragement and support of Dr Andy Low and other colleagues at Roke Manor and the practical assistance of Tanya Burge, Linette Sharp and Phyllis Bishop are also particularly noted. My thanks also go to Nicholas Pinfield and Linda Schofield of Springer-Verlag.

Finally, but primarily, my thanks and much appreciation go to my wife Helen, and to our children David, Joy and Stephen, for their constant positive encouragement and their understanding in foregoing time with their husband and father so that this book could come to fruition.

Romsey   Wally H. W. Tuttlebee
May 1990

Contents

SECTION II. CORDLESS TECHNOLOGY

SECTION III. The Future

Contributors

Dr. Dag Åkerberg
ETSI BP 152, Project Team 10, Route des Lucioles Sophia-Antipolis, F-06561 Valbonne Cedex, France

Brian Bidwell
Unitel, Elstree Tower, Elstree Way, Boreham Wood, Herts WD6 1DT, UK

Andrew Bud
Olivetti Systems and Networks, Via Tervis 13, 10015 Ivrea, Italy

Ed R. Candy
BYPS, Westbrook Centre, Milton Road, Cambridge CB4 1YH, UK

Dominic Clancy
Motorola, 16 Euroway, Blagrove, Swindon SN5 8YU, UK

Prof. John Gardiner
Dept. of Electrical/Electronic Engineering, University of Bradford, Richmond Road, Bradford, West Yorkshire BD4 1DP, UK

A. Peter Hulbert
Radio Communications Division, Roke Manor Research Ltd, Roke Manor, Romsey, Hampshire SO51 0ZN, UK

Dr. Heinz Ochsner
Ascom Autophon AG, Ziegelmattstrasse 1, CH-4503 Solothurn, Switzerland

Frank Owen
Philips Research Laboratories, Cross Oak Lane, Redhill, Surrey RH1 5HA, UK

Norbert Soulié
Matra de Communicaçiones, Apartado de Correos 115, 08420
Canovelles, Barcelona, Spain

Richard A. J. Steedman
Radio Communications Division, Roke Manor Research Ltd,
Roke Manor, Romsey, Hampshire SO51 0ZN, UK

Peter Striebel
Deutsche Bundespost TELEKOM, Section 332, PO Box 2000,
D-5300 Bonn, Germany

Bob Swain
RT 413, British Telecom Research Laboratories, Martlesham
Heath, Ipswich IP5 7RE, UK

Julian R. Trinder
Radio Communications Division, Roke Manor Research Ltd,
Roke Manor, Romsey, Hampshire SO51 0ZN, UK

Dr. Wally H. W. Tuttlebee
Radio Communications Division, Roke Manor Research Ltd,
Romsey, Hampshire SO51 0ZN, UK

Introduction

Wally Tuttlebee

The past few years in Europe have seen the beginnings of a quiet revolution in the way in which we view and use the telephone. The concept of a telephone permanently wired to a socket on the wall is being displaced by the concept of a lightweight pocketphone, with a telephone number allocated to a person rather than to an address. The explosive growth of cellular radio, the launch of Telepoint services and the imminent introduction of Personal Communications Networks (PCNs) illustrate the telecommunications industry's initial responses to the latent consumer demand for mobile personal communications.

The importance of telecommunications to the European economy has been recognised by the European Commission, who in this area have initiated standardisation activities, to regulate short-term developments, and research programmes aimed, amongst other things, at developing the "Personal Communicator" by the turn of the century.

Cordless telecommunications, unlike cellular radio, has to date received scant attention in books. Part of the reason for this has been the speed with which the field has developed. Also, those best qualified to write on the subject have until now focussed all their energies on product development, in order to realise the market opportunity. This book aims to remedy this gap in the literature.

The book presents the commercial background to the current scene as well as describing the technological issues underpinning the operation of cordless telecommunications systems. This blend has been sought in the twin beliefs that an understanding of the relevant technological issues provides those engaged in commerce with a solid foundation for their roles and similarly that an awareness of the commercial context of their work is essential to engineers. This interrelationship between the technical and commercial issues may be of particular interest to the undergraduate reader, to whom these two fields can often appear as very disparate. This book will also offer insights to the potential user of the emerging cordless services – domestic cordless telephone, wireless PABX and Telepoint – and will provide pointers for the future development of personal communications.

The early chapters outline the ways in which the cordless telephone market has developed, providing a historical and commercial background and describing the early proprietary digital cordless products and the European standards environment. Subsequent chapters examine the detailed techniques and technology which permit cordless communications. A final chapter addresses the challenging topic of "where hence?", outlining some ground rules and possibilities for the future evolution of personal communications.

Chapter 1 describes the emerging requirement for cordless personal communication, building upon the history of early analogue (domestic) cordless telephones and aspects of the cellular radio market in Europe. It describes the applications and markets for the new digital cordless systems, assessing their potential in Europe and beyond.

During the 1980s the UK and Sweden pioneered much of the development of digital cordless telephone products. The first offerings were brought to market in the UK in 1989 and in Sweden are expected in 1990. Chapter 2 describes these early proprietary products and the differing philosophies and approaches underlying their development.

An unspoken theme of this book, implicit in its title, is "1992" and the implications for the telecommunications industry of the Single European Act. It is this movement towards a unified European marketplace that is now focussing the future development of cordless telecommunications in the countries of the EEC, and indeed within EFTA, towards the Digital European Cordless Telecommunications standard (DECT). The role, problems and value of common technical standards are discussed in Chapter 3. This chapter also reviews the relevant standardisation structures within Europe and how these have been influenced by recent developments relating to the single market.

The year 1989 saw the launch of Telepoint networks in the UK and the decision of other European countries to implement trial Telepoint systems. Chapter 4 presents views on these issues from the UK, France and Germany as well as briefly reviewing developments in other countries. The operators' Memorandum of Understanding on a harmonised European Telepoint service (based upon CT2 CAI) is also described.

Chapter 5 presents an understanding of the underlying network issues associated with cordless systems, addressing particularly the management of user mobility and authentication.

Chapters 6 and 7 address the technical issues relating to the audio and the radio paths associated with a cordless telephone system. Issues of digitised speech coding, transmission plans, delay, echo control, privacy and security are explained in Chapter 6. Radio propagation, choice of spectrum, and micro- and picocellular techniques are then explored in Chapter 7, together with the techniques of multiple access, modulation, error control and communication protocols.

Chapter 8 considers the actuality and future potential of cordless data services. The potential importance of cordless data is reflected in the change of title during 1989 of the emerging DECT standard from Digital European Cordless Telephone to Digital European Cordless Telecommunications. This chapter initially describes the nature of cordless data services and their applications, and then explains how such services may be efficiently supported over the cordless medium.

The advanced capabilities and facilities offered by modern digital cordless telephones have been made possible by rapid progress in a range of technologies over recent years, not least in the area of digital silicon chips. Chapter 9 reviews the basic architectural requirements of a cordless telephone handset and then surveys the implementation approaches of the early analogue telephones and the current digital cordless products. The technology requirements for DECT and future technology trends are also considered.

It is always risky to attempt to predict the direction of future developments. Some observers would say this is doubly so in the field of personal communications given the speed of recent events in Europe. However, not to offer an informed view on this important topic would be unfair to the reader, and such is the purpose of Chapter 10. As well as reviewing current European research initiatives, an attempt is made to relate these to developments on the wider world stage.

Appendixes are provided which summarise the technical details of the CT2 Common Air Interface specification (CAI) and of the emerging Digital European Cordless Telecommunications standard, DECT. A more detailed description of the operation of the proprietary DCT900 system is given in a third appendix. A glossary of technical terms is also provided.

Many diverse concepts are involved in digital cordless communication technology and it would be impossible in a book of this size to do justice fully to each of these areas. Certain topics may already be familiar, perhaps in a different context, to some readers. An attempt has been made throughout the book to achieve a reasonably consistent level of treatment, although in some areas specific issues have been explored in a little more depth. For those new to the field, and also for those wishing to dig deeper on a particular topic, a selection of references has been included in each chapter, some providing general background and others addressing specific detail.

The contributors to the book are individuals who have shaped the development of cordless telecommunications in Europe in recent years. There is always a healthy tension in preparing an edited work of this type between the desire to produce a cohesive and fully consistent work and the wish to maintain the full diversity of expression and opinion representative of the individual contributors and their unique perspectives. As Editor I have sought to preserve a balance in this respect, but this inevitably means that the views expressed in any particular chapter do not necessarily reflect those of the Editor nor indeed those of some contributors. The contributors, the Editor and the publishers cannot accept liability for any errors or omissions which, in any work of this nature, may occur. It would be appreciated, however, if any errors could be brought to the attention of the Editor, for correction in future editions.

A final word. All too often these days we rush through books reading purely for information. This book will meet such a requirement – it contains much information. It is hoped, however, that it will also be palatable and enjoyable, providing the reader with a brief insight into the enthusiasm and excitement of the rapidly developing field of personal communications.

HISTORICAL AND MARKETPLACE CONTEXT

1 The Emerging Requirement

Dominic Clancy

This chapter looks at the commercial aspects of cordless telephony in Europe, and the opportunity for operators, manufacturers and distributors in servicing a large user base for the new products and services that will appear as a result of developments in this area.

The aim of the chapter is to set digital cordless telephony within the context of the generic mobile communications marketplace and to outline the most important characteristics of this particular market sector. As part of this process, this chapter will set out the differences between cordless telephone and other mobile technologies and will show how this affects the positioning of current digital cordless telephones against the new mobile systems that will emerge during the final decade of the twentieth century and the first years of the twenty-first. The comments made here apply to all cordless technologies as a generic group.

This chapter will also bring out the need for a firm commercial target when standards are developed, in order that the products of the future have the correct features and characteristics to find a ready market in an overcrowded sector. The European Telecommunications Standards Institute (ETSI) has now started to incorporate such a commercial element in its standards setting process, at least in the area of mobile communications [1]. An attempt is made to clarify the rationale for this in a wider context and to look at the future of cordless telephony in the overall European market. The aspect of standards setting is developed more fully in Chapter 3, which looks at the process of standards evolution within Europe.

1.1 The Cordless Telephone and Cellular Radio

1.1.1 The Emergence and Development of New Markets

The mobile telephone market in Europe has exploded over the last decade, from a position where there were only a few thousand users of mobile telephones to a position at the end of the 1980s where there were 2 million. This growth varies across the major markets, and Fig. 1.1 [2] shows the rate of growth of some of these markets in Europe. Later in this chapter

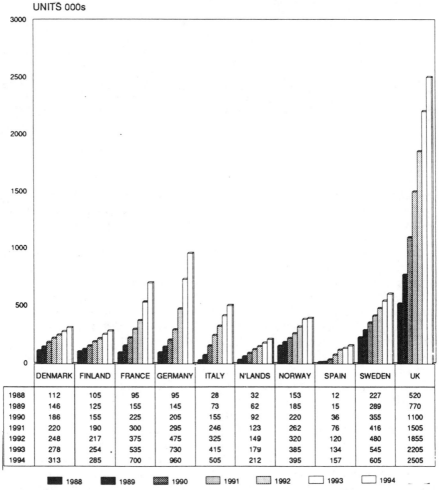

	DENMARK	FINLAND	FRANCE	GERMANY	ITALY	N'LANDS	NORWAY	SPAIN	SWEDEN	UK
1988	112	105	95	95	28	32	153	12	227	520
1989	146	125	155	145	73	62	185	15	289	770
1990	186	155	225	205	155	92	220	36	355	1100
1991	220	190	300	295	246	123	262	76	416	1505
1992	248	217	375	475	325	149	320	120	480	1855
1993	278	254	535	730	415	179	385	134	545	2205
1994	313	285	700	960	505	212	395	157	605	2505

■ 1988   ■ 1989   ▓ 1990   ▦ 1991   ▨ 1992   ☐ 1993   ☐ 1994

Fig. 1.1. Rate of growth of major cellular markets in Europe, 1988–1994 (includes GSM). (Source: E. Hardiman, BIS Mackintosh Mobile Communications Information Service, Europe, Financial Times Conference World Mobile Communications in the 90s, October 1989.)

we look at the important lessons from this market and ask to what extent these are transferable from the cellular market to that for cordless telephones.

Firstly it is important to appreciate what drove the rapid expansion of the cellular market and why cellular radio changed from being a status symbol for top management into an essential tool used by hundreds of thousands of businessmen all over Europe. Equally it is important to understand why cellular radio has still not become a consumer/domestic item and why it is unlikely that this will occur for some years.

Cellular Radio

Cellular radio was at first solely a telephone in the car, but was radically different from previous mobile telephone systems in that the telephone retained a unique number in the whole of the coverage area. Thus, it was no longer necessary to know the approximate location of the user in order to make a call to him using an appropriate area code. Cellular radio was also more attractive to the operators as the new system could support a much greater number of users than the earlier automatic mobile telephone systems. This meant that the network and administrative costs could be spread over a much larger user base with consequent economies of scale.

The ability to support a much greater number of users on the system also had consequences for the cost of terminal equipment, i.e. cellular telephones. Whereas the previous generation of mobile telephones had capacities of only a few thousand subscribers, cellular service could be made available to many times that number. This meant that development costs could be amortised over a much larger production cycle and that prices could accordingly be lower. The larger market potential also encouraged many more manufacturers to enter the market and the increased competition forced price reductions.

Cellular radio was initially positioned to attract executives for whom the price of the equipment and the cost of service could be justified in terms of the increased productivity and commercial gain that could be achieved by improved use of time away from the office when travelling to meetings etc. As prices were high at this early stage it was necessary to target cellular radio at an area which itself was a premium market in order to demonstrate significant gains. The target market changed as terminal prices fell and the cost benefits could be demonstrated to a wider market. At this point a horizontal market change also started to appear – as executives in one company in an industry sector adopted cellular radio as a business tool their counterparts in their competitor firms were forced to follow in order to retain their competitive edge, particularly in terms of customer service. It is interesting to note that at this stage target markets were confidently predicted by many industry experts. Doctors were seen as a prime market, yet even now only a small number make use of cellular radio. External factors played a large part in this.

The cellular operators all over Europe were happy to see a predominantly business market which was not sensitive to call tariffs as the benefits of cellular radio to the users became apparent. The operators were making large profits and were able to sell as much airtime as they could provide at peak times. Almost universally they adopted premium pricing approaches which made cellular radio too expensive for the consumer user. The average peak tariffs are shown in Fig. 1.2 [2]. It can be seen that they vary considerably from country to country and also from the standard tariff for the ordinary public switched telephone network (PSTN). In those countries where the difference between cellular and PSTN tariffs is least are found the greatest levels of consumer use of cellular radio. In these cases the level of tariff is politically influenced, whilst in others it is more commercially focussed.

Cordless Telephony

Cordless telephony has a rather different history in Europe as a whole and the market has been suppressed in many countries by the high cost of equipment which brought only limited benefit to the users. This meant that few could justify the outlay on the equipment, whether for business or domestic use, and that only certain market niches were found for the approved products in the early market. Over the last few years the price of equipment has started to fall and the demand has grown accordingly. The applications of the cordless telephone have until recently been limited to home use or to an area of cordlessness behind a single telephone line in an office. Concentrated use was not feasible because of either the limited number of channels or equipment cost. In addition the size of the early handsets was too large for easy pocketability, and battery life was too limited, for satisfactory regular use in an office. Furthermore, signalling characteristics in the specification in Europe caused regular breaks in the conversation, a feature which proved an irritating distraction for the users. In short, the satisfied market was relatively small and was severely limited by the technology.

The expanding use of cellular radio awakened users to the inadequacies of the existing cordless equipment as a business tool at the same time as increased awareness of mobility in communication was stimulating demand for mobility within the office and in the home. The development of digital cellular radio and the technological advances that had been achieved offered new opportunities for cordless telephones to move away from the basic residential or domestic cordless telephone to one that could be used in a number of different environments. These environments offered an exciting opportunity for manufacturers to develop new markets for telephone terminals with higher added value. A spin-off from the development of digital cellular radio telephones was the technology for digital cordless telephones that could offer enhanced (digital) voice quality in the home and behind existing PABXs (cordless or wireless PABXs), as well as the technology for the service that was to become known as Telepoint.

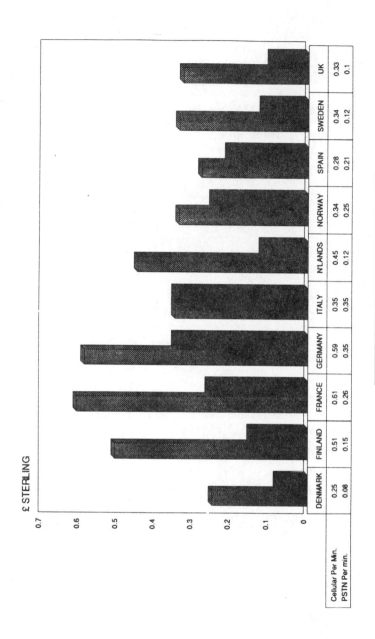

Fig. 1.2. Cellular radio and PSTN tariffs in Europe, 1989. (Source: E. Hardiman, BIS Mackintosh Mobile Communications Information Service, Europe, Financial Times Conference World Mobile Communications in the 90s, October 1989.)

1.1.2 Lessons from the Cellular Market

Two clear messages have emerged from the operation of cellular networks around Europe during the 1980s. These have implications for the positioning of cordless services of the 1990s and for the future marketing directions to be taken by the service operators and equipment vendors.

The first lesson is that demand for service climbs dramatically as the price of equipment falls, regardless of the fact that tariffs may remain unchanged or may increase. This implies that many users are ignorant of the cost of using cellular radio when they start to use the service. This means that airtime sellers have to be cautious about potential bad debt, as some users may be unable to meet their bills. It also implies that the economic need for mobile telephony is very strong, and that the cost of the service can be outweighed by the benefits it can bring to productivity and customer service. This prompted the high tariffs referred to above.

The second lesson is that, for a mobile service, users look for maximum coverage in order that they may use their mobile telephone in any area they choose. This was clearly demonstrated in Scandinavia, where the administrations had to introduce second cellular networks to meet the demand from the market. These networks initially covered only the main cities and towns and the routes connecting these, but the first system continued to grow more rapidly than the second, as users opted for a system that provided a service wherever they went. Even though the new services provided coverage that was adequate for 95% of customer needs, this was not perceived to be sufficient for a mobile service, and the operators had to expand the coverage of the network. North American readers should note that in Europe, cellular networks offer an average 80% geographic coverage within national boundaries, covering in excess of 90% of the population.

Which elements of these lessons are transferable to the domain of cordless telephony? The relationship of demand to the cost of service is less relevant than in the cellular market, except that the Telepoint operator may be able to win the marginal cellular users who can satisfy their mobile needs with a different type of mobile service, in particular the cordless payphone. The level of tariff is critical in setting the cross-elasticity between the two markets. It is important to remember that tariffing is a commercial process, and is not dictated by the technology of the system, although obviously relative techology costs have an influence on the tariffing calculation.

What is important is that the price of the equipment determines the entry price for a mobile customer, and that for a mass market, this price needs to be adjusted to the desired target market, rather than simply being as low as possible in order to win users at any price.

The second lesson is that the Telepoint operators have to position their service in such a way that the coverage meets the expectations of the target users. In this respect, for office use, the system must meet the functional requirements of coverage and handoff that an office environment imposes. It is important to note at this point that handoff can be provided with any cordless technology, as this is a feature not of the radio but of the network to which it is attached. In a public mobile network, the coverage has to match the perceived needs of the users. The requirement for ubiquitous coverage for a mobile user means that Telepoint is less likely to be a full mobile system in Europe, whether it uses DECT or CT2 technologies; the service will instead be positioned as a cordless payphone, with the consequent target market being radically different from the cellular market.

This leads on to the relative positioning of a number of services that will be appearing in the mobile and cordless arena over the next three to five years, and the relationship of these services to the future systems that are discussed in the final chapter of this book.

1.2 Market Positioning of New Services

The new mobile voice services that will appear by the mid-1990s in Europe are, in chronological order, likely to be:

CT2 CAI Digital cordless telephone
GSM   Pan-European cellular radio
DECT   Digital European Cordless Telecommunications
PCN   Personal Communications Network

These have to be positioned alongside existing services, particularly the analogue cellular networks that are operating now, or are scheduled to be introduced as interim networks in countries where demand is outstripping the capacity of the existing networks. They also have to take into account the paging networks, and the enormous user base for private mobile radio/land mobile radio. Future systems that will be introduced include digital short range radio and land mobile satellite services, but these are not considered in any detail here.

Fig. 1.3 shows the relative position of each service from a user perspective. It should be noted that services are in many cases able to compete functionally in areas that are not covered by their block, but the diagram is intended to show market positioning, not technology functionality.

Paging is the service that potentially has the lowest cost for the user. Because of its restrictions of receiving messages only, and in many countries requiring an operator to do this, the services have niche applications and are not used as a mass communication tool, although the population of pagers is very large in some countries. The introduction of the pan-European ERMES paging system will radically change the paging market.

The analogue cellular systems that have appeared in Europe are more expensive to use than a paging service but the target market is very similar to the target market for paging of five years ago. The market addressed is predominantly the business sector; personal use is restricted to the very wealthy, and even here business is often a prime motivation for use.

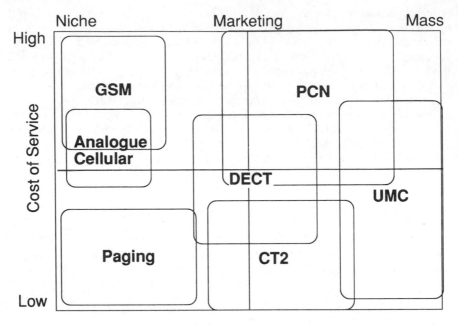

Fig. 1.3. Positioning of mobile technologies. (Source: K. Edmonds and D. Clancy, GEC Plessey Telecommunications, presentation to Mobile Communications Strategic Review Committee, Mobile Expert Group of ETSI, October 1989.)

In spite of the many claims that digital cellular radio service is a low cost, mass market service, this is not inherently so. Any reduction in the cost of terminals and/or service will result from continuing bundling of equipment and service as a consequence of competitive network operation, rather than from technical advances alone. Two operators are not a guarantee for reduced costs to the end user, as experience in the UK shows; there both operators have failed to take any strong initiative and, although the growth in this market has been strong and apparent terminal costs are very low, the overall annual user cost has changed little from 1987 to 1990. The market has grown spectacularly, beyond the ability of the network operators to satisfy demand at all times, but unstimulated demand cannot continue, and initiatives more like those used in North America will soon be needed further to stimulate growth in the 1990s when market demand will otherwise stagnate. These initiatives include usage-sensitive tariff plans, where users can choose whether to pay low call charges and high monthly subscription costs, or high call charges and low subscription costs. The first of these might appeal to the heavy cellular user such as a saleswoman on the road, the second to the occasional user such as a househusband!

The cordless systems have more to offer a mass market than their cellular partners. These are not networks, but rather access technologies. Their use does not require an expensive dedicated or parallel network, so their cost is lower for operator and end user alike. Their suitability for home, office and cordless payphone use extends the market for terminal equipment (handsets, base stations and handset parks) and service to a wide cross-section of the population in many countries.

CT2 is the first of the digital cordless technologies to reach the market and this will be used in the UK, Finland, France, Germany, Spain, Belgium, The Netherlands, Portugal, Italy, Canada, USA, Thailand, Singapore, Australia, New Zealand and other countries. CT2 is the subject of an operators' Memorandum of Understanding in Europe and will also now become an Interim European Telecommunications Standard (I-ETS).

CT2 is positioned as a low-cost product that bridges the market from paging users to a full mass market. DECT is similarly positioned but, by virtue of its additional features and ISDN functions, will be priced at a higher level. There is a further proprietary digital cordless technology used in Sweden, the A130 specification, which is promoted as being similar to DECT but which operates at 900 MHz. (This system is described in Chapter 2.)

PCN is still at the conceptual stage. It is clear even now, however, that the ideal of PCNs has been abandoned as the industry discusses low-power GSM terminals operating at 1.7 GHz. The original concept of a £50 portable telephone has been forgotten, and the service that was initially presented as the mobile telephone for everyone will not be PCN, but a later generation of network beyond PCN. This new service may start in the early twenty-first century, and for the sake of the present discussion is termed the Universal Mobile Communicator or UMC.

UMC is shown in Fig. 1.3 as the all-embracing mass market mobile telecommunications product. To achieve this goal the concept has to be driven by the market, and manufacturers and administrations must continually remember the goal of a truly low-cost network and terminals as they jointly determine the characteristics and specifications of this future network and its terminals.

Another simpler interpretation of the relative future positions of the different mobile systems appears in Fig. 1.4 [3]. This figure is valuable as it shows Telepoint, PCN and the different cellular systems on a cost–utility comparison, and includes the basic fixed network. The diagram shows a wide gap between Telepoint and PCN and analogue cellular radio on both axes and does not take into account the importance of positioning and targeting of products and services. In this respect it is oversimplified, but it is valuable as a rough indicator of the relationships between the different services. It is important to remember that the mobile market is no more homogeneous than, for example, the automobile market and that market requirements in each sector therefore have to be addressed with appropriate offerings.

With the relative market positionings of the future laid out, what are the consequences of this as the cordless telephone market adapts from its current structure and positionings? To understand this it is necessary to look at the market as it stands now.

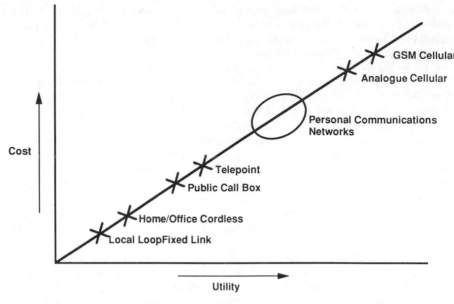

Fig. 1.4. Positioning of mobile and fixed services. (Source: R. Hooper, PA Consulting Group, Financial Times Conference World Mobile Communications in the 90s, October 1989.)

1.3 The Cordless Telephone Market

1.3.1 Structure and Requirements

Historically the cordless telephone market in Europe has been split into two areas, the first comprising France and the UK, the second comprising the rest of Europe.

In France and the UK, analogue cordless telephones operate in the HF/VHF region, and offer a low-cost product for domestic use only, as the voice quality is too poor to be acceptable for widespread use in offices and other business areas. A further limitation on widespread business use is the small number of channels available on these products, which leads to rapid congestion and interference if the concentration of cordless telephones rises above more than 8 in an area of 100 square metres. In the rest of Europe cordless telephones conform to a more elaborate specification set by the CEPT in 1983. They operate at 900 MHz and offer a voice quality that is greatly superior to analogue cordless telephones used in France and the UK.

If we look at the beginnings of cordless telephones in Europe, these were often poor-quality products, operating around 47 MHz, with a typical range of 150 metres in ideal conditions. Some products operated at different frequencies and had excessive operating ranges, of up to 24 kilometres in extreme cases! These were the first alternatives to the standard wired telephone offered by the telephone companies and, until the introduction of standards for cordless telephones, were the most advanced form of telephone available.

Although administrations at first sought to have these (imported) products banned, it was clear that the momentum of demand meant that the easier option was not suppression of the market but a controlled product that would not cause problems for either the telephone network or legitimate users of the radio spectrum.

Following moves to allocate frequency, the first approved cordless telephones soon appeared in the UK and France, imported from the USA, with modifications to national frequencies and with the addition of security features to prevent unauthorised access to the telephone base station. Cordless telephones became a domestic toy for the wealthy and those fond of gadgets and, since then, the market has developed strongly so that the cordless telephone is now found in many homes in these countries. In most of mainland Europe the specification is extremely complex, however, which makes the telephones expensive to design and manufacture. The result is that they have cost five or six times as much to the end user as the products sold in France and the UK. This means that, although their appeal is very strong, they are beyond the justifiable reach of most consumers. Unless they are rented from the telephone company, in mainland Europe most cordless telephones are used by businesses.

Any examination of the market for cordless telephones in Europe clearly indicates a number of criteria that are important if a new product is to succeed in its various market segments. If a simple, single-line cordless telephone is considered (such as the ones that we see in the shops at the start of the 1990s), it has to offer certain attributes for the domestic market and other attributes for the business market. These attributes are not exclusive and, from a manufacturer's perspective, the combination of these in one handset that can be used to target all market sectors and configurations has overwhelming attractions.

The following attributes are required for the domestic market:

Low cost product
Good voice quality
Security against unauthorised access

The following attributes are required for a business sector cordless telephone:

Good voice quality
Security against unauthorised access
Ability to provide high-concentration usage
Ability to operate in conjunction with existing PABX and key systems
Ability to work without interference in an office environment
Compatibility of equipment from different equipment vendors
Availability of handover between base stations
Availability of cordless Centrex

1.3.2 CT2 and DECT – Competitors?

These requirements for business cordless telephones are not met by any of the analogue cordless telephone specifications that have been in use in Europe, and CEPT decided to develop a new standard for digital cordless telephones that would address the problems of incompatibility, cost and voice quality: CEPT CT2. Early attempts at the development of this common standard were very slow and a second standard was developed in parallel in the UK in order to provide a digital standard for cordless telephones that would meet the demand for service that was perceived to exist already in the 1980s. This UK standard became known as CT2.

In Sweden during the 1980s another digital system was also developed, known as A130 after the specification reference of the Swedish PTT. The only implementation of this standard is one from Ericsson which is known variously as DCT900 or CT3. (The proprietary CT2 and DCT900 products are described in Chapter 2.) Neither the Swedish nor the early UK standards were accepted by ETSI as acceptable for the CEPT CT2 requirement, for a variety of political and technical reasons.

After two or three years of deliberations a new standard was formally initiated in 1988, built upon the earlier work. This was originally called CT3, but is now known as DECT – initially Digital European Cordless Telephone, the title being subsequently amended from Telephone to Telecommunications. The commitment to DECT as the future official common standard has been formally endorsed by all members of CEPT, even though it is not yet fully formulated.

Further developments in the UK during 1988 and 1989 led to the refinement of UK CT2 to produce the Common Air Interface (CAI) standard which is now to be adopted by ETSI as an Interim European Telecommunications Standard prior to the availability of DECT.

There has been a significant amount of debate about the relative merits of DECT and CT2. Many parties adopted extreme positions to prevent CT2 gaining a foothold in Europe, whilst others have sought to confuse the DECT standard in order to prolong the life of CT2. From a market perspective, however, all these activities fail to acknowledge that the market itself will decide in the long term which will succeed. The battle is likely to be akin to that between VHS and Betamax in the video recorder market. Both offer functionally similar features and services using different technological approaches. Although DECT will support ISDN – and this has been used as a lever against CT2 by the DECT lobby – users buy telephones to talk to people on other telephones and, from a marketing perspective, it is the features, functions and applications of the telephones that are important, rather than the technology used to achieve them. In the future it is possible that CT2 will be further developed to support ISDN.

ISDN will be important in some applications but completely irrelevant in others, and the users will choose according to their needs where the choice is available to them. Whether ISDN is required by users in a cordless environment is a question that has not been satisfactorily addressed in any study to date. ISDN is important as the first attempt to move away from the concept of service dedicated networks [4] and it should not be overlooked in the long-term development of cordless telephones. Any perceived increase in importance of ISDN will come about as the result of intensive marketing efforts, directed at raising consciousness of the potential of new services [2]. These marketing efforts have been attempted only in limited areas, and their success is limited, although their necessity is unquestionable if ISDN is to become a perceived essential in a cordless communicator (and, in this, both voice and data and combined products should be included).

What are the features of a digital cordless telephone of the near future? The attributes listed above are the core of these and are independent of the technology chosen. For office use the cordless telephone requires some extra features not necessary for other applications – essentially a recall function and the ability to move from one base station to another. These features can be designed into DECT systems and CT2 systems, although suggestions are often made to the contrary.

1.4 Market Segmentation and Interdependency

1.4.1 The Telepoint Market

There has been much confusion over what Telepoint is, and there are differing perceptions as to what it can provide either as a one-way or two-way calling service. Thus, a definition of a Telepoint service is required before the service can be sensibly positioned in a market with as many constituents as the mobile telephony market. This is necessary also to show why a Telepoint service still has a place even where there are other services such as PCN.

A Telepoint service is a cordless payphone, accessed with a portable terminal which has a long battery life and which is small enough to be carried at all times by the owner, either in a handbag or in a jacket pocket. A Telepoint system comprises a large number of points at which the PSTN can be accessed through a Telepoint base station, together with the necessary support, administration and billing systems.

A Telepoint system is not a network in the technical sense, only a collection of public access points for a cordless telephone. The system can have no greater functionality than the telephone network to which it is connected. This means that unless the telephone network has some form of mobility management or some ability to locate handsets in the public mode, it is not possible to make a call to the handset when used in a Telepoint mode. This is a limitation of the existing telephone network rather than of the CT2 or DECT technology used. This limitation obviously does not apply when the handset is used in a business or residential environment; there it will be used in conjunction with an identified base station which carries a telephone number by virtue of its fixed location, so two-way calling is possible. It is important to note that the DECT Telepoint will have a network compatible with the CT2 Telepoint networks.

A Telepoint service may therefore be different from a cellular service, with its full mobility management and ability to make and receive calls, but can be configured as a full mobile system with the addition of a mobility management or location register system. (Such an approach is to be adopted for the French Telepoint system, Pointel and for the German system, Birdie.)

The type of customer for a cordless payphone system, or Telepoint system, is not the same as for a cellular system, and Telepoint will attract only a limited number of customers from a cellular network. In most cases these migrating customers are not really in the cellular market. Rather, they use cellular radio merely because there was no service specifically designed to meet their mobile communication need precisely, and cellular was the most suitable one available to them. From a cellular network operator's perspective, these users are a liability in terms of potential bad debt, as they are more likely to default on payment (being able to do without the cellular service) than are those for whom cellular radio is an essential business tool.

The market for Telepoint as a stand-alone service has been the focus of much study and comment for the last three years. In all the in-depth market research that has been performed, it is clear that Telepoint will not succeed in attracting large numbers of users unless there is a substantial population of handsets in business and residential use.

1.4.2 The Wireless PABX Market

A number of manufacturers are developing cordless products aimed specifically at the business market, expecting that the market for business telephones will show a strong preference for cordless facilities within the next two to three years. This demand will be met by a range of products, such as cordless key systems and PABX equipment of various configurations with cordless facilities. The economics of a fully cordless or wireless PABX (WPABX) are uncertain and a satisfactory business case has yet to be developed for these products. There is much talk of the economies of not having to wire a building for telephones, but if cabling has to be provided for some telephones and for local area networks, then the business case becomes rather more difficult to sustain. Fig. 1.5 shows one analysis of the relationship between cellular and cordless PABX. It identifies professional and white collar workers as the prime groups for cordless PABX use, and shows how the two technologies overlap as mobility requirements change at the higher management levels, with users moving from office to public environments.

As a whole the cordless telephone market is very different from any of

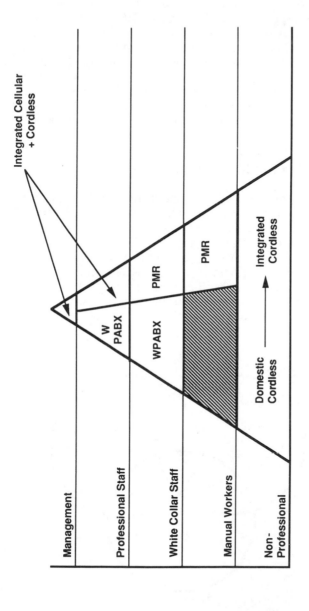

Fig. 1.5. Services: who will be the users? (Source: Norbert Soulié, Matra Communication.)

the mobile markets that we have seen to date. With the introduction of digital cordless telephones it is tempting to believe that all will continue as before, or that the market will emulate other mobile markets. The new market will be totally unlike the British or French CT1 markets, and may resemble certain aspects of the European CEPT cordless market, but will also embrace aspects of the PABX and key system markets, as well as the consumer market. Indeed, if a CT2 handset and base station package costs the same as a CEPT cordless telephone in Europe, the markets will be rather similar [4].

To expect a single distribution system to supply equipment to each discrete part of the cordless telephone market is unrealistic. What are the major elements of the market, and how do these relate to each other?

1.4.3 Market Sector Interdependency

Fig. 1.6 is a summary of market research that has been carried out by a number of companies in markets all over the world. It indicates the segmentation that is expected in a market five years after the introduction of CT2. In the earlier stages of the market, Telepoint as a stand-alone service will show as a much stronger sector and, although the number of handsets will grow, more and more handsets will be used in multiple applications. These figures are indicative and vary by a few percentage points from one market to another, but in every developed market the same message is clear: the main market for digital cordless telephones is in the

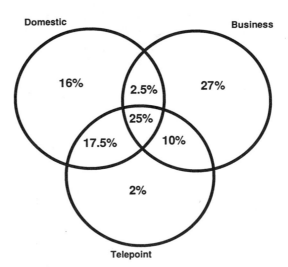

Fig. 1.6. Indicative segmentation of forecast CT2 user base five years after introduction to market. (Source: GEC Plessey Telecommunications.)

business and domestic sectors. The stand-alone Telepoint application is not
the bulk of the market. Any party entering the market must address the
domestic and business sectors to be a major player in the market overall.
At the same time, the Telepoint operators have to rely on the development
of a substantial population of handsets as potential subscribers for their
services.

The implications of Fig. 1.6 are important for engineers and marketeers
alike, in that they clearly indicate the priorities for commercial development
of cordless products for the future. Each sector has particular requirements
that have to be addressed in terms of features and functionality, and these
will vary from one country to another, as is the case with any product in
the telecommunications marketplace.

It is also clear that the Telepoint operators must be involved to some
extent with the distribution of cordless telephones to the business and
domestic sectors if they are to influence the growth of the handset population
which is key to their own long-term successes. If the operators are only
involved in Telepoint handset distribution their overall conversion rate of
handsets to active Telepoint users will be reduced. Fig. 1.7 shows the
potential distribution routes for all types of digital cordless telephones. For
the newly licensed operators in the UK this represents some departure from
their current activities, and no doubt some bonus structure will be developed

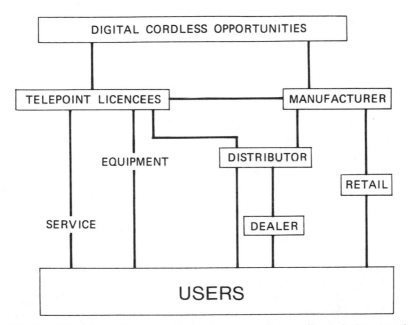

Fig. 1.7. Potential opportunities and distribution routes for cordless telephone products.
(Source: GEC Plessey Telecommunications.)

to encourage equipment retailers to sell subscriptions to the competing Telepoint systems.

1.5 Market Evolution

In the future it will also be important to continue the education of the user population, so that the more sophisticated products and services that will appear in the 1990s will be met with the level of understanding and demand required to ensure their success. This education will be an on-going process, and will encourage the migration of users to more richly featured and sophisticated products and services in the future. This migration will not occur on its own and will be stimulated by changes in the actual and perceived benefits of the new services.

In this market development, application will be the key, and more products will be developed that are application specific but which conform to a core technology (CT2, DECT, GSM, PCN and even UMC) to provide compatibility and minimise the development costs. It will be increasingly important to develop specifications that are commercially oriented and to keep the engineering development focussed to the end product required in the market, rather than that desired by the administrations. Commercial viability will be the watchword of the new generation of products in a market that is European and highly competitive.

In the future Europe will move to an increased use of radio-based communication equipment, including the Universal Mobile Communicator. The opportunity available for cordless products is immense, regardless of the technical battles and political manoeuvring that takes place. It is vital to ensure that standards enable the development of the market, rather than delay the introduction of new terminals and systems. In the end the customers select the product that meets their needs. Whoever makes the products that meet those needs best will be the ultimate victor.

1.6 Summary

The digital cordless telephone market is radically different from that for cellular radio and from the market for first generation cordless telephones. These differences may be exploited by manufacturers in a number of different ways to develop new markets for cordless terminals, and by operators to offer enhanced services to users. In both cases, manufacturers and operators will expect increased revenues from these services due to their higher added value.

It is important to consider the application requirements of the users when developing new cordless terminals, to ensure that the resulting product is appropriate for its intended market segment. Users will choose according to their needs. Any change in the perceived technology requirements will arise from intensive marketing efforts directed at raising the consciousness of users to the potential of new services. In this area, engineers and marketeers will have to work closely together to drive the evolution of the telecommunications market. Only then will we achieve the vision of the Universal Mobile Communicator within the framework of the future public land mobile telephone system that we have studied and debated in many of our companies. Whatever the technology, people buy telephones to talk to users on other telephones. All engineering and marketing efforts have to be directed to this end, with new applications developed to meet emerging needs in the market.

Acknowledgements. I am grateful to colleagues from GEC Plessey Telecommunications and many other companies for their assistance in compiling this chapter. I would particularly like to thank Ken Edmonds, Enda Hardiman, Andrew Bud, Peter Bauer, Norbert Soulić, Bill Jeffrey, Barry Turnbull, George Morris and Wally Tuttlebee.

References

1. Reports of the ETSI Strategic Review Committee and Mobile Experts Group, January 1990
2. "Pan European digital system - How is it developing?", E Hardiman, Financial Times Conference World Mobile Communications in the 90s, October 1989
3. "Will mobile communications compete with the fixed link?", R Hooper, Financial Times Conference World Mobile Communications in the 90s, October 1989
4. "Thoughts to the progress of cordless telephony", P Bauer, Philips Kommunikations Industrie (unpublished paper), Germany

2 Proprietary Digital Cordless Products

Wally Tuttlebee

Within European industry, particularly in the UK, the emerging requirement for digital cordless telephones described in the previous chapter was increasingly being recognised throughout the 1980s, with momentum gathering toward the latter half of the decade to agree international standards so that products could be brought to the emerging single European marketplace. In parallel with this standards activity a number of manufacturers independently had begun product developments. This was especially so within the UK, where a number of proprietary equipments were being developed under the umbrella of the 1987 UK standards, and also within Scandinavia, where a national standard was published in 1989. Thus, by the close of the decade proprietary digital cordless telephone products were becoming available.

In this chapter we review the background to these product developments, describing the early industry activity within Europe. In particular, three early proprietary digital cordless developments are described: those of Ferranti and Shaye, in the UK, and that of Ericsson, in Sweden.

It should be noted that in addition to these companies other UK manufacturers had also begun development of proprietary digital cordless systems in the mid- to late-1980s. With the emergence of the Common Air Interface (CAI) standard in the UK during 1988 these companies chose an alternative strategy of redirecting their developments to align with the CAI standard, as described below. Such products will also now be in the marketplace, but they are not described in this chapter.

2.1 Early Industry Collaboration

2.1.1 The Role of ESPA

Early discussions within continental Europe relating to digital cordless telephony centred strangely enough around the forum of ESPA, the European Selective Paging Association (now renamed the Association of European Manufacturers of Pocket Communication Systems), an association of paging equipment suppliers. The reason for this was that many of the members of ESPA already had significant markets in office systems and the potential market for cordless telephones within this business environment was recognised by these companies as early as 1984. Thus, in order to keep and develop their wire-less communications market in offices, ESPA decided to adopt a proactive role and initiated a study to compare the relative potential of the different possible technical approaches, namely Frequency Division Multiple Access (FDMA), Code Division Multiple Access (CDMA) and Time Division Multiple Access (TDMA). (These concepts are described in Chapter 7.)

The ESPA study report was published in late 1987 [1] and advocated a Time Division Multiple Access/Time Division Duplex (TDMA/TDD) approach. The emphasis within ESPA, reflecting the origins of the ESPA interest in cordless telephony, was to identify a system optimised to the office environment, capable of supporting a high density of users.

2.1.2 CT2

In parallel with these studies within ESPA, significant moves had been afoot within the UK. In the early 1980s a number of companies in the UK had begun independently to explore approaches to second generation cordless telephony and in 1984 several of these began to meet as a group under the sponsorship of the UK Department of Trade and Industry (DTI). This resulted in January 1987 in the allocation of 40×100 kHz duplex channels between 864 and 868 MHz for cordless telephone use. This was followed by the publication of detailed technical standards for cordless telephone equipment: MPT 1334 [2] in April 1987 and BS 6833 [3] in June 1987. MPT 1334 originally specified parameters associated with radio operation such as operating frequencies, transmitter power and spectrum, intermodulation, spurious emissions and receiver sensitivities. BS 6833 covered interconnection to the UK PSTN, speech quality, etc., as well as some further radio requirements such as susceptibility to interference. The CT2 system specified by these standards was an FDMA/TDD approach, built upon inputs from many of the UK manufacturers.

Whilst the business applications were seen as very relevant within the UK discussions, an important factor had been that the new digital cordless telephones should be priced so as to be accessible to the general public. To some degree this thinking reflected the participants' prior experience of first generation cordless telephones – the UK first generation (analogue) instruments had been one-quarter of the price of the equivalent analogue telephones built to the CEPT CT1 specification[1] [4], and had seen correspondingly greater market penetration. (Other sources quote a price differential of as much as six to one compared with CEPT CT1!)

2.1.3 The CEPT Initiative

A further product of the UK activity was an initiative which resulted in 1985 in the European Conference for Posts and Telecommunications (CEPT) beginning to address the concept of digital cordless telephones as a standardisation activity, initially examining services and facilities requirements (S&F) for a second generation system. In addition to the UK and ESPA work, considerable input to this CEPT activity came from another relevant European association, the European Conference of Telecommunications Manufacturers' Associations (ECTEL).

The UK DTI proposed to CEPT that the UK CT2 FDMA/TDD approach should be adopted as a European second generation cordless telephone standard. One or two CEPT administrations favoured this suggestion but not a majority [5]. Indeed, following objections from certain interests, the European Commission imposed a Standstill Directive in 1987 to slow down the UK CT2 whilst options for a common European standard were examined.

With the advent of the CEPT initiative, ESPA members including Ericsson, and also the Swedish PTT, wanted to optimise it for office applications. Thus the Swedish PTT launched to CEPT a revised version of the Ericsson TDMA/TDD concept operating around 900 MHz as an alternative candidate. The Swedish PTT contributed with solutions, especially for echo control and non-synchronised adjacent systems. This approach received ESPA support.

2.1.4 Early Manufacturers' Product Developments

Whilst these international technical discussions were progressing a number of manufacturers had independently chosen to initiate their own programmes of equipment development in advance of full European standardisation.

Ericsson began development of their TDMA/TDD concept, aimed primarily at the business cordless telephone market. A 900 MHz test system was built with three base stations with handover and a few "portables". The system functioned well with unnoticeable handover and was demonstrated

---

[1] This standard is described in Chapter 3.

to a meeting of the CEPT R22 committee (responsible at that time for cordless telephone questions) in Lund in September 1987.

Within the UK several companies had initiated proprietary developments in parallel with the emergence of the UK national specifications provided by the MPT 1334 and BS 6833 standards. Such companies included the larger well-established telecommunications manufacturers, such as STC, GEC and Plessey (later the joint venture companies GEC Plessey Telecommunications (GPT) and Orbitel Mobile Communications), as well as others for whom such products represented their *raison d'être*, such as Libera and Shaye. A prototype Libera product was also shown to the CEPT R22 committee at the same September 1987 meeting mentioned above.

2.1.5 CAI and Its Implications

Increasingly, as the CT2 standards were emerging within the UK, the potential value of public access Telepoint services was recognised. With this came the recognition that the use of a standard radio ("air") interface, to allow interworking between different manufacturers' handsets and base stations, would be desirable, since this would potentially allow users to access a larger number of base stations, thereby making the service more attractive. Thus, during the summer of 1988, an industry committee was established to define such an interface, now known as the Common Air Interface or CAI.

The CAI specification was developed during the latter half of 1988 and was formally published by the UK DTI as MPT 1375 in May 1989. This followed a series of consultation meetings organised by the DTI in London in the early months of 1989 to which all interested European industry and PTT players were invited. The technical substance of the CAI specification is described in Appendix 2.

In January 1989 four companies were licensed to operate Telepoint services in the UK. Within their licences was a proviso that such services should support the CAI by 1991. This presented to the UK equipment manufacturers an interesting dilemma – namely, given limited resources, should they continue to develop their proprietary non-CAI products, with a view to bringing these to the market quickly, or should they redirect their developments to reflect the CAI, which potentially had a larger and more secure future market?

As would be expected, different manufacturers adopted different strategies, shaped by their levels of previous investment and the maturity of their existing product development, as well as by less tangible factors such as their differing perceptions of how the market was likely to develop. Ferranti Creditphone (incorporating Libera) and Shaye chose to complete development and sell proprietary kit, the Zonephone and the Forum Personal Phone respectively, prior to possibly developing CAI product, whilst others redirected their development programmes directly to CAI product. Amongst these were GEC Plessey Telecommunications (GPT) and Orbitel Mobile

Communications, who both announced their CAI products in late 1989 (see Figs. 4.1 and 4.3).

2.1.6 The Conception of DECT

Both the early UK CT2 and the Swedish approaches proposed to CEPT in 1987 were recognised as having advantages and disadvantages, and there were many heated debates about the relative technical and cost benefits of TDMA or FDMA and about the relative maturity of the two techniques. Neither emerged, however, as the outstanding candidate for a common European standard.

Thus, despite the wish to agree a harmonised CEPT European standard, it was clear by late 1987 that the UK and Swedish solutions were sufficiently different for it not to be feasible to agree a common 800/900 MHz standard at that time. CEPT therefore decided in January 1988 to base the concept for a new European standard upon a TDMA/TDD/MC (TDMA/TDD/multi carrier) approach operating at just below 2 GHz, henceforth to be known as the Digital European Cordless Telephone (DECT). (This name was later changed, during 1989, to Digital European Cordless Telecommunications, to reflect an increasing emphasis on non-voice applications.) Also the European Commission noted this decision. It was agreed to allow interim solutions – CT2 in the UK and DCT in Sweden – and the Standstill Directive was lifted, permitting manufacturers to use their existing developments to meet the already-present market requirements. It was this decision that allowed the Ferranti and Shaye products to be launched in the UK in mid-1989 and the Ericsson product development to continue, with product launch in 1990. These three specific products are described in the remainder of this chapter.

2.2 UK – The Zonephone

2.2.1 Origins and Evolution

The Zonephone represents the fruition of the labours of staff within the Ferranti company [4]. The Ferranti interest in cordless telephony stems from around 1983, the year in which Ferranti applied for a licence to operate a cellular network in the UK. It was during the course of preparing this licence application that the limitations of conventional portable cellular telephones became apparent: battery life, wide area inconsistent radio coverage and capacity. Out of such considerations Ferranti began to explore and develop the concepts of low-power spectrally efficient cordless telephony. In conjunction with Telephone Rentals and institutional investors, a new corporate venture company, Libera Developments, was established in 1985 for this purpose.

Prior to this, in 1981, the PA Consulting Group had undertaken a market study for the Eurodata Foundation on the future of mobile telephones in Europe. In concluding that the cellular service would reach the limits of its capacity within a few years, this work had also indicated a potential market for a short-range, radio-based intermediate service positioned between conventional payphones and cellular mobile telephones. Thus it was that PA began working under contract to Ferranti in 1983 and later with Libera to establish the market and technical feasibility of a Universal Cordless Telephone System with low-power, low-cost handsets. Such a system would support handset radio access to a home base station, as a cordless extension, as well as offering public access to other PABX systems. It was concluded at the time that establishing a sufficient "critical mass" of cordless PABXs to make the service viable would not be simple. It also appeared at that time, however, that the provision of cordless extensions to the office PABX was a sufficiently attractive market in its own right to represent the first step of the universal product concept. Thus, early work was directed towards an office system, although the wider area of applications, including Telepoint, were central to the design team's goal.

In developing its cordless handset product, later to be known as the Zonephone, Libera continued to contract development to PA Technology in Cambridge. Early technical directions benefited from propagation research results from British Telecom Research Laboratories (BTRL) pointing towards the use of frequencies around 900 MHz. The benefits of digital as opposed to analogue technology were recognised. In particular, the FDMA/TDD approach was adopted because of simplicity and cost implications, vital to achieving the low cost that was implicit in the product concept. Throughout this period the early work of Libera, in common with that of other manufacturers, influenced the UK standards development activity via the UK industry group.

The potential competition from cheap imported equipments from South-East Asia within the UK market was an important factor in charting the subsequent evolution of the Ferranti concepts. Even with a digital TDD approach, it was concluded at that time that the likely price differential between second generation cordless terminals and existing first generation products could not be supported solely by the improved quality of service. Thus the potential to support extra facilities beyond the scope of first generation cordless telephony was examined.

It was concluded that the provision of public access (Telepoint) could transform the market perception of such second generation equipments. This hypothesis was borne out by a subsequent market survey which indicated that the prime role for a handset might actually be as a public access telephone, with the provision of a home base station as an add-on extra. It was this new perception of the UK marketplace, initially identified by Ferranti and subsequently supported by others, which to a large degree led to the early introduction of Telepoint services within the UK, in advance of other European countries. It should be noted of course that public perceptions and resultant market demands for such services across Europe are not homogeneous and that for other countries the business application (wireless PABX) may represent the more appropriate introduction strategy for second generation cordless telephones. As noted previously, such a position was implicitly taken within ESPA during the 1980s.

In 1987, following the publication of the UK standards, Ferranti Creditphone was established as a joint venture between Ferranti and Libera, to install and operate a Telepoint network in the UK. The term "zone" was conceived for the Telepoint radio microcell, to indicate that the cordless telephone could be used within the limits of a certain geographical area – implicitly explaining the concept to the potential user by virtue of the name of the service. Correspondingly the cordless telephone handset itself was called the Zonephone, a telephone capable of being used within a zone.

Public trials of the Zonephone service began in the UK in July 1988 under two temporary connection approvals and two licences, one covering operation of the Zonephone system and a temporary class licence for the handsets. The purpose of the trials was to explore the full range of engineering, operations and marketing issues.

Having identified the importance of the public access market in the UK, Ferranti/Libera were active participants, with the other UK manufacturers, in the development of the CAI during 1988.

In autumn 1988 Ferranti Creditphone applied for one of the Telepoint licences offered at that time by the UK DTI, with the intention of commencing service with the trialled Zonephone product and migrating to support CAI product as well in due course. The successful outcome of the licence application was announced in January 1989. British Approvals Board for Telecommunications approval ("green dot" certification) for its Zonephone equipment, necessary for the base stations to be connected to the UK PSTN, was granted in September 1989. This removed the final regulatory obstacle to the launch of public service, which occurred in October 1989.

2.2.2 Description of the Zonephone

Introduction

The Zonephone handset (Fig. 2.1) has been designed to be suitable for use in the office (connected to a PABX system), at home (with a domestic base station) and out-and-about (for use with the Zonephone Telepoint service). Each of these environments and applications added its own special constraints on the electronic, mechanical, acoustic and industrial design of the instrument, and a careful balance between the sometimes conflicting requirements has had to be struck by the design team. In this section we

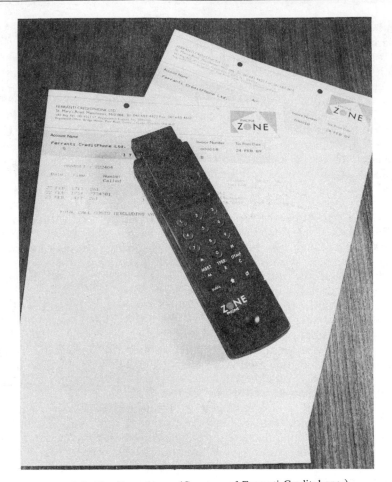

Fig. 2.1. The Zonephone. (Courtesy of Ferranti Creditphone.)

explore how Ferranti's and Libera's key design decisions were influenced by the various objectives.

For an office telephone, performance, reliability, convenience and security are dominant factors. For a domestic telephone low cost and simplicity of function are the overriding considerations. For use outside, ruggedness, easy portability, small size, long battery endurance and an acoustic performance adapted for noisy environments have all proved important.

Physical Format and User Controls

Mechanically, the telephone is a one-piece instrument in which hinged parts have been avoided, and moving parts minimised, in order to improve robustness and reliability. A sealed construction without hatches prevents the ingress of dust. Simplicity of line enables the handset to be slipped into the pocket or briefcase, or carried and used in its protective carrying pouch. The user controls are all on the front surface and comprise an 18-key keypad, using an advanced key mat construction for positive tactile feedback, and a three-position (Standby/Talk/Off) mode switch.

In "Standby" mode – the usual mode in which the handset would be operated at home or in the office – the telephone's receiver is scanning for incoming calls, and the ringer will be sounded if a call is addressed to the instrument. To answer such a call, or to initiate an outgoing call, the user would select "Talk", which has a similar function to taking a conventional telephone "off the hook". By selecting "Off", this same switch is used to turn the power off altogether to preserve the batteries indefinitely – as would be the normal case for a Telepoint user expecting only to make outgoing calls.

Power Source

It was the need for continual use in the office or at home which determined the choice of a rechargeable power source. This comprises four high-capacity nickel–cadmium cells which may be recharged through a purpose-built desktop, wall-mounted or in-car installed charger unit. The batteries can be fully recharged in 8 hours to allow a full 4 hours of talk time, or up to 40 hours on standby.

Speech Processing System

The demands of the office environment drove the policy of no quality compromises on perceived speech quality. Analogue cordless telephones had found their way into some offices, but the sensation of being "on the air" had proved unacceptable to professional users who were not willing to be distracted from their business by poor-quality reception. Apart from leading to the inevitable design decision to use a digital speech system, the office demands led to two other specific design considerations: the choice of a G.721 [6] codec system and the use of spatial diversity antenna systems, as discussed below.

Analogue networks can mask a host of impairments in the terminal equipment, but a modern digital exchange, or a fully digital network, reveals any inadequacy in the transducers, acoustics, radio path, coding and transcoding only too clearly. The need to transcode without degradation from the on-air digital speech to the network and PABX internal 64 kbit/s Pulse Code Modulation (PCM) schemes led to the choice of CCITT G.721 transcoder standards. (In CAI implementations, where the designer is no longer free to choose the coding scheme, G.721 coding has been specified: see Appendix 2.) The decision to use a full PCM combo and an implementation of the G.721 algorithm on a Texas Instruments Digital Signal Processor incurred a penalty in terms of cost, size and battery consumption when contrasted with other simpler coding techniques such as Continuously Variable Slope Detection Modulation (CVSDM), but Ferranti felt that the universality objective necessitated G.721 speech quality. (The principles of these different voice coding schemes are explained in Chapter 6.)

Spatial Diversity

No speech coding scheme can operate successfully if the radio carrier is unreliable. In practice, a radio signal in a typical office environment can be subject to large fluctuations in signal level, due to obstructions (shadowing) or destructive interference (multipath fading). Work carried out by Libera Developments during 1984–1986 and also by BTRL on the nature of a 900 MHz carrier propagation within buildings demonstrated the level of fades caused by the complex multipath regime which exists in a cluttered office or domestic environment. This work also demonstrated that such degradation could be effectively combated by using a spatially diverse antenna system. (Indeed, one of the reasons for choosing a TDD system as the basis for the British standard was that it permitted effective diversity to be applied at the base station end of the transmission path only while being effective for transmissions from portable to base and from base to portable, since the same frequency was used for both up- and down-link transmissions.)

The Zonephone system incorporates such antenna spatial diversity at all base stations. Two antennas separated by 10–15 cm – about half a wavelength – are mounted at each base station and either can be connected to the receiver. Algorithms have been developed which use the Received Signal Strength Indication (RSSI) and the Bit Error Rate (BER) to detect the characteristic deterioration of the signal from the portable as received by the active antenna at the base station as it approaches a null or an incipient fade. When the deterioration reaches a given level, long before any degradation of the speech path would be perceived by the user, the other antenna becomes active to ensure that the fade is avoided. Because of the reciprocity of the transmission path, detection and switching of the diplexed antennas at the base station ensures not only that the base detects fade-free performance from the portable, but also that the portable receives fade-free performance from the base transmissions.

Spatial diversity was originally developed for a cluttered interior environment, and what had not been anticipated before Ferranti's extensive system trials in 1988 of the complete Zonephone system was the extent and nature of the fading present in a street carrying heavy traffic, where the dynamics of the nulls were found to be more complex. The algorithm for managing the spatial diversity and the associated muting of any corrupted digitised speech has required considerable further optimisation.

In short, spatial diversity allows consistent speech performance right out to the nominal operating range, even in a complex fading environment.

Frame Structure and Signalling

Secure and rapid call set-up, and continuous monitoring of the call in progress, were important requirements of the Zonephone specification to meet the needs of office use where high call rates and high user densities are to be anticipated, and it is this application that has influenced the Zonephone frame structure and signalling. These aspects may be better understood by those new to the concepts after reading some of the later technical chapters of this book.

Fig. 2.2 shows the frame structure and timing used by the Zonephone when a call is in progress. A frame comprising 66 information bits is transmitted every 2 ms (nominal) for just under 1 ms, the intervals being occupied by transmissions in the opposite direction. The symbol transmission rate is 72 kbit/s, allowing the 66 bit frame with its prefix/suffix bits and the interframe gap to be accommodated and the "splatter" to be controlled within the BS 6833 specified limits with conventional Gaussian FSK modulation and without exceptionally onerous (and costly) demands being made upon the transceiver design. ("Splatter" in this context refers to the radio frequency energy generated in adjacent channels by the carrier modulation inherent in turning it on and off at the start and end of a TDD burst. It is also known as "spectrum splash".)

Each frame comprises 64 bits of digitised speech and 2 bits of signalling and control, giving full duplex speech at 32 kbit/s and a raw signalling channel of 1 kbit/s in each direction. In a TDD system the frame period is a trade-off – a longer frame period results in increased processing delay in the acoustic path whereas a shorter frame period increases the loss of capacity due to the transmit/receive turnaround. BS 6833 specifies that the round trip acoustic delay shall not exceed 5 ms. The choice of a 2 ms TDD frame period contributes 2×2 ms to the round trip delay due to the framing effects alone; the remaining 1 ms is just sufficient for delays in the codec and transcoding process, the filters, the transducers and acoustic propagation.

The raw signalling rate of 1 kbit/s is more than sufficient for all practical applications (although it is, of course, less than the ISDN D-channel). The Zonephone attaches considerable importance to enhancing the integrity of the signalling channel which forms the foundation of the security of the system as a whole. A highly redundant coding system incorporating error detection and recovery has been adopted which allows the signalling channel to remain usable for carrying channel control and handshake signals in bit error rates as poor as 1 in 10, including sustained burst errors – conditions in which the digital speech channel has long since failed to operate.

Access Security and Voice Privacy

All cordless applications require means of access control to prevent illicit access to an installation. In the USA, pirate users of first generation cordless

a

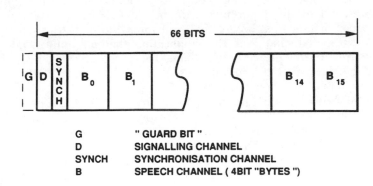

G	" GUARD BIT "
D	SIGNALLING CHANNEL
SYNCH	SYNCHRONISATION CHANNEL
B	SPEECH CHANNEL (4BIT "BYTES ")

b

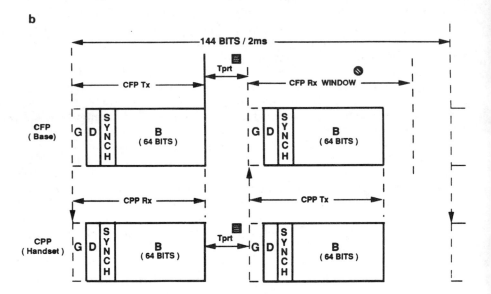

▤   Tprt is fixed and is the changeover time from receive to transmit
    in the handset

⊘   The CFP Rx WINDOW allows for propagation delay between the
    two units on the air interface

Fig. 2.2. Frame structure and signalling in the Zonephone. a Multiplex format; b Time Division
Duplex (TDD) framing.

telephones were able to make calls via subscriber base stations simply by accessing the correct channel. Considerably enhanced protection is provided by the Zonephone, which offers access control checks well beyond those specified in BS 6833. For private systems, the first check is to verify that the manufacturer's serial number of the handset corresponds to a legitimate enrolled handset on a domestic base station (which can recognise up to six enrolments) or business base station. Subsequent checks ensure that use of the handset to make outgoing calls is permitted and, if so, whether any call barring is to be applied.

A quite different process applies for Telepoint use. It is impracticable for every legitimate handset to be listed at each Telepoint. Instead, registered subscribers are given an authorisation code which is stored in the Zonephone in a scrambled way using the user selected Personal Identity Number (PIN) as a key. This authorisation code can be checked algorithmically and will only be accepted by the Zonephone Telepoint if the user has presented the correct PIN to the handset, if the correct handset is being used, and if the handset has not been disabled (for reason of payment default or due to the handset being mislaid or stolen). Even then, the Telepoint itself applies further checks before connecting the call. Certain classes of calls (such as emergency calls) can be made to bypass the access control processes.

Behind the network of Zonephone Telepoints there is an extensive management system, which is an essential component of the Zonephone system, providing intelligent functions to the user through a relatively dumb, general purpose handset – as well as policing the access system and collecting billing information.

The Advent of Common Air Interface

The Zonephone and the associated base stations described above, whilst being fully compliant with BS 6833 and MPT 1334, were originally developed long before the definition of CAI and so were conceived as proprietary protocol systems. However, the principal timing, frame structures and radio parameters are identical between CAI and the proprietary design. This has allowed dual standard base stations to be developed which can accept both CAI standard handsets and proprietary Zonephones.

This technical point had the important marketing implication of allowing the Zonephone system to be launched in a totally unrestrained way using proprietary Zonephones while maintaining the full capability of the system being upgraded to accept CAI instruments as well as Zonephones as soon as CAI equipment became available in the marketplace.

2.3 UK – The Forum Personal Phone

The Forum Personal Phone was designed and developed by Shaye Communications. The company's products include CT2 handsets, personal base units and Telepoint base stations. Two Telepoint systems in the UK are based upon Shaye technology – Phonepoint and Mercury Callpoint. The company has also supplied equipment to a number of systems worldwide.

In April 1982 the core team that would become Shaye Communications first started investigating opportunities for personal communications. The team at that time was employed by Sinclair Research and based in Winchester, southern England. In June 1986 Shaye Communications was established as a separate company by chief executive Bill Jeffrey and technical director Mike Pye. Shaye was successful in obtaining seedcorn funding from Fred Olsen and Timex, with major funding being achieved in the spring of 1987 from a group of international shareholders.

2.3.1 Technical Development and Standards

The development of Shaye Communications' technology occurred during a period of external standards development and ratification. Between 1984 and 1988 Shaye played an active part in the British Standards Committees. In December 1984 the Sinclair group was one of the participating companies investigating cordless technology that came together to form the DTI-sponsored industry group. Some time after Shaye Communications had been formed the first formal UK specifications for digital cordless telephones, MPT 1334 and BS 6833, were established.

The original concept in April 1982 was to offer a point-to-point personal communicator using selective call and trunking techniques, very similar to what has become the DSRR programme (Digital Short Range Radio, also known as Personal Advanced Radio Service or PARS). The objective was subsequently modified to be the development of a digital personal communicator which would transmit over short distances to a variety of base units and be connected to the PSTN. This concept in turn led to that of the Universal Personal Communicator, providing access to domestic, office and Telepoint systems.

Early research activity on the Forum project was concentrated on the signalling technology, frequency allocations and speech quality of personal communications devices. After original assumptions about availability of spectrum, systems studies were undertaken and performance evaluations conducted. It was determined that a specification could not be achieved at that time from a regulatory point of view. Therefore the team began to pursue actively the development of a specification for cordless telephones which eventually became CT2.

Identification of the target market and the corresponding need for a pocketable and portable 'phone led directly to the development of the

Forum Personal Phone concept. Before the radio specification was finalised by the DTI group, the Shaye team at Sinclair Research was already working on the design of the handset. Shaye's concept was for a single universal handset for use in the home, office and with the public Telepoint service and aimed at the broad cross-section of telephone users. The target for Shaye was that the Forum handset should fit comfortably into the pocket, and all technical developments were pursued with this end in mind.

By January 1985 the initial specification and operational strategy for what would become the Forum Personal Phone had been produced. These were enhanced and refined in parallel with the DTI radio and BS committee specifications, and followed by the design cycle of the product. This included bread-boards, a transceiver system, software simulation, rack-mounted development station and the development of two integrated circuits, one incorporating burst mode logic and codec, and the other all analogue functions associated with the speech path.

During this period Shaye determined that the speech quality requirements should be met by an adaptive delta-modulation digital voice coding scheme rather than an Adaptive Differential Pulse-Code Modulation (ADPCM) speech coder. Proprietary development of this took place within Shaye and the system was known as DVSD. This coding technique was economical in terms of power consumption and was to be a major factor in keeping the overall size of the Forum to a minimum and providing the best quality product to the consumer at a reasonable price.

Power consumption was reduced in all aspects of the circuit and scanning protocols. Lithium single cell batteries ensured long battery life when combined with low power consumption circuitry. These single cells provided high energy density whilst retaining their small size and light weight. The handset also incorporated a proprietary integrated aerial.

Further design refinement followed, with the handset industrial design eventually finalised during 1987. In mid-1988 Shaye began the first pre-production build of the Forum Personal Phone, with the company retaining complete responsibility for the design, engineering and control of the product. Initial product manufacture was subcontracted to Philips Circuit Assemblies in Dunfermline, Scotland. BABT approval for the Forum Personal Phone handset was secured in August 1989.

The programme for the development of Telepoint base units accelerated during 1988, in the run-up to the UK government's request for applications to create Telepoint services.

When the opportunity arose, in autumn 1988, to apply for a Telepoint licence, Shaye teamed with Motorola and was successful. Mercury Communications also joined the successful consortium to form the operating company now known as Mercury Callpoint. The Mercury Callpoint Telepoint service was launched in December 1989.

In addition to Mercury Callpoint, another successful consortium, led by British Telecom and involving STC, Nynex and France Telecom, also chose to adopt the Forum Personal Phone for its Telepoint service. This consortium, whose service has become known commercially as Phonepoint, launched its commercial service using Shaye Communications technology in September 1989.

In the three years since its foundation in 1986, Shaye Communications has developed from being simply a concept to a company involving almost 100 people. Future developments will involve close association with the growth in personal communications technology. These advances include the development of a CAI product. The CAI standard defines the radio interface between Telepoint base stations and CT2 telephones. Technically, using CAI, CT2 telephones from any manufacturer will be able to work with networks from any network provider. Developments beyond the introduction of CAI products may include products such as cordless PABX, allowing cordless extensions for business users.

2.3.2 Description of the Forum Personal Phone

The Forum Personal Phone (see Fig. 2.3) is the smallest and lightest first generation CT2 handset available. Designed in injection-moulded ABS, the microphone and keypad are protected by a flap when not in use. In its folded form it occupies only slightly more than $14 \times 6 \times 2$ cm, easily fitting into a pocket or handbag. Its weight, including battery, is only 130 g.

Operating from a 3.6 volt (nominal) supply, the telephone uses a single cell lithium or rechargeable nickel–cadmium battery. An indicator that the

Fig. 2.3. The Forum Personal Phone. (Courtesy of Shaye Communications Ltd.)

battery is low is also incorporated to provide advance warning of battery failure.

The product philosophy has been to minimise size and power consumption. This gives good battery life – 25–30 hours of talk-time from a disposable lithium battery, which is equivalent to some 3–4 months of domestic usage or 4–5 weeks in a business environment.

The user controls comprise a 15-key silicone rubber style keypad for dialling and other control features, an automatic on/off hook switch operated by the flap, and a flap release button. The standard features provided by the keypad include pushbutton digit dialling, memory storage of up to 12 (22 digit) numbers, last number redial and mute. When operated in Telepoint public access mode, user choice of service provider is available.

In domestic or business applications the facility is provided to select the telephone service provider (British Telecom or Mercury in the UK) and to use loop disconnect or DTMF (tone) dialling.

In the business environment the Forum Personal Phone can be used to make and receive calls via the office PABX. The Forum base unit can be linked into the PABX system using conventional telephone wiring, enabling calls to be transferred directly to individual handsets. Similarly it is possible to dial directly into the national and international network through the office PABX. It is also possible to transfer calls from one individual handset to another. For example, up to six handsets can be logged on to a single line Forum base unit, and can share a single PSTN or extension line, but users can be logged on to more than one base unit. Automatic transfer of a call in progress from one base unit to another as the caller roams between units is not possible with the initial products. However, greater user control is provided, in that the Forum Personal Phone system can be programmed so that outgoing calls from one or more handsets may be restricted. This feature is perhaps more applicable to domestic than business applications.

As with the Ferranti product, the Shaye Forum Personal Phone was designed to meet the UK standards, BS 6833 and MPT 1334.

2.4 Sweden – The DCT900

2.4.1 Origins

The DCT900 product has been developed by the Ericsson company in Sweden. During the years 1979–1982 Ericsson received numerous requests from different countries to offer single-channel analogue low-band cordless telephones, similar to those sold in the USA. These requests were treated at the Paging Division of Ericsson Radio Systems, which had long experience in on-site paging and office communication, and it was this which encouraged the idea of applying cordless telephone technology in the office environment. Experience from on-site paging indicated that many systems can coexist on the same frequency if all the receivers are close to their own base stations. Combining this observation with ideas of automatic Dynamic Channel Allocation (DCA) and handover could permit high-capacity systems requiring only a very limited frequency band. TDMA and FDMA concepts were compared in early studies; in Ericsson's view the requirements for quick DCA and handover and numerous simple low-cost base stations in offices favoured TDMA. Thus, early in 1983 a basic TDMA/TDD office communication system concept was presented, using 10 duplex timeslots on a single carrier, which created high internal interest. However, at that time investment was primarily focussed on mobile (cellular radio) telephones rather than on cordless products.

Further developments thus awaited the launch of the CEPT initiative in 1985 which resulted in Ericsson breadboarding a test system with handover. This was demonstrated to CEPT. The CEPT decision in January 1988 to base the CEPT system (now DECT) on TDMA, but around 1.6–1.9 GHz, did not include a firm timetable. Thus the Swedish PTT and Ericsson decided, like the UK, to make use of CEPT's option to allow interim national solutions of their system concepts, while actively participating in the DECT standardisation process. The Swedish specification [7,8], based upon the earlier proposal to CEPT, was issued (in part) in 1989, although the draft standard had been in preparation for some time previously. It is a coexistence standard[2] allowing residential, office and Telepoint applications, in the band 862–866 MHz, to which the Ericsson DCT system conforms. (Although in its title the specification refers to 862–864 MHz, extension of the band to 866 MHz is indicated within the specification.)

The product launch of the DCT900 system is expected in mid 1990 in a number of countries. Products offered will be office systems and Telepoint test systems. These will also be offered outside Europe in conjunction with manufacturing licences, which could give access to the full air interface specification for implementation. Important issues for the Swedish PTT and Ericsson are to gain market experience as well as to have early large-scale real-life tests of some of the concepts common to DECT.

2.4.2 System Features and Components

The main building block of the DCT900 system is a flexible cordless radio subsystem that, connected to or integrated with a PABX, offers cordless PABXs ranging from small to large systems for private or public use. To provide large private cordless systems, Telepoint systems and personal communication systems, network functions are being developed that interconnect cordless PABXs. The stated aim is that these network functions should support both DCT900 and DECT radio subsystems according to needs. The same cordless telephone handset that is used in private business and/or public systems can also be used in residential applications.

---

[2] The term "coexistence standard" is explained more fully in Chapter 3.

For small systems, i.e. a simple single cell, a single radio fixed base station will simultaneously provide external call connection and intercom functions for a number of handsets in a home or small office.

A typical DCT area coverage system will consist of one or more service areas that are completely covered by a number of cells. The total number of cells in such an area and individual cell-sizes depend on the traffic capacity needed at a certain location. The service offered to the user is two way – it is possible to initiate outgoing calls at the handset as well as to receive incoming calls whenever the handset is within one of the service areas belonging to the DCT system. When the handset is roaming between service areas, the system will keep track of its location. The system offers automatic in-call handover between adjacent cells that belong to one system. In order for a handset to access the system for outgoing calls an authentication procedure has to be completed. For security and privacy reasons the speech information is encrypted both for incoming and outgoing calls as a standard system feature.

The Cordless Radio Subsystem

The Cordless Radio Subsystem (CSS) is a microcellular cordless telephone system that can be integrated with or connected to a PABX or to the PSTN. The CSS basically consists of four building blocks: the radio exchange (Common Control Fixed Part, CCFP), satellites (SATs), base stations (Radio Fixed Part, RFP) and handsets (Cordless Portable Part, CPP). A block diagram is shown in Fig. 2.4.

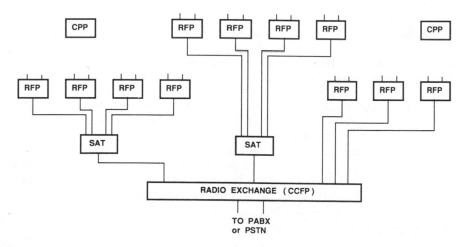

Fig. 2.4. The DCT900 cordless radio subsystem.

Every CSS contains one CCFP that forms the central control equipment of the system. To this a number of satellites are connected. Every satellite can serve a number of base stations (typically 4–10). Every base station covers one cell in the microcellular system; area coverage can be obtained using a multiple number of cells. It is also possible to connect base stations directly to the CCFP without using a satellite. The cordless system is based on digital transmission between base station and handset. Speech coding is done in the CCFP and the handset, using 32 kbit/s Adaptive Differential Pulse Code Modulation (ADPCM). The radio transmission between base station and handset uses Multiple-Carrier (MC) Time Division Multiple Access (TDMA). Full duplex operation is achieved by using Time Division Duplexing (TDD). One of the basic features of the system is decentralised DCA which optimises capacity distribution (the distribution of available channels per cell) according to changing needs.

A single standard type of simple radio base station is employed in the DCT900 system that can carry up to eight simultaneous calls. The standard base station provides one or eight calls for the same cost. This avoids the need for careful planning of the number of channels needed per base, and the system will automatically adjust to local variations in user density. If the total system traffic increases, extra speech processing units are needed only at the system trunk level in the central, CCFP.

DCT900 will operate in Sweden in the allocated frequency band 862–866 MHz, although in principle any band up to 8 MHz wide in the range 800–1000 MHz is possible. The radio frequency output power of the handset or base station is 80 mW peak and 5 mW average per channel. Modulation used by the handset is Gaussian Filtered Minimum Shift Keying (GMSK) with a bandwidth–time product of BT=0.5. The base station modulation is filtered Minimum Shift Keying (MSK). Receiver sensitivity at handset and base station is −90 to −95 dBm and the adjacent channel selectivity 40 dB, which is sufficient as each individual base station only transmits on one carrier at a time.

The DCT900 system uses antennal diversity in the base station, each base station having two antennas. The antenna to be used can be switched between timeslots. The base station determines which antenna to use for uplink reception whilst the handset determines which antenna to use for downlink transmission. This antenna spatial diversity has proved very effective against fading dips as well as against time dispersion. No time dispersion equalisers are needed in the receivers of the system, at least for envisaged ranges of less than 500 m [9].

Further technical details of the operation of the DCT900 system, including handover protocols, are presented in Appendix 1. The reader less well versed in the techniques of cordless telephony will find this Appendix easier to comprehend after studying the intervening chapters.

The Handset

The DCT900 handset, shown in Fig. 2.5, supports all the basic functions of a normal wired DTMF type of telephone. It has as standard an LCD (12

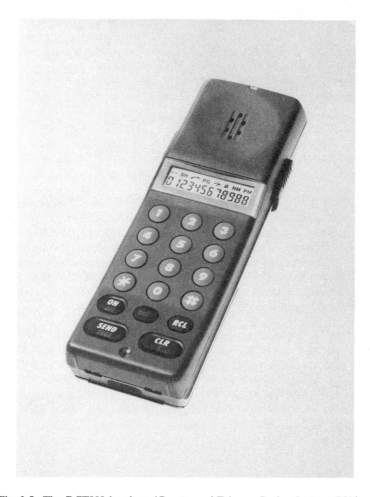

Fig. 2.5. The DCT900 handset. (Courtesy of Ericsson Paging Systems BV.)

digits and 8 indicators) and a keypad with 17 buttons (0 to 9, *, #, plus five other function buttons). This gives access to a number of functions such as check before dial, last number redial, scratchpad, abbreviated dialling (internal memory with 20 stores each of 24 digits maximum) and in-call dialling (DTMF).

Within one CCFP, paging functions are also available between handsets offering functions such as numeric message paging of a single handset or a group of handsets, delayed paging on programmed time, etc.

On the top of the handset a two-colour LED indicator (red/green, flashing/on/off) gives direct information on the status of the handset (within/outside service area, battery voltage OK/low, incoming call, ongoing call). This information is also available on the LCD.

The dimensions of the handset are approximately 53 × 155 × 25 mm and its volume is less than 200 cm³. Weight is approximately 190 g, including a battery pack of five AAA cells. A fully charged nickel–cadmium battery pack will give 30 hours standby time plus 3 hours talk time (or, for example, 40 hours standby time plus 2 hours talk time). It is also possible to switch off the handset completely.

2.5 Summary

This chapter has reviewed the early development of proprietary digital cordless telephone products within the UK and the wider European context. The commercial background to the parallel development of differing technical approaches in the UK and Sweden was explained. Descriptions were provided of the initial proprietary CT2 products launched in the UK during 1989 and of the Swedish DCT900 system, to be launched in 1990. Description of the Telepoint systems introduced in the UK in 1989 and with which the CT2 products operate is presented in Chapter 4.

Note: The inclusion or omission of any particular manufacturer's product in this chapter is for the benefit of illustrating the variety of approaches adopted and should not be construed as an endorsement or otherwise of any product. In particular it should be noted that other manufacturers' CT2 products, conforming to the CAI standard, are also now available in the marketplace. It is hoped to include such products in future editions.

Acknowledgements. The written contributions and other assistance provided by Chris Cant (Ferranti Creditphone), Jonathan Simnet (A-plus PR, on behalf of Shaye) and Dag Åkerberg (Ericsson) in compiling the background to and descriptions of the respective products is gratefully acknowledged.

References

1. ESPA, "Business cordless telephones", publication no. 5.2, September 1987 (Available from ESPA, c/o Willems Kapitelweg 10, NL-4827 HG Breda, The Netherlands)
2. UK Department of Trade and Industry, "Performance specification – radio equipment for use at fixed and portable stations in the cordless telephone service operating in the band 864 to 868 MHz", MPT 1334, London, April 1987
3. British Standards Institution, "Apparatus using cordless attachments (excluding cellular radio apparatus) for connection to analogue interfaces of public switched telephone networks: part I and II", BS 6833, London, 1987
4. H Bibby, "The future with phonezones and cellular", paper presented at the 1989 Pan-European Digital Cellular Radio Conference, 8–9 February 1989, Munich

5. RA Stewart, "A strategic view of CT2", in Mobile Communications Guide 1989, IBC Technical Services, London, 1988, pp 63–69
6. CCITT, "32 kbits/s adaptive differential pulse code modulation (ADPCM)", CCITT Red Book vol. 3, fascicle III.3, Rec G.721, 1984
7. Swedish Telecom, "Technical requirements for a digital cordless telephone", specification 8211-A130 (Swedish Telecom PRD, S-12386 Farsta, Sweden)
8. Swedish Telecom, "Swedish Telecom regulations on radio technical requirements on digital cordless telephones in the frequency band 862–864 MHz", TVTFS 1989:103, October 1989 (Swedish Telecom Radio, Frequency Management, S-13680, Haninge, Sweden)
9. D Åkerberg, "Tests of speech quality versus RMS delay spread for a digital TDMA cordless telephone system without use of time dispersion equalizers", report TY87:2091, Rev B, Ericsson Radio Systems AB, S-16480 Stockholm, Sweden

3 The Development of European Standards

Heinz Ochsner

As soon as the application of a technology results in a market which is big enough to attract the interest of many customers and several manufacturers the question of standards becomes extremely important. Today's mass markets such as television, compact discs or personal computers simply could not exist without standards. Particularly in the field of personal computers the problems of incompatibility or quasi-compatibility of equipment from different vendors still cost a lot of money and time.

Those involved today in the development of technology for cordless telecommunications and eventually personal telecommunications are indeed interested in creating a mass market for the new technologies, attracting a large number of customers and suppliers of equipment and services. It is therefore not suprising that in the international arena the creation of binding standards is one of the prime activities.

3.1 European Telecommunication Standards Procedures

The environment in which telecommunications standards are created in Europe has fundamentally changed since 1987. To understand a telecommunications standard it may be helpful to understand its creation. For this reason this section outlines the procedures which finally lead to a mandatory regulation with which the developer of a cordless telephone, for example, has to comply.

While the topic of this book is cordless personal communications, the explanations given in this section apply to most telecommunications standardisation projects which currently are, and in future will be, of public interest.

3.1.1 Who Creates Standards?

It is difficult to explain what a standard is without knowing who actually creates it, and vice versa. Here, we try to explain first who does it. Fig. 3.1 gives an overview of all the different bodies involved.

Worldwide Standards

Worldwide telecommunications standards usually grow out of the International Telecommunications Union (ITU) of the United Nations, the structure of which is outlined in Fig. 3.2. Founded in 1866 as the International Telegraph Union, its main purpose is to establish cooperation between member states in the field of telecommunications [1]. The Union's Plenipotentiary Conference is held every 6 years.

Standards within the ITU are created by two so-called Consultative

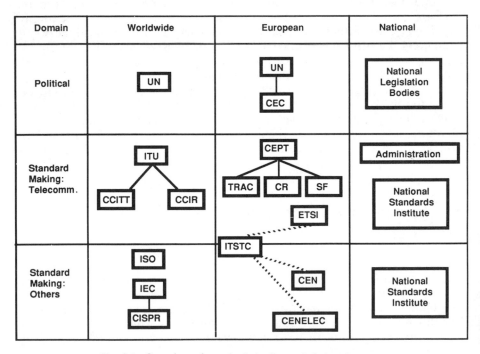

Fig. 3.1. Overview of standards bodies and their roles.

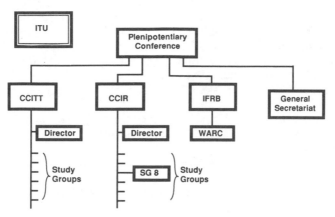

Fig. 3.2. Structure of the International Telecommunications Union, ITU.

Committees: the CCITT (Comité Consultatif International des Télégraphes et Téléphones) for the aspects of international telecommunications networks, and the CCIR (Comité Consultatif International des Radio-Communications) for the aspects of radio communications. Both committees have a similar structure consisting of a plenary assembly, which normally meets every 3 years, study groups set up to deal with particular questions, and a director supported by a technical and administrative secretariat. The Union may even set up laboratories and other technical installations, which are then available to the Consultative Committees. CCIR Study Group 8 is the most important one in the context of cordless personal communications, since it deals with the questions concerning mobile and personal radio communications.

The CCITT and CCIR create Recommendations and Reports which are not binding upon the member countries of the ITU. However, some of their work may later become part of international treaties.

The next important body within the ITU is the International Frequency Registration Board (IFRB). Its five board members are responsible for advising on and recording the worldwide usage of the radio spectrum. In particular it organises the World Administrative Radio Conference (WARC). For the allocation of frequencies the world is divided into three regions: region 1, consisting of Europe, the Middle East, the USSR and Africa; region 2, consisting of the North and South American continent plus Greenland; and region 3, consisting of the Far East, Australia and New Zealand. The current allocation table comprises all the radio frequencies between 9 kHz and 275 GHz. The next WARC will be held in 1992 and will discuss the allocation of frequencies to mobile services. It is therefore of prime importance for personal and cordless communications.

Frequency allocations defined by the WARC become mandatory for the Union's member states. However, changes in frequency allocations may result in the need for existing services to change their operating frequencies. Therefore, a reallocation of a frequency band to other services may take many years from the time of the decision to final implementation. The timescales associated with the release of a common frequency band for widespread geographical usage for a common application are obviously a major constraint in standardisation of products.

In addition to the CCITT, CCIR and IFRB, the Union maintains a General Secretariat.

With the growth of computer telecommunication the standards created within the International Standards Organisation (ISO) will increasingly gain in importance.

Finally the International Electrotechnical Commission (IEC) needs to be mentioned. Its CISPR (Comité International Spécial Perturbations Radio) dealing with radio interference substantially affects all systems and technologies using radio spectrum.

In many cases the recommendations and reports created by the above-mentioned committees serve as prime inputs for European or national standards.

European Standards

Europe is currently in a phase of rapid transition, with individual nations becoming integrated into a "Europe" which is far more than just the geographical description of a continent. As a result, the details of some of the text in this section may become rapidly outdated; it is the situation as of March 1990 that is detailed here.

The European Community (EC) should probably be mentioned first in the European arena. The Community's decision to implement a Single Market in Europe by 1992, and the recognition of the vital political and social, as well as economic role of telecommunications, has resulted in a major change in the telecommunications scene since 1987. The way for the Single Market to develop in the field of telecommunications is outlined in the famous Green Paper published in 1987 [2]; its proposed lines of action were endorsed by the Council of Ministers for telecommunications one year later. Amongst other things the Green Paper proposed:

• The reinforcement of the rapid development of standards, supported by the creation of a European Telecommunications Standards Institute
• The definition of the conditions needed for Open Network Provision to service providers and users
• The stimulation of the development of new services and the setting up of an information market

To do so, the Green Paper requested three major changes of the Community's telecommunications scene:

• Complete opening of the terminal equipment market, including the subscriber's first telephone set, to competition

- Opening of national networks to service providers of other member states, with the possible exception of a few basic services, such as voice telephony
- Clear separation of the regulatory and operational functions of telecommunications administrations

In addition to the Green Paper, with its purely political aspects, the EC is initiating, controlling and financing a variety of research programmes. Within the field of radio communications projects of the RACE, COST and ESPRIT programmes are important. Aside from the purely technical objectives, these programmes aim to promote collaboration between manufacturers across national boundaries. Furthermore, many of these projects in the past have led, and in the future will lead, to important knowledge finding its way directly into the standardisation process.

The Conférence Européenne des Postes et Télécommunications (CEPT) has as members the European PTT administrations and public telephone network operators. Provision of telephony services as well as of equipment was a state monopoly in all European countries for a long time. Therefore, standardisation of telephony was treated uniquely within the CEPT Comité de Coordination et Harmonisation (CCH). Because use of radio spectrum was administered by the CEPT, it was standardised by the CCH, too. However, after the creation in 1988 of the European Telecommunications Standards Institute (ETSI), with wider participation than just the telecommunications administrations (as requested by the Green Paper), all standardisation issues were moved from the CEPT to ETSI and CEPT/CCH was subsequently dissolved in early 1989.

Nevertheless, three committees with the CEPT "T" Commission are of prime importance to the creation of European standards. The Technical Recommendations Applications Committee (TRAC) turns recommendations of any body into NETs which are mandatory for all member PTTs and operators of CEPT (see Section 3.2 for further details concerning NETs). The Comité de Coordinations des Radiocommunications (CR) – previously the Radio Administration, Regulation and Frequency Management Committee (RARF) – develops strategies for the use of radio frequencies and assigns frequencies to services. Unless CR has assigned frequencies, there will be no European-wide service using common radio frequencies. Finally the Service and Facilities (SF) Committee defines the service capabilities of all public services or private services using public resources, such as radio frequencies. The subgroup SF2 has defined the services and facilities of the Digital European Cordless Telecommunications (DECT) system.

ETSI was established in 1988 [3]. Within this Institute all future standards relevant to European telecommunications will be created. The Institute consists of members which are classified into five categories: administrations, network operators, manufacturers, user groups and research bodies. Members pay a membership fee, which gives ETSI more possibilities for accelerating the creation of standards, e.g. by hiring technical experts. The structure of ETSI is shown in Fig. 3.3.

The ETSI General Assembly (GA) is the highest committee in ETSI.

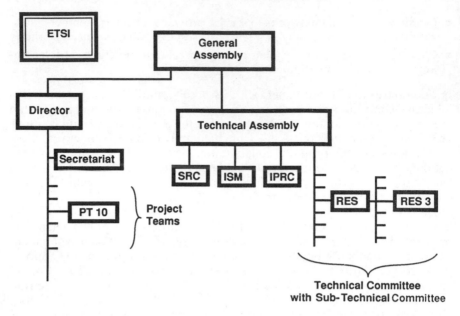

Fig. 3.3. Structure of the European Telecommunications Standards Institute, ETSI.

The GA's main tasks are to determine the ETSI policy, to elect new ETSI members and to manage the resources, in particular the budget. The GA is not, however, involved in technical activities. The administrative tasks of ETSI are performed by a permanent secretariat located in Sophia-Antipolis near Nice in Southern France. Headed by a Director, the secretariat also supervises the Project Teams (see below).

The Technical Assembly (TA) approves and issues European Telecommunications Standards (ETS). Approval is gained by voting. In addition the TA creates the Technical Committees (TC) and elects their chairmen. The TCs (twelve exist at the time of writing) actually create the standards and undertake the related drafting work. They may divide themselves further into Sub-Technical Committees (STC). The TC Radio Equipment and Systems (RES) deals with low-power radio applications. Its STC RES 3 is the body responsible for creating the standard for DECT.

Under the TA, committees other than TCs also exist: the Strategic Review Committee (SRC) studies and defines future possible tasks, the Intellectual Property Rights Committee (IPRC) deals with problems arising from patents which apply to certain standards, and the ISDN Standards Management Committee (ISM) controls and coordinates the creation of the ISDN standards which are the responsibility of many TCs.

As mentioned earlier, ETSI may hire experts to constitute Project Teams (PT). Such PTs are allocated to TCs or STCs and support the creation of the standard. The work on DECT is supported by such a team, formed in autumn 1989, called PT10.

The ETS are still voluntary standards not binding on national telecommunications administrations. Nevertheless, administration members of ETSI will not introduce "competing standards" once ETSI has started to work on a new ETS. Furthermore, once an ETS is established, existing national standards will eventually be withdrawn.

The ISO and IEC have their European counterparts in CEN (Comité Européen de Normalisation) and CENELEC (Comité Européen de Normalisation Electrotechnique). Since the work done in ETSI, CEN and CENELEC may conflict, the Information Technology Steering Committee (ITSTC) has been established to coordinate the work of the three European standardisation bodies.

National Standards

Even though there are mandatory European standards (NETs) or European regulations to apply standards (Directives), implementation and enforcement of standards is a pure national matter. Therefore, the mechanisms of standardisation are different in each country. National Governments, PTT administrations, network operators and national standards institutes share the responsibility for telecommunications standards and their implementation.

3.1.2 What is a Standard?

There exist a vast variety of terms for documents which describe a standardised telecommunications system or, maybe more exactly, a telecommunications technology. Two types of documents must be distinguished: the technical description of the standard, and those documents, or Acts, which legally enforce the use of the standard.

Standards, Specifications, Recommendations and Reports

The terms "standard", "specification", "recommendation" and "report" usually denote a technical description. It is nearly impossible to assign different meanings to the different terms since which is used depends mostly on the organisation which created the documents. Here the term standard will be used for the complete system description while specification may be used for different parts of it. The ISO defines a standard as follows:

Standard: A technical specification or other document available to the public, drawn up with cooperation and consensus or general approval of all interests affected by it, based on the consolidated results of science, technology and experience, aimed at the promotion of optimum community benefits and approved by a body recognised on the national, regional or international level.

Standards generally define interfaces between different modules of a system, e.g. the radio interface specification between the cordless handset and its associated base station. Standards must, however, avoid describing (or even implying) possible technical realisations of modules. A standard usually will also contain rules on how to verify the compliance of a particular product to a mandatory standard (type approval). It must be noted, though, that for most standards in effect today the interface descriptions and the type approval procedures have been created by different bodies. As an example, the CEPT CT1 interface specification for analogue cordless telephones (see Section 3.3) has been created by CEPT while each country which has introduced CEPT CT1 has its own national type approval specification.

Regulations, Directives, NETs and MoUs

Because it has great impact not only commercially but also socially and politically, telecommunications has been regulated by the national authorities from the very beginning. Therefore, in addition to the technical recommendations there are regulations which enforce the introduction of the recommendations. To quote the ISO again:

Regulation: a binding document which contains legislative, regulatory or administrative rules and which is adopted and published by an authority legally vested with the necessary power.

Within the EC, a special kind of regulation is the directive. A directive is usually proposed by the Commission of the European Communities (CEC) but finally issued by the Council of Ministers. A directive may, for example, instruct the member states to perform certain actions, usually by issuing regulations themselves, or to notify the EC on certain national actions. Member states are free to choose the way in which they implement the directive. It should be noted that directives are issued not only to implement standards but to perform actions in any area in which the EC can direct its member states. Some actions thus fall outside the powers of the EC. In this situation the EC may issue a recommendation. (Such an EC recommendation has nothing to do with a recommendation for a standard, in the sense of a technical description, as just described.) As an example, the EC will issue a recommendation proposing actions for a coordinated introduction of DECT in the Community, and a directive requesting member states to free the necessary frequencies by 1992. In particular the recommendation proposes:

- That prospective operators of DECT Telepoint services sign a Memorandum of Understanding by June 1991
- That ETSI completes the standard by October 1991
- That DECT be introduced by end 1992
- That DECT be widely available by 1995

The Directive requests from the member states:

- That the frequency band 1880–1900 MHz be assigned to DECT by CEPT/CR
- Recognition that the band may be extended in the future

Another important tool of regulatory character is the Norme Européenne de Télécommunications (NET). A NET is an interface standard for connection of telecommunication terminals to public networks. Once the TRAC Committee has decided to turn a standard into a NET, it becomes obligatory for all nations which are members of CEPT. NET33, for example, describes the approval requirements for digital telephones connected to an ISDN. It is expected that once the DECT standard is completed, the approval requirements for DECT equipment, which are part of the standard, will become a NET as well.

An agreement to undertake a concerted course of action is called a Memorandum of Understanding (MoU). Operators of public telecommunications networks may sign such an MoU and agree to, for example, introduce a Telepoint service by a certain date. Since the MoU is a contract between the signatories it becomes binding for them. An example of an MoU is that between Telepoint operators, PTTs and PTOs signed in March 1990, described in Chapter 4.

3.2 The Need for Standards

The Greek mythical footpad Procrustes used to invite exhausted travellers to take a rest in his bed. For some the bed was too long; for others it was too short. If the bed was too long Procrustes used to stretch the traveller to a size to fit the bed; if the traveller was too long Procrustes would take an axe and cut his legs to the appropriate size. In all cases the travellers were equally long and equally dead.

Standards which are too rigorous limit the application for which they were designed. The standard and its makers are in permanent danger of being the modern Procrustes by killing the application through tight and inflexible standards. In order not to create the "bed of Procrustes" a standards maker has to make sure, firstly, that only those areas are standardised that need to be, and, secondly, that standards are sufficiently flexible to fit the application rather than forcing the application to fit the standard.

The need for standards has already been mentioned in the introduction to this chapter. In the case of public telecommunication networks the need for standards is obvious. In addition, however, big markets, in particular the European Single Market, need standards to allow even small manufacturers to create equipment which may be used with other manufacturers' systems. By allowing a system to be assembled from modules produced by different manufacturers, the standard thus gives small manufacturers access to big markets. Finally, standards may lead to large volumes of components and hence to cheaper equipment.

On the other hand standards always restrict developers of equipment because given rules have to be followed. The reduced freedom of implementation of new features into products may reduce the potential of new developments and in the worst case result in nearly identical products from all manufacturers. A further general disadvantage of standardisation is the long gestation time of standards. Since standards have to be verified after their creation, several years may elapse between the first ideas of a new system to be standardised and its commercial introduction. The result is a system which is no longer state-of-the art. To ameliorate this problem standards makers often attempt to forecast technological progress in order to define a technology intercept at the anticipated introduction date of a new standard – i.e. the standard is based upon the expected technology which will be available at the time of its completion, rather than that which is already available. Such an approach was adopted in the UK in the context of the CT2 standard.

Seeing the benefits as well as the dangers of standardisation, the concept of a two-stage implementation of standards has been developed: Coexistence (CX) specifications and Common Interface (CI) specifications. Whilst this concept has been in use implicitly for some time, an explicit distinction between the two separate specifications has been made for the first time in the case of DECT.

3.2.1 Coexistence Specifications

Since we are talking about radio communication systems, the radio interface specification will be discussed here. A coexistence specification makes sure that equipment from different manufacturers can operate and coexist in the same environment. Coexistence means that if, for example, one system uses two radio channels, then the number of channels denied to a second system from a different manufacturer would be the same as though the first system were another of his own. A CX specification does not, however, treat the communication between the two peers in detail, the communication protocols being proprietary to the manufacturer of the equipment. Coexistence specifications are needed where equipment is used only privately. The best example of such equipment is the current analogue cordless telephone product – all existing analogue cordless telephone specifications are essentially coexistence specifications.

3.2.2 Common Interface Specifications

If equipment of different manufacturers has to interoperate then an exact description of the radio communication is needed. Interoperability is needed for public services such as the Telepoint service. As explained above, interoperability also enables small manufacturers to participate in a market by allowing them to produce only parts of the system. A large number of manufacturers are believed to result in a big market with a large variety of different products. A CI specification may further allow high volumes of standard components and eventually cheap equipment. This, however, is only true if the standard is wisely designed and no "bed of Procrustes".

A CI standard for cordless telephony of course needs to define the exact format of all signals being transmitted. Furthermore, the protocols for some procedures need to be defined. Such defined protocols ensure that one end of a communications link will know what response to expect in reply to a message sent to a peer at the other end of the link. Nevertheless, in order to allow freedom of implementation, the standard must not specify how these functions should be implemented. DECT, for example, will define the type of modulation but not the demodulation technique to be employed. Furthermore, the standard must not say how certain decisions are to be taken. It should, for example, be within the product designer's province to choose a preferred algorithm for handover or for call curtailment in bad propagation conditions – although the standard may place requirements upon the performance of such algorithms.

A major danger exists if a standard such as DECT allows systems designed to the CX specification and those designed to the CI specification to operate within the same area. To prevent confusion of the CI system it must be able to recognise the CX system as such. Hence the positive differentiation of the CX system by CI systems is a prime requirement of the DECT standard.

3.3 Standards for Analogue Systems

This section presents the analogue standards for cordless telephones being used in Europe today. The intention is to describe the standards and their application rather than the technical details of the systems they cover. The only system parameters presented here are the frequency bands and the number of channels, because these touch upon regulatory issues.

Dates of introduction and plans for system trials quoted here are based upon the situation in March 1990. Of course introduction of a standard may be delayed and plans may be changed.

3.3.1 The European CEPT CT1 Standard

CEPT released the first version of its CT1 standard in 1983. The standard T/R 24-03 [4] describes the technical characteristics, test conditions and methods for radio aspects of cordless telephones. However, as T/R 24-03 is a recommendation only, each of the national versions is different. This was not a great problem when PTTs were the only buyers of equipment and used to purchase equipment uniquely from national manufacturers. Today, though, a manufacturer has to design a slightly different product for each country in which he intends to sell it. Nevertheless, CEPT CT1 cordless telephones are in use in 11 European countries: Austria, Belgium, Denmark, Finland, West Germany, Italy, Luxembourg, The Netherlands, Norway, Sweden and Switzerland. Yet more countries are expected to open their markets for CEPT CT1.

CEPT CT1 uses 40 channels spaced at 25 kHz intervals in the range 914.0125 MHz to 914.9875 MHz (portable transmitting) and 959.0125 to 959.9875 MHz (base transmitting). Channels are selected dynamically, i.e. one of the 40 channels is chosen at call set-up.

CEPT CT1 is a coexistence specification. It does not allow the cordless handsets to communicate with base stations of other manufacturers. However, like any other telephone, a CT1 set has to be type-approved against national specifications of the line interface. This specification is a CI specification.

The 40 channels do not provide enough capacity for business applications. In addition the frequencies will need to be released by about 1995 for the GSM cellular radiotelephone service. Therefore, Belgium, Germany and Switzerland decided to open a new band from 885.0125 MHz to 886.9875 MHz and 930.0125 MHz to 931.9875 MHz offering 80 channels. This system is sometimes called CT1+.

Trials with a Telepoint service based upon CEPT CT1 or CT1+ are planned in several European countries, in particular in West Germany, Switzerland and Italy.

3.3.2 ELSE, The West German Common Interface Specification for CEPT CT1+

In order to provide a Telepoint service based on CT1+, West German industry is currently working on a CI specification for CT1+. This specification is called ELSE (Einheitliche Luftschnittstelle). The standard is expected to be completed by mid 1990 and products based on ELSE may be available shortly thereafter.

3.3.3 The UK Analogue Standard UK CT1

In the UK it was felt that CEPT CT1 was not suitable for a free telephone equipment market because the standard resulted in expensive products as compared with, for example, the units sold in the USA. Therefore, CEPT CT1 was not introduced in the UK, but a UK CT1 standard was published instead: MPT 1322 [5]. This standard is very similar to that being used in the USA.

UK CT1 offers eight channels: 47.45625 MHz to 47.54375 MHz (portable transmitting, spacing 12.5 kHz) and 1.642 MHz to 1.782 MHz (base transmitting, spacing 20 kHz). Any apparatus is either tuned to one of the channels or allows switching between two channels.

MPT 1322 is again a CX specification. As for all telephones, the requirements for connection to the PSTN are a mandatory CI specification, found in [6].

3.3.4 The French Analogue Standard F CT1

A system similar to UK CT1 is in use in France. The specification NF C 98-220 allocates 15 channels spaced at 12.5 kHz from 41.3125 MHz to 41.4875 MHz (portable transmitting) and 26.3125 MHz to 26.4875 MHz (base transmitting). However, only 10 channels are really in use today. As with CEPT CT1, products conforming to this standard have proved to be expensive considering their limited capabilities, and the market take-up has been correspondingly low.

3.4 Standards for Digital Systems

Future systems with a wide area of application will undoubtedly be digital. First national digital standards already have come into effect in the UK and Sweden, and products based on these standards have been described in Chapter 2.

3.4.1 The European CEPT CT2 Service Definition

While the relevant CEPT committee (R22 at that time) was finalising its CT1 specification, the CEPT SF (Services and Facilities) committee was already studying CT1's successor. The draft CEPT SF2 recommendation dated 1985 specifies CEPT CT2 as a system providing enhanced services such as wireless PABX. Being a pure service definition it does not state the transmission technique; however, nobody really doubted that the new system would be digital.

During 1988 and 1989 the service definition for CEPT/CT2 was extended and became the service definition for DECT.

3.4.2 The UK Digital Standard CT2

In the UK the poor capacity of the eight channel UK CT1 was recognised very early. Consequently a digital system was developed. Its radio characteristics and requirements are found in the UK specification MPT 1334 [7].

This system, called UK CT2, uses 40 channels spaced at 100 kHz from 864.15 MHz to 868.05 MHz accessing the radio medium by Frequency Division Multiple Access (FDMA). Unlike all the analogue systems it separates the two directions of communication using the Time Division Duplex (TDD) technique rather than Frequency Division Duplex (FDD). In this way duplex separation is achieved with cheap switches rather than with expensive filters.

MPT 1334 is a CX specification. In addition to the radio specification the mandatory requirements for connection to the telephone networks are issued in a separate document BS 6833 [8].

3.4.3 The Common Air Interface Specification, CAI

In order to allow a Telepoint service based on UK CT2 a common interface specification, a refinement of the existing specifications MPT 1334 and BS 6833, had to be created. This specification is available as MPT 1375 [9], better known as CAI (Common Air Interface).

While the UK Telepoint service at its introduction in 1989 was based on proprietary versions of UK CT2, all the Telepoint networks will support CAI by 1991.

There are plans to trial a CT2 CAI based Telepoint service in several European countries, notably Finland, Spain, France, Italy and Germany – in Germany alongside the CEPT CT1 system. CAI is to be adopted as an Interim European Telecommunications Standard. Chapter 4 discusses these issues in greater detail.

The technical details of CAI are summarised in Appendix 2.

3.4.4 The Swedish Digital Standard

Another digital approach to cordless telecommunications was undertaken in Sweden. It was recognised that CEPT CT1, which is introduced in Sweden, is not particularly suitable for high-capacity applications, in particular for cordless PABX. The radio characteristics of the Swedish DCT (Digital Cordless Telephone) are specified in the document TVTFS 1989:103 [10].

DCT uses the Time Division Multiple Access/Time Division Duplex (TDMA/TDD) radio access technique. The frequency band between 862 MHz and 864 MHz may be used with either one carrier offering 16 duplex channels (a total of 32 time slots) or two carriers bearing 8 duplex channels (16 time slots per carrier) each. The band may be expanded to 866 MHz at a later date. DCT would then provide a total of 32 duplex channels.

TVTFS 1989:103 is a CX specification. The mandatory telephony requirements are given in [11].

3.4.5 The Digital European Cordless Telecommunications Standard, DECT

None of the standards presented so far currently is resulting in, or ever will result in, pan-European systems. This should change with DECT, currently being developed within ETSI.

As mentioned earlier, a CEPT service description for CEPT CT2 has existed since 1985. Both the UK CT2 and the Swedish DCT were proposed for CEPT CT2. The CEPT, however, was of the opinion that neither system was suited for a wide variety of applications and decided that a new system should be developed. This system is called Digital European Cordless Telecommunications (DECT) and will offer services which will go significantly beyond those available with current systems. In particular the DECT radio environment can be used for:

- Cordless telephones for use in private residences
- Telepoint scrvices
- Cordless PABX applications
- On-site cordless data services

The standard will allow design of a handset for use at home, in the office and outdoors.

The system will use frequencies on 10 carriers between 1880 MHz and 1900 MHz. Each carrier may bear 12 telephone conversations by using a TDMA/TDD approach. A high degree of flexibility will allow DECT to support everything from simple cordless telephones to complex wireless PABX networks integrating voice and data services.

Further technical details of the standard as available in March 1990 are summarised in Appendix 3.

3.5 Summary

This chapter has covered the evolution of standards in Europe. First the environment in which standards are created in Europe was discussed. The important bodies, ranging from the ITU's Consultative Committees CCIR and CCITT to the new (but most important) ETSI were detailed. Next, the benefits of standardisation and its dangers were considered. The concepts of coexistence and common interface specifications were shown to give manufacturers the possibility of compromise between these benefits and dangers. Finally the existing standards for cordless telecommunications were briefly presented. The variety of different national systems will in time be replaced by the emerging unique standard for Europe, called DECT.

References

1. RCV Macario, "Mobile radio telephones in the UK", chapter 4, Glentop Press, UK, 1988
2. Commission of the European Communities, "Towards a dynamic European economy – Green Paper on the development of the common market for telecommunications services and equipments", COM(87) 290, Brussels, Belgium, 1987
3. D Gagliardi, "The development of standards", paper presented at the Pan-European Digital Cellular Radio Conference, 8–9 February 1989, Munich
4. CEPT, "Radio characteristics of cordless telephones", recommendation T/R 24-03 (revised), Jersey, 1987
5. UK Department of Trade and Industry, "Performance specification – angle modulated MF and VHF radio equipment for use at base and handportable stations in the cordless telephone service", MPT 1322, London, August 1982
6. Office of Telecommunications, "Provisional code of practice for the design of private telecommunication branch networks", London, UK, December 1986
7. UK Department of Trade and Industry, "Performance specification – radio equipment for use at fixed and portable stations in the cordless telephone service operating in the band 864 to 868 MHz", MPT 1334, London, April 1987
8. British Standards Institution, "Apparatus using cordless attachments (excluding cellular radio apparatus) for connection to analogue interfaces of public switched telephone networks: parts I and II", BS 6833, London, 1987
9. UK Department of Trade and Industry, "Common air interface specification to be used for the interworking between cordless telephone apparatus including public access services", MPT 1375, London, May 1989 (amended November 1989, February 1990)
10. Swedish Telecom, "Swedish Telecom regulations on radio technical requirements on digital cordless telephones in the frequency band 862 to 864 MHz", TVTFS 1989:103, 1989
11. Swedish Telecom, "Technical telephone requirements for a digital cordless telephone", 8211-A:130, June 1989

4 Telepoint et Pointel: European Perspectives

Ed Candy, Norbert Soulié, Peter Striebel and Wally Tuttlebee

The first two chapters of this book explored the emergence of the digital cordless telephone marketplace during the late 1980s and the resulting proprietary products. The Telepoint concept, which formed an integral part of these developments, is a major step towards bringing mobile communications services to the mass market. This chapter presents perspectives on Telepoint from different European countries.

The first contribution, from the UK, reviews the events which led up to the award of licences in January 1989 to operate Telepoint networks in the UK, the implementation and rollout of those networks and their expected evolution. The French perspective is then presented, outlining the reasons for the adoption of CT2 in France, the Pointel[1] requirements and the anticipated market development. The development of cordless telephony in West Germany is then reviewed and the Deutsche Bundespost's plans for Telepoint trials of CT2 and CT1+ systems described. Brief reviews of developments in Italy and Finland, where CT2 based systems are being implemented, are then presented. Finally the background to, purposes and content of the Memorandum of Understanding on a Harmonised European Telepoint Service, which was signed in March 1990, are described.

---

[1] 'Pointel' is the name given to the emergent French Telepoint service.

4.1 Telepoint Networks in the UK
Ed Candy

Public cordless telephony (or Telepoint) is the first example of a personal communicator destined for use by the general public and as such is a significant breakthrough. The cost of implementing the Telepoint base station and the Telepoint handset is relatively low, providing the opportunity for establishing a public network with a comparatively low cost infrastructure and thereby providing a low cost personal public telephone service. Furthermore, Telepoint offers a unique utility – a handset user is by definition able to use the handset in the home, the office or public places. It is these two points that make Telepoint different from cellular radio. The evolution of the CT2 product into the Telepoint concept is well described in [1,2].

4.1.1 Network Licences

By the late 1980s manufacturers and prospective network operators were in a position to request the UK Government to issue licences for the operation of public Telepoint services (all public telecommunications services must be licensed by law in the UK). Following the success of the UK mobile communications industry and confident of the maturity of the CT2 technology, the Government invited applications in July 1988, the closing date for submissions being 21 October 1988.

The invitation provoked a host of applications. Eleven high-quality replies were received for up to four network licences. The applicants included the British Telecom led Phonepoint consortium; a Callpoint consortium comprising Motorola, Storno and Shaye; Ferranti Creditphone; Marconi Communication Systems; Mercury Metrophone; Millicom Telepoint; Philips Telecommunications and Data Systems in conjunction with Shell and Barclays; Plessey Telecommunications; Racal Telecommunications; Telepoint Retailers consortium; and the Telecom Corporation.

The UK Department of Trade and Industry and Office of Telecommunications (OFTEL) assessed the applicants for their ability to create a successful business enterprise and quality Telepoint service. They were looking for commercial acumen, a high degree of network and operating skills, and for companies which could demonstrate both technical and financial resources.

On 26 January 1989 Lord Young, then Secretary of State for Trade and Industry, announced that four licences would be granted to: Ferranti Creditphone; the Philips, Shell and Barclays consortium; a consortium comprising STC, British Telecom, France Télécom and Nynex; and a fourth consortium involving Motorola, Shaye and Mercury.

The successful consortia had between them a variety of characteristics, such as European partners, strong consumer marketing skills, network and operations design experience, the ability to source, manufacture or design equipment, and the ability to market Telepoint to the business community. There is, however, a different emphasis on each of these characteristics between the different operators and it is expected that these differences will heighten the competition between the four operators, so promoting a successful Telepoint industry within the UK.

In formulating the policy to allocate Telepoint licences, the DTI believed the success of the service would depend on a large geographic distribution of base stations and on users being able to use any of the base stations provided by any of the network operators. Under the original BS 6833 specifications, different proprietary and incompatible interface standards had emerged which (whilst adequately providing the necessary technical specifications for Telepoint) would ultimately lead to separate networks with users unable to exchange handsets between the various networks. As a result, a group of manufacturers and operators were brought together in October 1988 under the guidance of the DTI to produce the so-called Common Air Interface standard (known as CAI for short). The objective was to provide a uniform standard for public Telepoint which would enable handsets to be transferred between networks and operators.

Lord Young's statement on 26 January 1989 set out the requirement of the licencees to adopt CAI so that Telepoint users had freedom of choice of equipment, a sentiment he made explicit in his statement when he added:

So, from the end of 1990, the licencees will be required to support a common standard which will allow the customers of any one service operator to make their own choice of handset from amongst those available on the market, and, from mid 1991 or such later date as the Director General may determine, the user registered with one system must be able to communicate via base stations of any of the others.

This clearly set out the responsibilities of the Telepoint licencees to adopt the CAI specification by the end of 1990 and to form "roaming" agreements with other network operators to provide the broadest possible service to the user throughout the UK. To encourage the Telepoint service to start as quickly as possible, all the licencees were given the option of commencing the initial service with proprietary equipment so long as they met the requirement to support the CAI standard from 1990 onwards.

4.1.2 Service Implementation

Following the award of licences, establishing the service itself required a combination of equipment and potential base station locations, as well as the foundation of companies and their manpower resources to implement the system. Two of the four licencees – the Ferranti Creditphone consortium operating the Zonephone service and the Phonepoint consortium (STC, British Telecom, France Télécom and Nynex) – announced that their services would commence in the summer of 1989. As it transpired, they both came into operation in the latter part of 1989.

The equipment and call charges for both services were broadly similar. The Zonephone service was launched in October 1989 using proprietary equipment supplied by Ferranti. The handset and charger was initially priced at around £230, home base stations at around £270, a connection fee was set at £30 and a monthly access charge at £10. Phonepoint launched in September 1989 using a proprietary standard originally developed by Shaye Communications, using Shaye handset equipment and base station equipment modified by British Telecom from Shaye sub-modules. The prices quoted for Phonepoint were £195 for the handset, a home base station of around £195, a connection fee of £20 and monthly access of around £8. Call tariffs were to be similar to public payphone tariffs.

In the spring of 1989 the third consortium, Callpoint (Motorola, Shaye and Mercury), announced its intentions to launch in December 1989, again using Shaye proprietary equipment.

On 19 October 1989 the Barclays Philips Shell consortium (known as BYPS for short) announced they would commence service in 1990 using handsets, base stations and network equipment manufactured by GEC Plessey Telecommunications to the CAI standard (see Fig. 4.1).

By choosing to launch immediately with CAI, the BYPS consortium argued that CAI equipment guaranteed freedom of choice for the customer as well as guaranteeing that equipment purchased would not become obsolete when the proprietary services were required by the terms of their licence to convert to CAI. It was further argued that a CAI network would provide customers with an opportunity for roaming between networks.

There are, of course, additional benefits of CAI. A network operator who launches with this standard does not have the complexity of supporting both proprietary and CAI standards, nor the expense of converting and upgrading a network. As CAI is a common standard, it should encourage higher volumes of manufacture and therefore result in a lower product price for the consumer. It is becoming apparent that the CAI standard is being taken up by various international and European operators, again because of the availability of high volumes of handset equipment and infrastructure products.

The two proprietary handset products on offer at the end of 1989, from Shaye and Ferranti, have been described in Chapter 2. Both are compact, pocket-sized products. The Telepoint networks employing them use synthesised voice messages (generated in the base station) to prompt and inform the user of the progress of a call.

Two of the CAI product manufacturers, GPT and Orbitel, also announced details of their CAI products in late 1989 with product delivery during 1990. Both handsets include liquid crystal displays (LCDs), volume controls and can take standard penlite or rechargeable cells. The LCD can be used for displaying the call status and for recalling telephone numbers previously stored. The volume control makes the handset suitable for use either in offices with low levels of ambient noise or in busy streets with high levels of noise. The use of standard-size removable cells means that customers will find power sources readily available in high-street shops.

Fig. 4.1. The GPT CAI cordless pocketphone to be used with the BYPS "Rabbit" Telepoint system. (Courtesy of GEC Plessey Telecommunications.)

Each of the Telepoint operators announced rollout plans for 1990. The BYPS consortium plans to install 7000 CAI base stations throughout the UK by the end of 1990. The Ferranti Creditphone consortium announced its intention to install 5000 proprietary interface base stations, commencing in London, by the end of 1990, with dual standard stations supporting CAI by the end of 1990. The Phonepoint consortium has rollout plans for several thousand proprietary base stations by the end of 1990 with up to four channel capacity per base station, with plans for the installation of CAI base stations in the first quarter of 1991. Callpoint planned to install 1000 two-channel proprietary base stations by Easter 1990, with a target by the end of 1990 of 4000 two-channel base stations covering all the towns of population greater than 100 000.

The successful implementation of Telepoint requires the acquisition of sites for the installation of Telepoint base stations. All four Telepoint operators have been engaged in commercial discussions with a range of property owners to provide the necessary distribution of base stations throughout the UK. A Telepoint user needs to be able to identify the location of a Telepoint site quickly to make a call. Thus, each of the operators has developed distinctive signage or site acquisition policies which, to a lesser or greater extent, simplify the task of the user in finding a site. For example, the BYPS consortium acquires this visibility through popular and well-known brand names such as those provided by the consortium members itself.

For the customer, Telepoint provides a low-cost personal communications service. By supplementing the Telepoint network with paging and voice messaging, users are never out of touch and are spared the irritation of incoming calls at inconvenient moments.

For a great many customers Telepoint will provide an excellent service. Customers will typically be those with small businesses, the cost-conscious businessperson, the self-employed or members of the general public. These people will be able to buy a cordless handset to suit their pocket and taste from the many different brands readily available in the high-street shops or from specialist dealers. The first handsets to have gone on sale are about one-tenth of the price of the first cellular handsets, and cordless handsets should fall quickly in price.

Those in business can also buy a wire-less PABX (switchboard), eliminating the need for expensive telephone wiring and giving more convenience and flexibility in use. CT2 technology will allow the design and manufacture of cordless small PABXs, which account for about 80% of all PABX sales. The domestic customer can also buy a domestic cordless base station, allowing calls to be made from the living room, bedroom, garden or kitchen, as well as allowing extra extensions to be added easily when wanted. These systems, as witnessed by the large sales of analogue cordless telephones in the UK, are very attractive in their own right, but it is the addition of public Telepoints that really creates a personal communications service.

To become a Telepoint user a customer merely has to buy (or already have) a CT2 cordless telephone, take it to the nearest Telepoint and call the network operator, when all the registration details will be automatically supplied. There will be no need for lengthy delays in application and connection.

Ultimately, Telepoints will appear everywhere. The stated goal of several of the UK Telepoint operators is that the great bulk of the population should never be more than 2 to 5 minutes away from a Telepoint. For the pedestrian, Telepoints will be installed in high streets, shopping malls, railway stations, entertainment centres and so on. For the motorist, Telepoints will be in car parks, lay-bys, motorway and main-road service areas, and so on. In the UK, where large chains of these types of sites are available through well-known and visible companies, it will be very easy to find the nearest Telepoint as the user will not have to look for the Telepoint itself, merely the nearest brand of shop, petrol station, car park, etc., known to provide the Telepoint. In some places, such as large shopping malls or railway stations, Telepoint can provide blanket area coverage so that the user need not look for a particular brand of shop, but can make a call from anywhere on the complex.

While office and domestic cordless telephones can both make and receive telephone calls, Telepoint users may make only outgoing calls. However, the system could be enhanced so that a subscriber can nominate a specific Telepoint when expecting a call, and the UK Department of Trade and Industry (DTI) in early 1990 indicated an intention to allow the network operators to adapt their systems to permit this. By supplementing Telepoints with paging and voice mailboxes, a quasi two-way calling service can be provided. For example, when a person is called at the office but happens to be out, the call can be automatically diverted to his or her voice message box, the caller will leave a message and the person will be paged. The call can be returned from the nearest Telepoint if necessary. For many people the ability to return the call at the time of their own choice is preferable to being forced to stop and answer the insistent ringing of a mobile telephone whenever somebody chooses to ring them.

It is obvious from the above that a Telepoint system together with the office, domestic, paging and messaging systems has all the features and facilities needed to provide a market previously excluded from the benefits of mobile communications with a service that it needs and can afford. This is the real position of the Telepoint system.

Some commentators choose to compare Telepoint with cellular radio, and jump to the conclusion that cellular systems will dominate cordless systems. Indeed, cellular systems do provide a very good service, but there is a high price to pay. In the UK and USA there is a market phenomenon whereby users can receive heavily discounted and apparently "free" cellular telephones but are in turn locked into long service provision contracts. Customers thus seduced are often unaware of the high cost of calls until they receive the first bill. This causes many to leave the service or become bad debtors. The stable customers on cellular systems are mostly business customers for whom time is money or who are unaware of the high cost of cellphone calls. As the number of cellphones increases, the bill for cellular calls is becoming a significant cost and company communications managers are starting to give close attention to the costs being generated. The Telepoint system has no pretensions to being a cellular system – instead it provides a great many people with an equally useful service at a greatly reduced cost.

The Telepoint system itself is a network of a large number of public cordless telephone base stations. Each base station is a small, easily installed piece of equipment about the size of a briefcase that is connected by ordinary telephone lines to the public switched telephone network (PSTN). Handsets can be used up to about 200 m away from a base station, which is about the distance from which one could see a Telepoint sign on a location known to provide the service.

As a call is made the base station records the details of its duration and destination. Each call is individually authorised before it is allowed to proceed. The handset sends the user's account and personal identity number (PIN) and the system verifies that they match correctly. The system also checks that users are creditworthy. These two checks can be performed either locally in each base station or in one central computer. Performing these functions locally requires that the base station be updated each night with the latest information, but also avoids delays while the central computer is contacted. Performing the functions centrally is a secure and easily managed method but involves a call to the central computer for every customer call made.

In short, while each Telepoint base station is quite simple, it is the sheer number and spread of all the base stations which will allow Telepoint systems (in conjunction with office, domestic, paging and messaging systems) to provide an effective and affordable service.

4.1.3 Service Evolution

The evolution of the Telepoint service can be examined over two timescales. In the long term the role of cordless telephones in the progression to fully featured personal communications systems can be seen. In the short term the immediate plans for upgrading Telepoint systems can be described.

It is generally accepted in the mobile communications industry that cordless telephones and handheld cellular telephones provide, in essence, the same service. Moreover, the systems will eventually converge into a unified form of service [3,4]. For a mass market service, cordless systems with their low cost and high spectrum efficiency are probably the best starting point. Following the development of the markets for domestic, office and Telepoint systems, it is easy to predict the development of higher power cordless telephones. These would be the equivalent of mini cellular phones, with a coverage of 1–2 km as opposed to today's 200 m. These larger cells could provide complete coverage over entire cities and would overlay the Telepoints.

As such a system would develop progressively, these large cells would first be installed where required and installed step by step in major cities and towns. This system would be much more spectrum efficient than a pure cellular system using cells of the same size, since the great mass of customers, encouraged by the tariff structures, would continue to use the very efficient Telepoint and office systems. Cordless telephones could also be used inside cars, buses, trains, etc., which were connected to the public network by cellular or other radio systems.

In the short term, as all the network operators make the transition to CAI equipment, the user of any network will be able to use all the base stations provided by all the operators. This will multiply the number of locations providing Telepoint service to a customer. Telepoint will probably also be increasingly used to give blanket coverage over entire complexes rather than in the vicinity of a particular shop. As this develops, it should be possible for users intending to stay in these locations for a reasonably long period to register their location and so be able to receive incoming calls. When data communication standards are agreed, Telepoint users will be able to access a variety of data or ISDN-type services such as fax, E-mail and remote logging on to computers.

To put it simply: if all goes to plan, and there is no real reason why it should not, Telepoint systems could become one of the most effective and popular mobile communications services.

4.1.4 Summary

Telepoint systems in conjunction with domestic and office cordless systems constitute the first potential mass market for personal communications. Installing extensive networks of Telepoints in popular places and complementing these with paging and messaging services will ensure users a high-quality and effective service. The relatively low cost of the infrastructure means that call charges will be modest.

In the UK the process of building up Telepoint networks has already begun. By the end of 1990 extensive networks conforming to the CAI will be in place. From this time onwards, as networks are further developed, as the associated domestic and office cordless markets develop, as equipment prices fall and as users become familiar with the Telepoint concept, the service can be expected to gather a tremendous momentum.

4.2 Pointel: A French Perspective
Norbert Soulié

To British readers it may be preposterous to assert that Telepoint is a French idea. They may only know the British Telepoint concept. How is France involved? Why can French interests, and among them manufacturers, claim a bit of paternity on a digital cordless service?

Surprisingly enough, Pointel raised interest in France even before British counterparts sat around a table to specify the Common Air Interface (CAI). In late 1985 engineers at the Centre National d'Etudes des Télécommunications (CNET) were considering the microcellular "communication area" concept which had been proposed by Matra Communication to France Télécom. In November 1986 various papers were presented at the IDATE conference in Montpellier [5] on that subject and the concept was officially presented at the France Télécom stand at Telecom 87 in

Geneva in October 1987. At approximately the same time, the "Mission Lestrade", initiated by the then Minister of Posts and Telecommunications, Gérard Longuet, was prompted to study, amongst other subjects, the potential deregulation of future Telepoint and payphone services. This initiative did not come to fruition however.

In early 1989, press releases were issued by various companies interested in manufacturing Telepoint equipment, as well as by France Télécom. A request for proposals for equipment supply was launched in July 1989 by France Télécom, and around ten offers, some from Franco-British consortia, were made. The intention is to implement a pilot Pointel network during 1990, prior to opening the service on a commercial basis in mid-1991 [6].

4.2.1 Why a CT2 in France?

This question covers two issues: firstly the need for the microcellular service and secondly the choice of standard.

As regards the need for the microcellular service, following the implementation of the Radiocom 2000 cellular radio system various analyses showed that there would still be an unanswered need in France from mid-income professionals and mid-high-income consumers, not only "yuppies". It was also argued that location registers did not need to be updated for outgoing calls provided users were able to initiate an outgoing call at any Telepoint base station, regardless of whether or not they had previously registered on that particular base station.

On the choice of standard, three technical approaches were considered: analogue, Frequency Division Multiple Access (FDMA) and Time Division Multiple Access (TDMA). The analogue one was rejected because neither the French standard nor the CEPT CT1 standard were judged adequate to meet the requirements of high user density anticipated over the next 10 years. The FDMA solution was judged acceptable in terms of density, technology and maturity, but the need for a CAI was a prerequisite before it could be accepted. The TDMA solution was often preferred as more spectrum efficient but was considered more risky and too long-term oriented to fulfil the immediate needs of a network operator. In the end, in spite of a strong international lobby in favour of TDMA, France Télécom decided, for various technical and commercial reasons, to join the CT2 club, or at least to launch an experiment.

Considering initially the technical issues, frequencies allocated to CT2 in England (864–868 MHz) were in France used by the French Army. Between the years 1986 and 1988 all interested parties wondered whether they would ever be released. During 1988, however, the climate changed such that, although no formal announcement had yet been made even by mid-1990, it is now widely expected that these frequencies will be made available for second generation cordless telephony.

In spite of various requests from French manufacturers to join the British CAI group, such discussions only took place during the first half of 1989 as part of the international CAI consultation exercise initiated by the UK Department of Trade and Industry. During this consultation period a study was conducted by CNET experts, the results of which led to some revisions to the CAI.

Finally, various manufacturers had promised assistance to France Télécom in 1987, with various types of proposals and suggestions. Alcatel, Matra Communication and Secré made public at that early stage their interest in implementing microcellular systems.

4.2.2 Pointel Infrastructure Requirements

The Pointel infrastructure asked for by France Télécom is being defined at the time of writing (March 1990); requirements are to be kept confidential by tenderers. However, it is clear from France Télécom that some basic decisions have already been taken, namely that authentication will be centralised and "on-line" and that evolution to ISDN is judged to be very important [6].

New solutions such as smart cards, integration with paging, incoming call transfer, etc., will be welcome. In other terms, although France Télécom had chosen the CT2 concept, there was a will to evolve to upgraded solutions.

At the end of 1989, the solution offering incoming calls (PSTN to Telepoint user) was under close scrutiny – all the more interesting that British manufacturers had not included that service in their initial considerations and perhaps a reflection of the new Personal Communications Network (PCN) concept conceived in early 1989 (see Chapter 10).

The main interest in providing a bi-directional Pointel reflects the possibility of offering a better service. Market surveys in France suggested that outgoing-only Pointels were perceived simply as an enhanced version of public payphones and would thus face competition from payphone cards. They also suggested that bi-directional Pointels would be a threat to hand-portable cellular phones in urban areas if the price differential were sufficient.

Two options were considered: that of combining Pointel with paging and that of implementing a call-rerouting infrastructure.

Many advantages supported the first alternative: miniaturisation of pagers, better coverage of "calling areas" on paging networks and the high autonomy during standby, such that the Pointel handset itself could be turned off, enhancing battery life. However, various problems remain to be solved, notably interfacing the paging to the Pointel handset, delays introduced by the transmission of the paging message and the perceived low probability, at that time, of a common (France–UK at least!) paging system. (It should be noted that such a system is now in hand – Euromessage in the short term and, beyond that, the European Radio Messaging System, ERMES.) The second alternative was favoured by the idea that appropriate infrastructure can in principle support rerouting of incoming calls to the actual Telepoint base station.

At the end of November 1989 the envisaged network solution consisted of the following steps. Firstly, the owner of a handset wishing to receive calls in a specific place issues a specific message (manual registration) informing a Home Location Register (HLR) that he or she can be contacted at that Pointel base station or, even better, at a certain location (e.g. station, exhibition) covered by a group of base stations. The user would be invoiced a certain amount for this service, i.e. the registration facility would be provided as a value-added service. Any call for this person subsequently arrives at the HLR, which reroutes the call to the registered base station. The base station then rings through a specific code for the required handset. It is envisaged that all registration files would be erased regularly, i.e. after 12 or 24 hours or every night at midnight, rather than a de-registration facility being provided.

4.2.3 The French Market: Now and in the Future

So far, the only publicly available data concerning the French CT2 market have been published by Matra Communication [7], assessing an installed base of 2.5 million users, of which 1 million are anticipated in Ile-de-France, after 5 years. These figures include residential, small business and street (Pointel) applications (Fig. 4.2). To reach such figures, the numbers of Pointel base stations proposed were 2000 in Paris, inside the "Boulevard Périphérique", 6000 in the Paris suburbs and 25 000 in the provincial cities.

Most of the attention in France at the time of writing is currently focussed on the French CT2. Indeed France Télécom is a member of the Phonepoint consortium, operators of one of the first Telepoint networks, which was introduced in summer 1989 in the UK. In addition to this, however, France Télecom and some manufacturers continue to work on DECT as members of ETSI RES 3 committee, the French company Alcatel being a signatory to the Memorandum of Understanding between manufacturers strongly supporting DECT. Also, Matra Communication was a participant in the British Aerospace led consortium bid which was successful at the end of 1989 in securing a licence to operate a PCN in the UK. Thus, whilst France is actively establishing a CT2 based Pointel system, it is doing so very much with a view to the evolution of PCNs over the next decade.

As in the UK, French manufacturers are proposing Telepoint/Pointel systems on several continents. Some time in the future we shall see Telepoint services in planes, trains, buses – the Channel tunnel linking France and the UK will have to be equipped, *bien sur*!

Acknowledgements. The author expresses his thanks to France Télécom and CNET, in particular MM Brussol, Maziotto and Veilex, Mrs. G. Wilson and Mr. J. Baker from Orbitel, and ECTEL TCS group members for the continuous exchange of views leading to the present definition of Pointel.

Fig. 4.2. Pointel in use in the street. (Courtesy of Matra Communication.)

4.3 The Views and Plans for Telepoint in Germany
Peter Striebel

4.3.1 The Development of Cordless Telephony in Germany

Until 1985 customers looking for cordless telephones in West Germany could only buy imported, non-approved equipment and connect it, illegally, to their access lines. As these phones had problems with, for example, frequency band, privacy and security, and as the demand for cordless telephony was steadily growing, Deutsche Bundespost – the sole (legal) supplier of telephone sets at that time – asked for cordless telephones which were designed according to CEPT and CCITT recommendations. These phones were to provide 40 channels in the frequency range 914–915/959–960 MHz. Delivery of this apparatus (CT1) started in 1985/1986.

Based on technical experience and on user requirements – one of which was for greater channel capacity on the "Black Friday" of 1987 in the Stock Exchanges – an enhanced version (CT1+) was developed providing for 80 channels and using the frequency band 885–887/930–932 MHz. Distribution of these sets commenced in early 1989.

Type-approved cordless phones were excepted from the Bundespost monopoly from the very beginning, i.e. they are available from Bundespost or from any retailer. The features of these cordless phones comprise memory functions for abbreviated dialling, last number redial facility and (with some) an LCD. Originally it was aimed to provide a modern cordless phone which could replace any ordinary or enhanced phone connected to an exchange, or PABX, line. Some CT1+ manufacturers are now about to introduce base stations which can serve more than one handset, typically up to six, and there are first steps towards wireless PABXs.

4.3.2 The Telepoint Idea

Deutsche Bundepost became aware of the Telepoint subject when licensing discussions for such kinds of service started in the UK in 1988. This led to the basic decision in early 1989 to carry out Telepoint field trials in West Germany. But the tricky question was "Which technique could best meet the requirements of a Telepoint application?"

There is on the one hand the well-tried, reliable but still proprietary CT1+ technology with a high standard of the system-parameters and a double channel-capacity (compared with CT2). This has a disadvantage, though, on the handset side – its size and weight would not encourage people to carry it around for Telepoint applications! On the other hand there is the new CT2 system that uses advanced technology (e.g. digital speech transmission) and has been tailored to Telepoint use from the very beginning (e.g. pocketability of the handset) but carries all the risks accompanying the first generation of a new system.

Deutsche Bundespost TELEKOM was (and is still) of the opinion that neither of these systems is so far ahead of the other that it should focus on one of them only. This led to the decision to run field trials with both systems.

In autumn 1989 the plans for the trials were announced and a call for tenders was published. It is envisaged to implement a CT2 system in Munich, a CT1+ system in Dortmund/Meschede and both systems (CT2 and CT1+), working side by side, in Münster. This gives the opportunity to test two products of both techniques. Each of the four trial systems will include around 150–200 Telepoint channels and up to 2000 handsets.

The bidders submitted their offers to Deutsche Bundespost TELEKOM by mid-January 1990 and field trials are expected to start in autumn 1990.

4.3.3 Market Approach

One of the aims of the field trials, apart from testing how failure-proof and reliable the technical system is, is to find out whether customers are satisfied with the kind of service that will be offered. Deutsche Bundespost TELEKOM wants to take the Telepoint service as it stands at present, i.e. there are no plans for enhancements or add-on features such as the ability to take incoming calls, or even handover facilities. To put it simply, the handsets are, of course, capable of receiving calls, as this is necessary when they are used on home base stations or wireless PABXs, but this capability will not be a feature of (public) Telepoint stations. The slogan is "Keep this system simple", as it is felt that only by doing this will it be possible to address a reasonable market share. The equipment price and service fees (subscription, call charges) will be a decisive factor in the success of the service, and to draw the service features of Telepoint close to those of the cellular telephone service would cause a considerable increase in costs. The price difference would then become too small to segment the market from that of mobile telephones. This factor is particularly important given the future (optimistic) price forecasts for the new GSM cellular telephone equipment and service. That is why Deutsche Bundespost TELEKOM intends to avoid features which will increase the cost of Telepoint handsets or stations and why it plans to apply charges which will be around two-thirds (>100 km) to one-tenth (local) of the call charges of the cellular telephone service.

Deutsche Bundespost TELEKOM hopes that this policy and the economies of scale will help the manufacturers to reduce the equipment price. The size and price of the handsets, a reasonably priced service which is good value, and sufficient availability of areas covered by the service will together determine the success of the Telepoint services. Deutsche Bundespost TELEKOM will do its best to meet these challenges.

4.3.4 Further Steps

If the field trials turn out to be successful in terms of both the technique involved and market acceptance, a basic decision on the general rollout of the Telepoint service will probably be taken in early 1991.

For a regular service Deutsche Bundespost TELEKOM would like to see handsets which are able to operate with smart cards. This would offer many advantages. It would separate registration for the service from a specific piece of equipment – thus the usage of different handsets by the same customer would become possible. The network operator (service provider) could keep full control of the identification modules, thereby avoiding the need to allocate identification numbers to different manufacturers. If the security algorithm were to be broken the handsets could remain unchanged, and just new cards provided. With respect to roaming, smart cards might also be able to operate several authentication and validation procedures adopted by different service providers and, if not, different procedures could probably be supported simply by inserting the appropriate card.

Although there might be a sizeable number of people who would want to decide themselves when to phone, and would therefore accept the lack of an incoming call capability, to others this could be a considerable disadvantage. Deutsche Bundespost TELEKOM thinks that paging could bridge this gap. A first approach could be to have a single charge for those registering for both services – Telepoint and paging. At a later stage designers and manufacturers could provide a single integrated piece of equipment capable of supporting both services.

4.3.5 Conclusion

It is Deutsche Bundespost TELEKOM's opinion that Telepoint will only become a successful service if the requirements stated above are met. There is also another important factor to be considered, that of timescale. If it is not possible to place Telepoint as a widespread and moderately priced service within the next 2 or, at most, 3 years the threat from GSM cellular telephones and perhaps PCNs could prevent any further success. For the same reason it makes no sense to delay the first implementations of Telepoint services until DECT equipment will be available.
Deutsche Bundespost TELEKOM hopes that the 1990 field trials will provide a successful take-off for Telepoint services in West Germany. Its Telepoint service will be called BIRDIE.

4.4 Italy
Wally Tuttlebee

As in France and West Germany, there has been strong interest in Telepoint in Italy and plans for a large-scale experiment during 1990 were reported at the Pan-European Digital Cellular Radio Conference in February 1990 [8]. Trials began in early summer 1990.

The initial Telepoint trials in Italy are expected to involve around 250 base station sites, with each base station supporting four traffic channels. The trial Telepoint system will provide coverage for the cities of Rome and Milan, as well as for the airport and train stations of some dozen or so cities and the main traffic sites along the Rome to Milan motorway route.

The initial experimental networks use two proprietary air interfaces: CEPT CT1 and CT2 (Zonephone). For subsequent commercial service the use of the Common Air Interface (CAI) is envisaged, subject to the availability of the appropriate spectrum between 864 and 868 MHz, in order to support the possibility of international roaming (see Section 4.6 below).

4.5 Finland
Wally Tuttlebee

Surprisingly, perhaps, the second country in the world to implement a Telepoint network, after the UK, was Finland, with the establishment of a trial CT2 system based on proprietary Shaye equipment in September 1989 by the Helsinki Telephone Company (HTC) in collaboration with Nokia Mobile Telephones [9].

The regulatory situation in Finland is somewhat different from that in many European countries, in a way which has encouraged both competition and the usage of radio technology for telephone access. Liberalisation of the market has led to the current situation where there exist over 50 private regional operating companies providing telecommunications infrastructure within mainly the urban areas of the country. In addition, the Finnish PTT provides the national long-distance network, international connection, some local operation and the NMT mobile cellular radio telephone network. Unlike some countries, regulatory restrictions do not preclude the regional companies from using new technologies for connection of customers to the network. This framework has encouraged early experimentation with the Telepoint concept, and indeed with CT2 PABX applications. Thus it is predicted that within 10 years more than 50% of new voice connections into the public network may be wireless [9].

The initial trial Telepoint network established by the HTC used proprietary CT2 technology; this was upgraded to a full commercial service in April 1990. The project began in 1987 with the intention of starting a pilot Telepoint service and also a wireless PABX trial. Having now proved the Telepoint concept, it is anticipated that during 1990 larger Telepoint networks will be established using CAI compatible products. Indeed, the Finnish PTT, PTL-Tele, and the Cooperative Society of Private Telephony Companies in Finland, which represents Finland's 54 privately owned local telephone operators including the HTC, have both issued tenders for Telepoint equipment and both plan to implement nationwide Telepoint networks. PTL-Tele has stated that it hopes to provide service cover for Finland's main cities over the next 3 years.

In due course it is possible that a transition to DECT could occur, although this is likely to depend on how the Telepoint service develops across Europe as a whole.

A more rapid growth of CT2 Telepoint in Finland is anticipated than may occur in the UK, since the CT2 equipment is entering the market at prices comparable to the CEPT standard CT1 telephones currently used there, whilst offering a Telepoint service in addition to the ordinary domestic cordless telephone facility – i.e. additional benefits for a comparable price. (By contrast, domestic analogue cordless telephones in the UK are presently much cheaper than the newer digital CT2 telephones.) Thus an early high growth in market share is predicted for CT2 in Finland.

4.6 The MoU on a Harmonised European Telepoint Service
Wally Tuttlebee

In parallel with the various national developments already outlined in this chapter, discussions were in hand in late 1989 and early 1990 between Telepoint operators, national PTTs and PTOs of several European countries with a view to facilitating the development of a harmonised European Telepoint service based on CAI [10]. These discussions came to fruition on 14 March 1990 with the signing of a Memorandum of Understanding, (MoU) by some 12 Telepoint operators representing six different countries, namely Finland, France, West Germany, Portugal, Spain and the UK [11]. (Further signatories from other European countries, including Belgium, the Netherlands and Italy, have followed in the subsequent months.) The basis of the MoU was the common recognition of a number of factors relating to the current and potential development of Telepoint services in Europe as summarised below.

Firstly, the signatories recognised that Telepoint services were already being introduced in a number of European countries. Harmonisation of standards for these services would prevent the proliferation of incompatible standards in the interim period, prior to the availability of equipment to the emerging DECT standard. Such harmonised standards would also facilitate international roaming. This would require common frequency bands and agreement between operators on key issues such as authentication, billing, etc., and the MoU was seen as providing a mechanism by which such issues could be addressed. The growth of a European Telepoint service was also seen as promoting demand for European paging (reinforcing initiatives in this area) as well as making low-cost mobile communications more widely available to the general public.

The MoU was intended to provide a framework of cooperation such that Telepoint services, to a harmonised CAI, could be introduced in each of the signatory countries by the end of 1990, with a view to widespread service availability (cities, railway stations and airports) by 1993. To this end the signatories agreed to support the adoption of the CAI as an Interim European Telecommunications Standard (ETS) for Telepoint applications and to contribute within ETSI to any necessary standards refinement activities arising from this. At the subsequent ETSI RES meeting in Jersey at the end of March 1990 it was agreed that CAI should become an Interim ETS.[2] This decision coupled with the availability of CAI equipment, such as the GPT and Orbitel products (see Fig. 4.1 and 4.3) is likely to accelerate the introduction of Telepoint services in other European countries in the next couple of years.

---

[2] To be ratified by ETSI in October 1990.

Fig. 4.3. The Orbitel "Contact" CAI cordless telephone. (Courtesy of Orbitel Mobile Communications.)

Initially, the MoU was open for signature by any suitably qualified telecommunications administration, public telecommunications operator or Telepoint operator within any CEPT country; it was anticipated that in the future operators from outside the CEPT area might be invited to become signatories. The signatories assumed the title of the Association of European Telepoint Operators, with the intention of holding regular meetings in order to further the goals of the MoU.

Standardisation on the CAI for European Telepoint carries with it the requirement for access to the specified frequency band, 864–868 MHz, and the various signatories agreed to make attempts to secure availability of this band within their own countries for the Telepoint application by the end of 1990.

All the parties to the MoU also agreed to promote greater public awareness of Telepoint services and in particular to promote services in other countries, once international roaming becomes established. With this in mind, the possibility of some kind of common European-wide logo is under consideration. It was intended that the principles necessary for inter-system roaming should have been agreed by the end of 1990, with a target of implementing a European roaming service in 1992.

References

1. G Vincent, "Telepoint: the way ahead", 1989 Telepoint/CT2 Conference, Communications Educational Courses, London, 12 May 1989

2. G Vincent, "Telepoint and CT2: a new approach to mobile communications", National Communications, Chicago, 1989
3. J Cummings, "The market opportunity for Telepoint systems", Financial Times Conference on Mobile Communications, London, November 1989
4. G MacNamee, S Vadgama, R Gibson, "UMTS – a personal and mobile communications service", ITU COM 1989, 1st World Electronic Media Symposium, Geneva, October 1989
5. IDATE conference, November 1986, Montpellier, France, proceedings documented in bulletin no. 25, Les Services de Futures, published by IDATE
6. M Brussol, "Cordless communications in France", Digital Cordless Communications for Europe, a one-day conference organised by IBC Technical Services, London, June 1989
7. "Telecommunications" (French industry newsletter), published by A Jour, Paris, issue no. 51, 9 February 1989
8. "European implementation plans – Italy", R Failli, 1990 Pan-European Digital Cellular Radio Conference, Rome, February 1990
9. "The Finnish experience", J Alho, 1990 Telepoint/CT2 Conference, Communications Educational Courses, London, 29 January 1990
10. UK Department of Trade and Industry, "Common air interface specification", MPT 1375, London, May 1989 (amended November 1989, February 1990)
11. "Memorandum of Understanding on a harmonised European Telepoint service", Association of European Telepoint Operators, (published in English and French), London, 14 March 1990

CORDLESS TECHNOLOGY

5 Cordless Networks

Andrew Bud

Networks based specifically on cordless telephones are a development of the mid 1980s. At that time, simple cordless telephones, mostly manufactured in the Far East, were flooding into the USA and Europe, satisfying the huge market for cheap domestic telephones the main value of which lay in bringing calls into the garden or bathroom. They had no potential or pretension to offer any functions beyond those of an ordinary wired telephone set.

Yet it had already been recognised that the cordless telephone could also offer real mobility to the user – a service that was already showing its commercial value in the cellular and paging markets. So, as described in Chapter 2, the development of a new generation of cordless systems began. Work on the radio interface between handset and fixed part was complemented by the creation of new kinds of fixed control and switching networks, capable of offering mobility and security. As the 1990s begin, these systems are about to enjoy their first real commercial existence. The value and growth of cordless telephone markets will now increasingly depend upon the power of the networks offered to the customer by equipment suppliers and service operators.

Those familiar with the design of public land mobile cellular systems will recognise many features, albeit in modified form: whilst cordless systems are evolving towards increasingly sophisticated mobile services, they will always differ from cellular networks due to the anarchic and individualistic ways of a handset-controlled system free of central planning, often co-habiting with totally uncoordinated neighbours.

Within this framework many important characteristics of the cordless network are independent of the exact cordless standard used on the air interface. This chapter does not, therefore, dwell at length upon the differences between, for example, CT2 and DECT, although these will be

noted where they are important. It does review the principal types of
cordless telephone networks that exist or are foreseen. Key strategic network
design issues are highlighted and discussed. Finally the relationship with and
implications for the critical process of standards development are reviewed.

5.1 Types of Network

To structure a review of cordless systems it is essential to understand the
different types of network. Networks can be classified by many parameters
– number of lines, area covered and technical performance are examples.
For present purposes, the best way to distinguish between different types
of system is to ask "Who owns the fixed part?". The answer implies a
conveniently clear definition of the services and the technical implementation.
Falling costs and administrative de-regulation are nevertheless blurring even
these boundaries. Using this approach leads to the study of cordless networks
in three main groups:

• Domestic systems: typically owned by individuals or families
• Business systems: owned by work organisations such as companies or
  Government offices
• Telepoints: owned by Public Telecommunications Operators (PTOs)

Each of these systems is now briefly described and its key features
highlighted.

5.1.1 Domestic Networks

It perhaps might sound a little exaggerated to describe the single base station
of a home cordless telephone as a "network". However, any cordless
telephone, particularly a digital system, requires some important network
functions from its fixed part in order to interface correctly to the public
switched telephone network (PSTN), and to offer some basic services to
the user. Even the simple domestic base station must thus include a number
of such features, now reviewed.

Protocol Conversion

Most residential subscriber lines in Europe still rely on simple electrical
techniques for signalling between the subscriber and the PSTN. Pulse
disconnect dialling and ring tones are common. By contrast, modern cordless
telephones communicate such information over the radio channel using
protocols based upon the ISO OSI model.[1] Messaging for processes such

---

[1] See Chapter 7 for a brief explanation of the protocol concepts of the ISO OSI model.

as dialling occur as logical elements at level 3 of the OSI stack (the network layer). Hence the base station of even a simple domestic unit requires the inclusion of a full set of protocol entities, and a protocol conversion to translate between PSTN and digital cordless signalling methods.

Speech Conversion

Modern digital cordless telephones transcode speech for transmission – typically using CCITT standard G.721, an adaptively compressed version of PCM. Since PSTNs use analogue transmission, a decoding function is required in the base station. This is often interfaced to the radio controller, to stop unpleasant effects on the line arising from bursts of noise or reception difficulties.

Newer generations of systems will also require simple echo-cancellation to compensate for longer transmission delays.

Registration

Systems such as CT1, CT2 and DECT associate unique identities with handsets, to prevent unauthorised use of the PSTN line. Many domestic products permit a handset to be "logged-on" to the base, registering its unique identity as a permitted user.

Features

The signalling power of modern digital cordless telephones is such that clever system features can be added to the base station at relatively little extra cost. These include the attachment of multiple handsets to the same number, simulating the case of multiple telephone sets wired in a house. Such an arrangment also usually includes an intercom capability, enabling two users to speak to each other without using a PSTN line. In future, it is likely that such network features of the residential product will be developed until it is virtually indistinguishable from a small office system.

5.1.2 Business Systems

A domestic cordless telephone can of course be used in an office, and indeed this has been particularly common in West Germany. This is not, however, what is really meant by a "business system". Instead the definition applies to a network designed specifically to serve office needs using cordless extensions. In general, business networks have three principal characteristics:

- Several lines of attachment to the public network
- Considerable traffic between internal extensions

● Usage by people who are very often mobile

Normal non-cordless business networks are either key-systems, for small numbers of users, or PABXs for 50–5000 extensions. The main functions of these systems are the switching of calls between extensions, and the management of access by users to the limited number of outside lines.

Cordless business systems must offer these functions and, in addition, the management of mobility, and the problems of security and identification. These aspects are developed in more detail in Section 5.2.

Architecture

A typical larger business network is illustrated in Fig. 5.1. It consists of a number of radio base stations, connected to a centralised switching and management resource.

Each base station provides radio coverage over a restricted area. Within

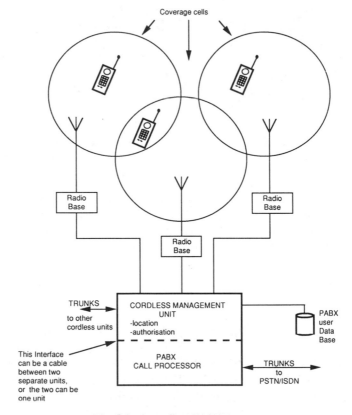

Fig. 5.1. A cordless business system.

this area the base station can offer access to a number of cordless handsets simultaneously, the number being determined by the technology of the system and the number of radio subsystems in the base station. Any handset can gain access to the network via any base station, although privileged areas can be specifically defined in the central management resource. The base stations have high-speed signalling links to the central resource, which manages and supports them.

The central resource needs switching capabilities to make a double association, particularly for incoming calls (see Fig. 5.2). This association can be made in two distinct steps: a standard PABX is used to select an individual subscriber's extension line and a second switching system then routes the call for the subscriber to the correct base station. Such an approach is, however, rather wasteful of costly switching power and is normally adopted to retrofit cordless capabilities to an existing system.

The more cost-effective approach (for new installations) is to integrate the two processes into a single network. A database is required to contain the information relating to this double association and it controls a single call switching network. This database may also contain the information necessary to ensure that a handset is authorised to use the system. Aspects of the management of this database are discussed in Section 5.2.1.

As the use of cordless business systems grows, companies will inevitably seek to provide their employees with access to cordless PABXs on several different sites. This will require the development of methods to exchange information between the databases of the separate PABXs and the signalling systems to support such transactions. These signalling methods will require standardisation. This issue is revisited in Section 5.3.2.

Such issues will also arise as the power of the fixed public network grows and as mobility begins to be offered as a standard feature. This scenario is developed further in Section 5.1.4.

5.1.3 Telepoint

Telepoint is a new service, developing in many different implementations in Europe at the beginning of the 1990s. In principle it is the provision of base stations in public places by PTOs, enabling any subscriber to the service to gain access to the fixed telecommunications network.

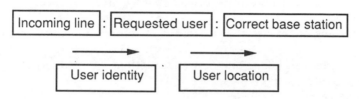

Fig. 5.2. Switching capability requirements for incoming calls in a cordless system.

This service developed first in the UK, driven by pressure from companies who had invested in the CT2 standard. For regulatory and political reasons, such services developed independently of the operators of wired and mobile cellular networks, and therefore did not have favoured access to their existing network resources. The services were also developed by private companies, whose access to capital required a cautious, low investment approach to the development of the new networks.

Such considerations defined the character and topology of the UK Telepoint networks. In other countries, such as France and Italy, the development of the Telepoint network is more closely integrated with existing network resources, and different technical strategies have been adopted.

Early Telepoint in the UK

In the UK, four companies have been licensed to offer Telepoint services. The service they offer has initially been limited by the licence to outgoing calls only (that is, calls originated by the owner of the cordless handset). The service they require from the PSTN is limited to the rental of business subscriber lines on normal terms and their initial investment in network support, other than the base stations, consists only of billing and administration facilities. The large investments in central support and the advanced use of the network required to offer two-way, fully mobile calling remain to be developed.

The network structure is shown in Fig. 5.3. In the early 1990s each network operator expects to install several tens of thousands of bases. Each base is connected to between one and ten PSTN lines.

The base stations include the following general functions:

- Support for the radio connections
- Authentication of a handset, autonomously
- Collection of billing information
- Downline loading of billing information to the network centre upon request
- Management of data on fraudulent handsets
- Reporting of traffic, fault and maintenance information

The network management centre includes the following functions:

- Polling of base stations to collect billing, maintenance and traffic information
- Downloading to base stations of current information about fraudulent users
- Administration of billing and new subscriptions
- Other security functions

The operation of such a Telepoint network is somewhat similar to that

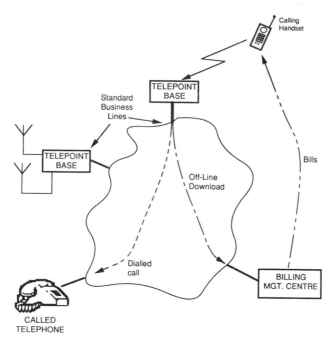

Fig. 5.3. UK Telepoint structure (1990).

of a credit or debit-card point-of-sale system using smart cards. When a subscriber wishes to make a call, a radio link is established over which the subscriber identifies himself, and the base station locally authenticates this identity. The subscriber then makes a call, effectively buying network units, the cost of which is measured in the base station. The billing information for a day's traffic is stored in the base station and later downloaded in bulk to the billing and management centre. There are very many ways to operate a Telepoint network, and to implement authentication and security functions. These are further discussed in Section 5.2.2.

One peculiarity of the UK situation is the presence of multiple competing operators. This has three principal implications:

- The radio system must be adequately robust to enable independent co-located base stations to operate without serious degradation of service
- The signalling system must enable arbitration between call set-up attempts heard by all operators but destined either for only one or, in the limit, for all
- The network architecture and information flows must permit roaming, that is, the use of the base stations of one operator by a subscriber of another operator when necessary. This has proved to be particularly difficult commercially and for security management

Such issues will be faced more widely with the development of Open Access Networks (Section 5.1.4).

Development of Telepoint

With the signature of a Memorandum of Understanding in March 1990, many European PTOs committed themselves to building Telepoint networks. Each such network will have different characteristics.

The Pointel network in France, for example, is intended to integrate full two-way calling, by means of central location databases and on-line authentication. In Italy network development is based on the structure of the existing public payphone credit-card network. In Germany there is a notable emphasis on the use of separate subscriber identity security modules. These national variations reflect different approaches to the issues discussed in more depth in Section 5.2 and will be subject to the rapid evolution characteristic of the mobile communications field.

A further development which is probable is the use of cellular networks as support for Telepoint base stations. Clear applications are the Telepoint in a train or on a boat. A number of technical issues arise, relating to the mapping of identities between the cellular and Telepoint networks. These are clearly resolvable and such development is expected in the near future.

5.1.4 Open Access Networks

The evolution of Telepoint and networked cordless PABXs and the development of intelligence in the fixed public network seem likely to converge on the creation of new Open Access Networks. These will have the form illustrated in Fig. 5.4.

The main feature of such networks will be that any subscriber will be able to access the fixed network via almost any base station, public or private. Base stations usable via Open Access may belong to a huge range of commercial entities, including PTOs, employers, third-party PABX owners and even owners of domestic cordless telephone bases. By connecting such otherwise private installations into an intelligent wide-area network, the network operator will be able to offer coverage and access far beyond anything envisaged for Telepoint, with very limited investment. Services may range from simple one-way Telepoint to full two-way calling.

Such a development is widely anticipated, and has been taken into account in the design of recent European cordless standards. In fact, it represents more of a commercial and regulatory change than a technical revolution, although there are certain technical prerequisites. These are:

- The existence of cordless air interface protocols which support the signalling and authentication needs of such a service
- The existence of authentication mechanisms flexible and secure enough

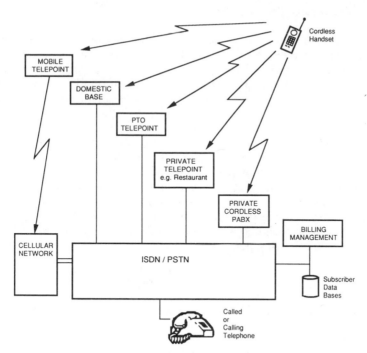

Fig. 5.4. Open Access Network.

to support the presence of perhaps thousands of different service providers, the majority of whom are private

- The development of a common signalling protocol for the communication of mobility and billing information between different local cordless networks

- The diffusion of ISDN or other digital means by which private systems can connect and signal to a wide-area intelligent network

Such issues are topics of active study in Europe.

The result of Open Access is likely to be that, in the medium term, the functional differences that initially distinguished the various types of network will fade, whilst the issues reviewed in Section 5.2 will become of ever more general importance.

As noted, the development of such networks will, leaving technical factors aside, depend upon the willingness of operators to invest in the central network control, and on the position of the regulatory authorities who have the responsibility to licence such services.

5.1.5 Advanced Private Networks

The development of cordless networks is taking place in the same time frame as the introduction of ISDN and the diffusion of networked personal computing in business. These trends will force the progress of cordless telephones to incorporate data carriage facilities of rapidly increasing power. Chapter 8 deals with the transmission aspects of such performance in more detail.

The advent of such powerful cordless multi-media standards will lead to the development of networked computing environments in which the client/server relationship takes account of the fact that the user terminal may be mobile and perhaps pocketable. Since many functions of a cordless portable network, such as authentication, are to be found in existing data networks based on constrained open media such as Ethernet, a very close integration may become possible. In the first instance, however, the use of cordless telephone technology simply to provide user-to-network bridges is a most probable development.

5.2 Network Functional Issues

Having discussed the character of specific kinds of cordless networks, we now go on to look at key issues that affect the design of almost any advanced cordless network. These are:

- The management of mobility
- Authentication and security

5.2.1 Mobility Management

The management of mobility needs to be considered at two levels in a cordless network: servicing incoming calls and offering in-call mobility.

Incoming Calls

There are several ways in which incoming calls can be serviced by a cordless network, depending on the network size and architecture.

Small Networks. In a small network, the number of cells and the rate of incoming call alerts is low enough to permit paging of a handset in all cells using the cordless paging mechanism. No modern cordless system incorporates a specific channel for paging, so such a paging mechanism consists of transmitting the handset identity for a finite period of time on a channel to which the handset could reasonably be expected to listen. If entirely random, this process would require power-consuming attention from the handset and would occupy significant system capacity. For this reason systems such as DECT define a low duty-cycle schedule over which a particular handset may be paged. Such a page must, however, always be transmitted in all cells, in the absence of some location mechanism. In large systems this becomes impracticable.

Medium Networks. In a medium-sized network, some form of location registration must take place. This means that a central data base holds the current location of the user and by reference to this database incoming calls can be directed to the appropriate zone. The location registration procedure is a high-level protocol function, which can take place either manually, periodically or automatically.

Manual registration implies that the users must take the initiative actively to inform the network of their whereabouts. It simplifies both network and handset. It is most suitable in systems with discontinuous, clearly defined cells such as isolated Telepoints.

Periodic registration means that the handset automatically connects to the network and notifies its presence at pre-defined, regular intervals. This has the virtue of simplicity but can lead to waste of precious battery power and system spectrum, and generates unnecessary network traffic if the handset is largely immobile.

The most sophisticated solution is automatic registration, by which the handset periodically awakes, listens to network broadcasts in order to determine its location, and, if its location has changed, connects to and notifies the network. Such a solution requires a base station broadcast beacon; these beacons cannot occupy a specific or fixed channel in a cordless environment. This feature is present in a sophisticated, standardised form in DECT but is less readily implemented with CT1 and CT2.

Some flexibility can be added to the system by optimising the registration zones, which can consist of one or more cells. The choice will be determined by a trade-off: small zones cause extra registration signalling traffic, whilst large zones lead to redundant paging traffic across the zone.

Large Networks. Large networks, such as Open Access Networks, with very large numbers of subscribers, could be faced with an enormous amount of location registration traffic originating from a huge coverage area and many small cells. Such a network will have to fall back upon manual registration, or else use a more sophisticated approach.

One such approach is the hierarchical structuring of location databases. Thus the frequent location updates are confined to local databases, with centralised databases informed only of less frequent changes of zone.

A more innovative method, proposed by the InTouch PCN consortium, uses separate networks for alerting and call carriage, optimising each independently. Alerting is performed using a wide-area paging technique, operating with 200 km cells in the VHF band. When a handset receives an alert, it automatically registers on the nearest accessible cordless base station, completing the connection before actively alerting the user. With this approach, incoming calls are converted to outgoing calls and registration traffic is practically eliminated, as is most of the mobility management infrastructure.

Initiatives in this direction date from the beginning of UK Telepoint operations, with the combination of pagers and CT2 handsets. Due to the lack of network switching power and the limited coverage of Telepoint, such a service relies upon manual response to a pager alert.

Multiple Mobile Networks. Some special care has to be taken in the structuring of mobility services that rely upon more than one mobile network. An example would be a mobile Telepoint, based upon a cellular infrastructure such as GSM. Poor partitioning of databases or mapping of identities, for example, can lead to an intolerable increase in overhead signalling on one or other of the networks.

Roaming. Roaming implies an administrative or commercial separation between the network with which the subscriber is enrolled and the network by which an in-coming call may be delivered. Delicate commercial issues arise regarding such questions as:

• In which network is the user's current location registered?
• On what terms does the visited network maintain the location register or forward location-registration messages?
• Should a customer be informed that s/he has roamed and is registered on a costlier network?

The chief technical issue is the need for an agreed inter-operator mobility signalling protocol, an issue discussed further in Section 5.3.2.

In-Call Mobility

Since a cordless telephone is a low-power, low-range device, coverage radii of more than 50–200 m are normally impracticable; within some buildings the cells may be much smaller. Thus a conversation initiated in one cell may continue into another if the user walks around. Indeed, coverage patterns inside a building can be such that cells may actually interleave over a distance of a few metres. In these circumstances it is desirable to have some facility to hand the call over from cell to cell during the call.

The implementation of such a facility differs between standards. DECT and DCT900, for instance, have low-level radio protocols that make the process very rapid and clean. CT2 and CT1 have no such provision and the process is therefore more complex, if implemented.

The process is normally initiated and controlled by the handset, which autonomously chooses the base station onto which to hand over. With a

TDMA system such as DECT, it is possible to establish a connection to the new base before closing down the connection to the old one, ensuring almost seamless handover. Such a process calls for very careful design of the fixed network, however, since the presence of two separate protocol links to the same end-point, routing via different paths, has very significant implications.

In order for the process to be fast, the handset must also be able to recognise very rapidly a base station belonging to the same system. This implies the need for an effective identity structure.

5.2.2 Authentication

The issue of authentication of handsets, which originally arose in the context of Telepoint, is now recognised to be of equal importance for all other systems as well. The problem may be summarised as being the prevention of unauthorised handset owners stealing telephone time and, in particular, setting up a call in the first place.

Threats

The need for secure authentication of cordless telephones must be stressed. In a Telepoint network, a fraudulent user cannot merely steal large amounts of costly telephone time, but can also cause commercial difficulties through the appearance of false transactions on the bills of honest users. Cordless PABXs also have a definite need, since their location and coverage areas can make it easy for a thief to make unobserved calls. Residential users too may discover a growing need as cordless systems become more widespread.

Whilst the very complexity of even unauthenticated formats, protocols and handshakes over the air interface might seem to make modern cordless systems quite secure, this is in reality an illusion. These protocols are all publicly available as national or European standards. It therefore requires no secret knowledge for a bright hacker to build and sell a microprocessor-controlled gadget capable of listening to the transmissions of others and either masquerading as a genuine user or waiting for a genuine call set-up and then simply stealing the channel by broadcasting with greater power. Such gadgets could diffuse quickly and cause real chaos.

Such attacks are repelled relatively easily by the authentication techniques described below. More difficult to protect is secret authentication knowledge stored in base stations, since there may be many hundreds of thousands of bases distributed throughout a nation or continent, in the hands not just of network operators but of private site-owners or PABX owners. Methods of dealing with such threats will be discussed below, but ultimately a judgement is required balancing security against cost. Each operator has a different point of view.

Authentication Techniques

The general approach to the authentication of cordless handsets is the challenge and response technique. The base station issues a random number over the radio interface to the handset; the handset uses this to calculate a response which is also based upon its own identity and some secret information known only to the network operator. The network operator can also calculate what the response should be and can therefore check the validity of the handset response. This process is illustrated in Fig. 5.5. The notable differences arise in the method by which the handset generates the response from the challenge and the way that the network verifies the authenticity of the response.

In systems based upon extensive telecommunications networks, typically owned by major network operators, the validating calculation (#2) within the network can be carried out at some central point, such as a telephone exchange, which is well protected and secure. This means that the secret data (which may be a key or a process) do not need to be distributed too widely. However, several messages have to pass rapidly across the network simply to set up a call and these have an implicit or explicit cost. Central databases capable of fast transaction handling are also required. Such "on-line" authentication techniques are typical of the systems installed by the major PTOs in France and West Germany.

In the UK, the Telepoint operators' licence defines a strictly arms-length relationship with the fixed network operators. Telepoint base stations initially have had to use normal dial-up business telephone lines, with standard tariffs, since the use of leased lines has not been economic. The delay and cost involved in dialling-up a central database for each call would be unacceptable and so an "off-line" approach to authentication has been adopted.

The "off-line" approach involves performing the validating calculation (#2) in the Telepoint base station. The base station must therefore be proof against tampering and the secret data (typically an encryption function) must not be accessible. The off-line approach also presents difficulties in

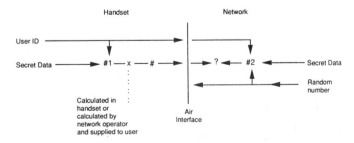

Fig. 5.5. Calculation of authentication information.

the implementation of roaming, since each operator would like to have different secret data.

Off-line operators also have to take precautions against the customer who is in default or has been struck off the system for some other reason. Blacklists of unauthorised customers are downloaded regularly by the network centre to the base stations. In some systems, a ZAP function is implemented. This recognises when a blacklisted customer attempts to gain access and sends a command to the handset which effectively suspends or destroys the subscription number. This reduces the network load caused by bad debts.

Handset Aspects

Two principal approaches are used for the calculation #1 (Fig. 5.5). In UK Telepoint, the calculation is carried out by the network operator, and the result is sent by post to the user. The user must then type the number into the handset, in which it is stored permanently. This number is strictly related to the user ID. In the case of UK CT2 this is the manufacturer's serial number, so the number is related to the equipment. (DECT has a different and more flexible ID structure.) In order to avoid unauthorised use of the handset, therefore, a Personal Identification Number (PIN), has been incorporated by some operators into the validation process, whereby the user has to type in the 4-digit number each time a call is made.

The other approach is based on intelligent identity modules such as smart cards or Telephone Identity Modules (TIMs). These are small, usually detachable units containing microprocessors sealed in plastic. The calculation #1 is carried out in real time within the module, which also contains the subscriber information and the secret data. The advantage of this approach is that both the identity and the validity of the subscriber are contained in a cheap, portable, ultra-secure unit which is separate from the handset. Validation comes much closer to the *owner*. The problems of subscriber billing and authentication are therefore totally decoupled from the manufacture and distribution of telephones. The subscriber can potentially use his identity elsewhere in the network, on other apparatus; authentication functions do not have to be provided to handset manufacturers, thus increasing security. The disadvantage is that the cost of the handset is significantly increased by having to include a robust module reader. Countries such as France and West Germany are inclined towards the use of this technique.

5.3 Standards Implications of Network Aspects

The development of cordless networks is closely associated with the development of standards for these networks. These standards can apply to the air interface or to the fixed network.

5.3.1 Air Interface Signalling

In the design of air interface signalling standards, a difficult trade-off must be made between three main factors which affect the cordless system as a whole:

- Openness
- Flexibility
- Complexity

These factors are important in any telecommunications system; they are of special relevance to European cordless systems, where the objective has always been to enable handsets to be used on different networks at home, in the office and in the street, and where for national reasons those networks may differ enormously in their constraints and requirements.

Openness relates to the compatibility between a handset from one manufacturer and a network supplied by another; clearly, the customer will get better service with greater reliability if many features are specified explicitly and tightly in a standard. This is of particular interest to those promoting open markets for telecommunications equipment and to operators of public networks who wish to see the largest population of compatible handsets.

Flexibility is the degree to which the standard permits the effective implementation of fixed networks with different architectures, implementation and features. There is always a close relationship between the architecture of a protocol and that of the network it was designed to serve. A signalling structure which has been shrink-wrapped onto an implicit network topology and service set will be inflexible, and will not work very effectively with a different one. Manufacturers tend to favour flexible standards.

Complexity is the price paid to introduce flexibility into a fully specified open system. By introducing enough options, choices and set-up parameters, a wide range of networks can be served. Unfortunately, such complexity directly affects handset cost and weight, since it is the handset that must adapt to any network. Fortunately the impact of complexity is declining as processing power and memory plummet in cost.

The two major digital standards in Europe, CT2-CAI and DECT, provide an interesting study in these trade-offs. Judgements are difficult and necessarily subjective, but taking together the signalling protocol and the application which controls it, CT2-CAI tends to trade openness for flexibility while DECT places more emphasis on openness across the range of applications and is consequently somewhat more complex.

In the European cordless field, such trade-offs are in reality determined as much by political constraints as by market factors.

5.3.2 Other Network Standards

As was noted earlier, islands of cordless mobility such as cordless PABXs or Telepoints can be connected only if there are standards for communication of cordless mobility information between them. Such information includes location registration, authentication and handover information. These standards are related to but quite separate from those of the cordless air interface.

At present there are two major standardised digital signalling systems in Europe for communication between digital switches. One is the CCITT Signalling System No. 7 (SS7), used in public integrated digital networks. The other is DPNSS, a standard used for communication between PABXs in the UK. Another standard for inter-PABX signalling, based on the ISDN standard Q.931, is due to be standardised by ECMA and adopted throughout Europe.

Signalling System No.7

A standard for the communication of mobility information exists for SS7. This was designed as part of the GSM development of Pan-European Digital Cellular Radio and is known as MAP (Mobile Application Part). CCITT is now working on a similar standard known as MSAP.

Unfortunately, MAP is not ideal for cordless systems, since it is based on cellular requirements. For example, inter-cell handovers are assumed by MAP to be managed by the network, whereas in cordless systems the handset manages the process. However, it provides a basis from which a cordless mobility signalling standard could certainly evolve. Such a development will be of particular interest to Telepoint and Open Access Network operators.

Private Networks

At the time of writing, there is no accepted Europe-wide inter-PABX signalling standard analogous to SS7, so there has been no platform upon which to construct a private network MAP. Consequently, two branches of action are evolving.

A short-term approach proposed by some manufacturers involves the use, with slight modifications, of existing features in DPNSS and other proprietary signalling standards. Such features include call forwarding and call transfer. When activated from third extensions, these become effective means of routing incoming calls within a cordless network. Developing standards for Computer-Integrated Telephony (CIT, a means of controlling PABX functions by a separate computer) are also being looked at for their suitability as a provisional solution.

A number of standards bodies in Europe are beginning to recognise that in the longer term, however, inter-PABX signalling must acquire explicit mobility signalling elements. Some private studies of such functions for DPNSS are in progress, but the definition of application parts for Q.931 is perhaps of greater importance and is not yet under way.

5.4 Summary

This chapter has offered an introduction to some of the principal network issues raised in the specification and design of cordless telecommunication systems and networks in Europe. It described the continuum that exists between the simplest cordless telephone set and the Open Access Network, and showed that the network is becoming the key component in the development of cordless personal telephony.

Many early customers for cordless networks will not initially dream of multi-cell mobility, inter-system roaming and Open Access. But the capabilities of the standards now emerging in Europe should ensure that their investment in handset hardware will continue to serve them well when such features come to be viewed as basic necessities. As this chapter should have intimated, as progress on intelligent networks chases developments in European cordless communications, that day is not far off.

References

Since the technology of cordless networks is so new and has been spawned almost entirely in the development laboratories of private industry, there are at the time of writing very few detailed technical references in the public domain. Some public references are listed below.

1. Specifications of CT2-CAI layer 3 may be found in the MPT 1375 specification from the Department of Trade and Industry, London, UK
2. Specifications of DECT layer 3 may be found in the proceedings of ETSI Technical Sub-Committee RES 3 and its output document "DECT common interface specification"
3. A detailed description of the DECT network and signalling aspects will be found in the proceedings of the Fourth Nordic Seminar on Mobile Radio (DMRIV), Oslo, June 1990: "System and network aspects of DECT", A Bud, Olivetti Systems & Networks, Italy
4. A description of a business cordless system is to be found in the proceedings of the conference Digital Cordless Telephones and PCN, London, May 1990, organised by Blenheim Online: "Adding cordless capability to existing PABXs", M Ward, GEC Plessey Telecommunications, UK
5. A description of a UK Telepoint network is to be found in the proceedings of the conference Digital Cordless Telephones, London, September 1988, organised by IBC Technical Services: "The future with phonezones", H Bibby, Ferranti Creditphone

6. Background on Open Access Networks may be found in numerous papers published by Cox et al., Bell Laboratories/Bellcore, in the years 1984–1990.

6 Audio Aspects

Dag Åkerberg and Julian Trinder

Cordless telephones use radio to provide the telephone user with the benefit of mobility. Conventionally, users of mobile radio have tolerated the poor speech quality often associated with an analogue radio channel. However, to today's consumer the cordless telephone is viewed simply as another telephone and the same high speech quality associated with the fixed telephone network is expected. This chapter on audio aspects considers the requirements for, and outlines the approaches adopted in, the provision of good speech quality. It addresses in particular the special requirements arising in a Private Automatic Branch Exchange (PABX) environment and/or over local, national and international Public Switched Telephone Networks (PSTNs) when one or both telephones use digital cordless rather than wired links.

Digital speech and transmission, compared with analogue, provides constant levels, less noise, more delay and requires a higher transmission bandwidth. The distortion is partly of another kind: quantisation distortion. Thus traditional methods for evaluating the link quality are not completely satisfactory for digital speech links and new methods are under development within standardisation bodies. The latter problem is emphasised when it comes to the evaluation of speech coding techniques suitable for radio transmission. For example, compliance with a frequency response mask requirement can have limited correlation to good results in a subjective perception test in a radio environment. The choice of speech coding method and evaluation of its performance, including transmission over a varying radio channel, is a complex task with no "right" answers, although a convergence towards 32 kbit/s Adaptive Differential Pulse Code Modulation (ADPCM) is apparent at the present time, being the standard for the CT2 CAI and emerging DECT specifications.

For mobile radios a subjective speech quality lower than that for wired telephones has been accepted to date as the price of mobility. For modern digital cordless telephone systems the requirements are higher. The cordless handset is designed to be the only or prime telephone used. Thus the subjective quality under adequate radio conditions should ideally be on a par with that of wired apparatus. Other main requirements for speech coding for cordless systems with lightweight handsets are low cost, low current consumption, effective use of the limited radio spectrum and low delay. Generally a more frequency-efficient coding technique is more complex, needs more processing power, has more delay and lower quality. Delay and/or lower quality can be improved by higher complexity. The different schemes for digital speech coding which have been used or proposed for cordless telephony are reviewed in Section 6.1.

In telephony a voice transmission plan is used to specify acoustic and electrical levels and limits, and other network characteristics, in such a way that correct audio levels are received at the handset and that quality degradation due to distortion, noise, echoes and delay is kept under control. The quality depends very much upon the transmission network. Analogue two-wire networks, especially older ones, have large variations in attenuation, delay and audio characteristics, while modern digital four-wire networks are much more tightly defined. The transmission plans for modern cordless telecommunications systems are based on well-defined digital transmission. From this base, modifications can be made to fit analogue network specifications, which presently are not uniform across Europe. The voice transmission plan requirements for cordless systems are discussed in Section 6.2.

Networks for ordinary telephony are recommended to contain a means of echo control when the (one-way) delay exceeds a certain limit (25 ms). For example, international gateways are equipped with echo control devices when satellite links, which introduce long delays, are used. Modern cordless telephone systems introduce additional delays compared with an analogue, or digital, telephone. The radio multiple access method and/or the duplex operation uses time division, which introduces delay, and the digital speech coding method contributes further delay. The cordless system has to be specified, including possible internal echo control means if needed, so that this extra delay does not violate correct operation of the echo control at international gateways, or otherwise significantly reduce the subjective speech performance. These issues of delay and echo control are discussed in Section 6.3.

Finally voice security and speech encryption are discussed briefly in Section 6.4.

The topics treated in this chapter are intimately related and the requirements and solutions are dependent upon existing standards, standards work in progress, technological possibilities and the constraints of the existing older and modern networks. The aim of the chapter is to give a broad understanding of the basic principles and how to apply them. For further details or more exact definitions the reader should consult the references.

6.1 Voice Coding

The evolution of the telecommunications industry has been shaped by a great number of market pressures, of which perhaps the most paradoxical is the pronounced affinity for voice communications, despite an extensive range of alternative telecommunications services. To meet the diversity of market demands, technology is increasingly moving towards digital transmission for all kinds of services. Digital format can offer rugged and reliable communications despite complex network routing without fear of signal degradation within or between the network nodes. In order to integrate improved telephony services within the newly evolving digital telecommunications industry, great emphasis has been given to the digital representation of the voice signal, which has hitherto largely been handled in its analogue form.

Within the telephone unit the microphone and pre-amplifier circuits form a continuous linear electrical analogue of the incident sound pressure. The function of the voice coder is to convert the continuous analogue signal into a discrete digital representation suitable for digital transmission. At the remote location a complementary voice decoder regenerates the continuous electrical analogue signal, which can then be amplified and converted back to a sound pressure wave by a linear acoustic transducer.

The complementary coder–decoder pair is often referred to as a codec. Within each digital telephone unit the codec device usually handles two different signals: the coder handles the outgoing voice signal and the decoder handles the incoming voice signal. Depending on the type of codec and the signal characteristics, the two parts of the codec may at any one time be performing dissimilar and non-complementary signal processing functions. In a full-duplex telephone link the true codecs, which perform the complementary signal processing functions, are in fact divided between the two ends of the link.

Voice coding techniques for radio-based telephony (cordless and cellular) divide into two main groups: waveform coding and parametric coding. The principle of waveform coding is to reproduce as closely as possible the waveform of the continuous sound pressure analogue. It can be argued that since the human hearing mechanism is largely insensitive to waveform details and responds chiefly to short-term power spectra, waveform coding conveys a great deal of redundant information. Parametric coding on the other hand is designed to convey sufficient parameters of the voice signal such that at the remote location a waveform can be reconstructed the short-term spectral characteristics of which closely match those of the incident signal. Significant savings in information rate can be made by using parametric coding rather than waveform coding, whilst still preserving excellent speech intelligibility and subjective quality. Examples of waveform coding are Pulse Code Modulation (PCM) and Delta Modulation (DM). Examples of parametric coding are Linear Predictive Coding (LPC) and its many variants.

The principles underlying some of the more popular voice coders will be outlined below. We start by describing PCM in some detail, since this is the staple digital voice coding scheme employed in the fixed PSTN; it also forms the basis for an explanation of Adaptive Differential PCM (ADPCM), the emerging standard for cordless telephony (CT2 and DECT). We then discuss DM, a fundamentally simpler form of speech coding which has been used in one of the first commercial digital cordless telephone products.

The DECT specification leaves an option for the addition of a second, more frequency-efficient codec, when such becomes technically and commercially available. Parametric coding is likely to be used in this future codec. Some discussion of parametric coding, exemplified in the form of LPC, is therefore also included within this section. Finally the issues of assessment of speech quality and the (non-)requirement for channel coding of the speech data are addressed.

6.1.1 Pulse Code Modulation, PCM

PCM coding is a method of waveform coding that can represent any band-limited analogue waveform to a specified precision in digital format [1]. The waveform is sampled at a uniform rate at least twice that of the highest frequency component in the waveform to be coded. Each sample is then quantised to the nearest level against a series of uniform steps. Each step is assigned a unique digital code, usually binary. The PCM digital format is a series of such codes which define the sequence of levels selected by the quantiser at each sample in time. The decoder simply reconstructs each waveform sample on the basis of the digital codes received and then band-limits the result to half the sampling rate in order to recover the analogue waveform.

A useful figure of merit for PCM coders is the Signal-to-Quantising-Error Ratio (SQER), which is the ratio of the root-mean-square (RMS) of the signal to the RMS of the quantising error. It differs from Signal-to-Noise Ratio (SNR) in that the quantising error is a function of the signal itself, and is absent when the signal is zero.

If the range of the signal values to be represented is $\{+A$ to $-A\}$, optimal quantisation in uniform steps to α bits yields a resolution of

$$q = \frac{2A}{2^\alpha}$$

If the quantiser operates by mapping each signal component to the nearest quantum level, the quantisation error function (ξ) will have a uniform distribution over the range

$$-\frac{q}{2} \leqslant \xi \leqslant \frac{q}{2}$$

with probability density function

$$P(\xi) = \frac{1}{q}$$

Accordingly the mean quantising error power is

$$(\xi_{rms})^2 = \int_{-\frac{q}{2}}^{\frac{q}{2}} \xi^2 \cdot P(\xi) \cdot d\xi = \frac{q^2}{12}$$

so that

$$\xi_{rms} = \frac{q}{2\sqrt{3}} = \frac{A}{2^\alpha \sqrt{3}}$$

Thus the Signal-to-Quantising-Error Ratio in decibels (dB) is given by

$$SQER_{dB} = 20 \cdot \log_{10} \left(\frac{\Sigma_{rms}}{\xi_{rms}} \right)$$

where

$$(\Sigma_{rms})^2 = \frac{1}{T} \int_0^T S(t)^2 \, dt$$

For the voice signal it is normal to allow for $A = 4\Sigma_{rms}$ to avoid excessive clipping (probability $< 10^{-4}$). Substitution in the above equations thus yields a value of $SQER_{dB} = 6.02\ \alpha - 7.27$ dB. The quantisation error has uniform (non-Gaussian) distribution characteristics, is roughly white in spectrum and is correlated to the main signal. A PCM codec with range A, well matched to the optimum value of $A = 4\Sigma_{rms}$ and $\alpha = 11$, will thus have an SQER value of 59 dB. This is generally felt to be adequate precision for reasonable voice quality. For a 4 kHz bandwidth the sampling rate needs to be 8 kHz, which would imply a bit-rate of 88 kbit/s.

There are two main problems with linear-PCM as described above. Firstly it requires high bit-rates to achieve adequate precision, and secondly the peak signal level needs to be carefully matched to the quantiser input range to avoid excessive clipping or poor resolution. Both of these problems are overcome in a refinement of PCM, log-PCM, which is described below.

Log-PCM exploits the fact that the large peaks in the voice signal are generally infrequent and have short duration. Increasing the quantisation for large signals therefore does not have a significant effect on perceived quality. Smith [2] has shown that using non-uniform quantisation the performance of 11-bit linear-PCM can be approached with only 7-bit resolution. Practical telephony systems usually standardise on 8-bit log-PCM at a sampling rate of 8 kHz (64 kbit/s), which is roughly equivalent to 12-bit linear-PCM (96 kbit/s).

Another variant of log-PCM is A-law PCM, in which the central region of the logarithmic function is approximated by a linear section.

6.1.2 Adaptive Differential PCM, ADPCM

In seeking to understand ADPCM, we firstly discuss ordinary (non-adaptive) differential PCM. These topics are reviewed in greater depth in [3].

In differential PCM the correlation between successive samples of the voice signal is exploited. The main effect of this positive correlation is a reduction in the variance $\langle \cdot \rangle$ of the first difference between samples. Since the variance is reduced fewer bits are needed to code the first difference than would be required to code the raw sample, thus facilitating a lower bit-rate. The quantisation of the first difference may be either linear-PCM or log-PCM.

If $X(r)$ represents the signal sample value and $D_1(r)$ the first difference, i.e. $X(r) - X(r-1)$, this reduction in variance may be easily derived, since

$$\langle D_1^2(r) \rangle = \langle [X(r) - X(r-1)]^2 \rangle$$
$$= \langle X(r)^2 \rangle + \langle X(r-1)^2 \rangle - 2\langle X(r) \cdot X(r-1) \rangle$$

i.e.

$$\langle D_1^2(r) \rangle = 2(1 - C_1)\langle X(r)^2 \rangle$$

Hence the variance of the first difference between samples is less than the variance of the raw samples when the first correlation (C_1) is greater than 0.5. The variance would actually increase for a first correlation (C_1) of less than 0.5.

This restriction on first correlation (C_1) range can be lifted if a weighted difference is taken:

$$D_1(r,a_1) = X(r) - a_1 \cdot X(r-1)$$

gives

$$\langle D_1^2(r,a_1) \rangle = \langle [X(r) - a_1 \cdot X(r-1)]^2 \rangle$$

i.e.

$$\langle D_1^2(r,a_1) \rangle = \langle X(r)^2 \rangle (1 + a_1^2 - 2a_1 \cdot C_1)$$

Differentiating the variance factor by a_1 yields a minimum for $2a_1 - 2C_1 = 0$:

$$\langle D_1^2(r) \rangle_{min} = \langle X(r)^2 \rangle (1 - C_1^2)$$

The principle of weighted differences can be extended to exploit higher-order correlations:

$$D_n(r,a_1,a_2,\ldots,a_n) = X(r) - \sum_{i=1}^{n} a_i X(r-1)$$

It can be shown [3] that the variance $\langle D_n^2(r,a_1,a_2,\ldots,a_n) \rangle$ is minimised for

$$[A] = [\Gamma]^{-1}[\Sigma]$$

where

$$[A] = [a_1,a_2,\ldots,a_n]^T$$

and

$$[\Sigma] = [C_1, C_2, \ldots, C_n]^T$$

and

$$[\Gamma] = \begin{vmatrix} 1, C_1, C_2, \ldots, C_{n-1} \\ C_1, 1, C_1, \ldots, C_{n-2} \\ C_2, C_1, 1, \ldots, C_{n-3} \\ \cdots \\ \cdots \\ C_{n-1}, C_{n-2}, \ldots, C_1, 1 \end{vmatrix}$$

Because the correlation matrix $[\Gamma]$ is symmetric, it can be inverted by triangular decomposition, using various recursion algorithm techniques. Alternatively gradient algorithms can be used to obtain the weight vector $[A]$ directly.

The optimum linear combination of previous samples for the weighted difference will vary with the correlation matrix of the voice signal. It is therefore important to update the matrix regularly in order to achieve minimum variance in the signal being presented to the quantiser. Such a scheme is called an adaptive predictor, since the weighted sum of previous samples is essentially trying to predict what the next sample will be.

DPCM that uses an adaptive predictor and an adaptive quantiser is called Adaptive DPCM or ADPCM. The adaptive predictor keeps track of spectral characteristics (correlation between samples) and the adaptive quantiser keeps track of level changes by adjusting its step size or resolution to match the level of the difference signal, as discussed in the previous section on PCM.

Since its inception in the early 1970s [4,5,6] ADPCM has been adopted by the CCITT as an international standard [7]. Because of its historically envisaged application in conjunction with 64 kbit/s PCM in the PSTN, the G.721 coding algorithm is defined in terms of a transcoding function to be implemented in tandem with standard G.711 64 kbit/s log-PCM codecs (μ-law or A-law) [8].

The processes of ADPCM encoding are presented diagrammatically in Fig. 6.1. The first process within the transcoder is conversion to linear (or uniform) PCM. A difference signal is then obtained by subtracting a signal

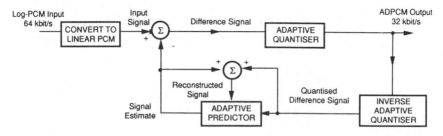

Fig. 6.1. ADPCM encoder.

estimate that has been derived from earlier input samples. An adaptive 16-level quantiser codes the difference signal to 4 bits every 125 μs, thus halving the original data rate (8 bits every 125 μs).

The inverse function of the adaptive quantiser then produces a quantised version of the difference signal, which is added to the signal estimate to give a reconstructed version of the input signal. Both these latter signals are used to update the signal estimate in the adaptive predictor. The adaptive predictor is based on a second-order recursive filter and a sixth-order non-recursive filter:

$$s_e(k) = \sum_{i=1}^{2} a_i(k-1)s_r(k-i) + \sum_{i=1}^{6} b_i(k-1)d_q(k-i)$$

where $s_e(k)$ is the new signal estimate at time (k), $s_r(k-i)$ are the earlier samples of the reconstructed signal and $d_q(k-i)$ are the earlier samples of the quantised difference signal. Both sets of predictor coefficients, $a_i(k-1)$ and $b_i(k-1)$, are updated using gradient algorithms [7].

Many of the functions within the ADPCM decoder (Fig. 6.2) are very similar to those in the encoder. The inverse adaptive quantiser reconstructs the quantised difference signal, and the adaptive predictor forms a signal estimate based on the quantised difference signal and earlier samples of the reconstructed signal, which is itself the sum of the current estimate and the quantised difference signal. The synchronous coding adjustment function is an extra refinement which makes minor adjustments to the log-PCM output values, so that quantising errors do not accumulate when ADPCM transcoders are concatenated.

As explained, ADPCM coding is fundamentally based upon PCM and as such retains a reasonably high quality of speech reproduction, comparable to that expected of the PSTN. It is for these two reasons of quality and implicit compatibility with the digital PSTN that ADPCM has emerged as the main standard for cordless telephones, e.g. CAI and DECT. The penalty associated with this, however, is complexity of implementation and corresponding power consumption. This aspect is discussed further in Chapter 9.

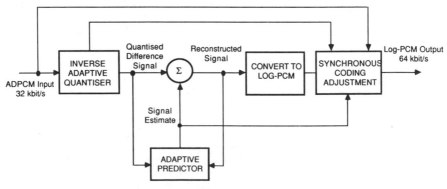

Fig. 6.2. ADPCM decoder.

6.1.3 Delta Modulation, DM

There are a great number of variants of delta modulation: Linear Delta Modulation (LDM), Adaptive Delta Modulation (ADM), Continuously Variable Slope Delta Modulation (CVSDM), Continuously Variable Slope Delta Modulation with Syllabic Companding (CVSDM-SC), Digitally Variable Slope Delta Modulation (DVSDM), etc. [3,9,10].

Delta modulators operate by sampling the analogue signal at very high rates, but with only 1-bit (two-level) resolution. Their main virtue is simplicity, which reflects primarily in cost. At low bit rates (16 kbit/s) voice quality begins to suffer, and the sound becomes rather rough in character, marginally acceptable for military communications but certainly not up to the public's expectation of a toll quality link.

We shall start by describing the basic principles of the linear delta modulator, illustrated in Fig. 6.3. The band-limited input signal X_r is sampled at a rate f_0 which is much higher than $2W$, where W is the highest frequency component of the input signal. At each sample the analogue accumulator holds a previous estimate Y_{r-1} of the input signal, and the sign of the difference $X_r - Y_{r-1}$ is used to update the accumulator by an amount $\pm\Delta$.

With careful selection of f_0 and Δ the accumulator can be made to track the input signal closely. The maximum signal gradient that can be tracked is $\pm\Delta\cdot f_0$, any gradient outside this range resulting in a slope overload. All features of the input signal will be lost during the slope overload condition. If Δ is too large then the smaller details of the signal will be masked. For a specific bandwidth W and sampling rate f_0 the quantisation Δ must be carefully selected according to the signal level.

The LDM decoder is particularly simple and is shown in Fig. 6.4. The received data ($+1$ or -1) is multiplied by an appropriate step value Δ to produce $\Delta\cdot b_r$, which is then accumulated to give a reconstruction Y_r of the original signal. This is then lowpass-filtered to its original bandwidth W, to remove components around the sampling frequency f_0.

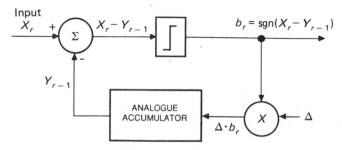

Fig. 6.3. Linear Delta Modulator encoder.

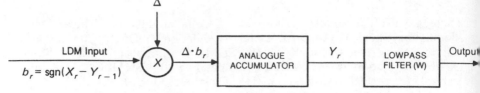

Fig. 6.4. Linear Delta Modulator decoder.

Adaptive Delta Modulation (ADM) is a method of scaling the step size Δ or slope in order to accommodate variations in signal level. ADM techniques fall into a number of groups depending on whether the companding function (step size adaptation) is instantaneous or gradual, and whether the function is driven by analogue signals within the encoder (CVSDM) or by the digitally encoded representation of the signal (DVSDM). The overall encoding function is equivalent to LDM of an input signal with compressed dynamic range. Within the ADM decoder a similar step size algorithm ensures that the original dynamic range of the signal is restored.

A DVSDM scheme has been adopted by Shaye Communications for their proprietary cordless telephone product, the Forum Personal Phone. The reasons for this are undoubtedly cost and size, since a DVSDM codec is much simpler and cheaper to produce than an ADPCM codec or transcoder.

6.1.4 Linear Predictive Coding, LPC

LPC is a parametric representation of the voice signal – only the principal features of the signal, such as short-term power spectrum and excitation function are coded. This type of coding offers low data rates; for military communications 2.4 kbit/s (LPC-10) is common, whereas for commercial applications 8–16 kbit/s is typical.

To achieve low data rates a very simple model of the voice signal is employed. The voice signal $S(z)$ is modelled as the output of a time-varying autoregressive filter $H(z)$ driven by an idealised impulse-like source $E(z)$:

$$S(z) = H(z) \cdot E(z)$$

$S(z)$ is the z-transform of the signal time-series:

$$S(z) = \sum_{n=0}^{\infty} s(n) \cdot z^{-n}$$

$H(z)$ is the z-transform of the impulse response:

$$H(z) = \sum_{n=0}^{\infty} h(n) \cdot z^{-n}$$

$E(z)$ is the z-transform of the excitation time-series:

$$E(z) = \sum_{n=0}^{\infty} e(n) \cdot z^{-n}$$

We can now expand $H(z)$ in terms of a pth-order non-recursive predictor $P(z)$:

$$P(z) = \sum_{k=1}^{p} a_k \cdot z^{-k}$$

and

$$H(z) = [1 - P(z)]^{-1}$$

so that

$$S(z) = H(z) \cdot E(z) = \frac{E(z)}{1 - P(z)}$$

i.e.

$$S(z) = P(z) \cdot S(z) + E(z) \tag{6.1}$$

The signal $S(z)$ is thus represented by a prediction term, $S'(z) = P(z) \cdot S(z)$, plus an error term $E(z)$, which is the excitation function. Equation (6.1) may be regarded as the LPC voice synthesis equation.

· The predictor coefficients a_k best fit the speech production model when the expectation value of the mean square error $\langle E(n)^2 \rangle$ is minimised, tending to give a more idealised impulse source.

From the LPC synthesis equation

$$\langle E(n)^2 \rangle = \sum_{n=1}^{\infty} \left[s(n) - \sum_{k=1}^{p} a_k \cdot s(n-k) \right]^2$$

this function can be minimised by setting the partial derivatives to zero:

$$\frac{\partial \langle E(n)^2 \rangle}{\partial a_j} = 0, \qquad j = 1, 2, \ldots, p$$

from which

$$r_{j0} - \sum_{k=1}^{p} a_k \cdot r_{jk} = 0, \qquad j = 1, 2, \ldots, p$$

where

$$r_{jk} = \sum_{n=1}^{\infty} s(n-j) \cdot s(n-k)$$

or in matrix form

$$r - [R] \cdot a = 0,$$

i.e.

$$a = [R]^{-1} \cdot r$$

where **a** is the vector of predictor coefficients a_k, **r** is the vector of autocorrelations r_{j0}, and $[\mathbf{R}]$ is the matrix of autocorrelations r_{jk}.

Fortunately the matrix is symmetric, positive definite and approximately Toeplitz for quasi-stationary signals, so that a number of efficient techniques can be used to invert the autocorrelation matrix $[\mathbf{R}]$ and find the best vector for the linear predictor **a** [11].

In a practical LPC system the predictor coefficients are often re-coded into alternative, more robust forms. One such scheme re-models the synthesis filter as an acoustic tube having "p" coupled segments of equal length, but with different cross-sectional area for each segment. The filter coefficients are then re-coded as the reflection coefficients between segments. An alternative re-coding scheme uses log-area ratios to describe the acoustic-tube model and hence the synthesis filter.

In addition to specifying the recursive filter an LPC coder must also convey sufficient parameters relating to the excitation function $E(z)$ for an adequate re-synthesis of $E(z)$ at the LPC decoder. There are a great variety of ways to code the excitation function. Simple LPC codecs use only amplitude, fundamental frequency and voicing (a 1-bit parameter to distinguish between periodic and non-periodic excitation). Some of the more complex LPC schemes use PCM-type coding of the residual $E(z)$. Other LPC schemes reduce the residual coding still further by adding a long-term predictor to reconstruct the excitation function, rather like ADPCM. The synthesiser excitation function is then the sum of the long-term predictor output and a lesser signal, the innovation sequence, which is derived from a part of the LPC code format. An example of codec using LPC is the GSM codec.

The reader is referred to [11] for a fuller treatise on LPC techniques. As noted earlier, DECT will have an option for future introduction of a second coder. The advantage of using a parametric coder would be its relatively low data rate, less than that of 32 kbit/s ADPCM; this could potentially permit an effective doubling of capacity over the radio interface once the technology allows the speech quality, cost and power consumption requirements to be met.

6.1.5 Speech Quality

The measurement of speech quality is a non-trivial issue. One useful metric of quality is the Quantising Distortion Unit, qdu, based on a reference point of 1 qdu for a 64 kbit/s log-PCM codec, with higher qdu ratings corresponding to progressively poorer speech quality. In a system containing a number of codecs the overall qdu rating is calculated by adding the qdu ratings of the individual codecs. Qdu ratings for a range of speech coding techniques, collated from the published literature, are presented in Table 6.1.

In the UK the maximum quantising distortion permitted in any private branch network connecting into the analogue public network in the UK is 3.0 qdu, which would appear from the Table 6.1 to rule out all but log-

Table 6.1. Qdu ratings for various speech coding techniques

Coding scheme	Qdu rating
64 kbit/s log-PCM codec (8-bit sample)	1
56 kbit/s log-PCM codec (7-bit sample)	3
64 kbit/s log-PCM codec (+32kbit/s ADPCM transcodec)	3.5
32 kbit/s CVSDM	6
13 kbit/s GSM RPE-LTP	7–8
16 kbit/s CVSDM	10

Sources: [12,13].

PCM. Curiously, for this purpose, cordless telephone units to BS 6833 Parts 1 and 2 are deemed to have distortion values of 2.0 qdu [12], despite their use of ADPCM!

For low bit rate speech codecs, measuring speech quality is much more difficult, due to the non-linear distortions of the speech signal, and has to be carried out using subjective tests. Two types of testing are often performed, measuring quality and intelligibility. The most widely used intelligibility test is the Diagnostic Rhyme Test (DRT), which uses pairs of rhyming words. The listener is asked to decide which of the two words was spoken. Not only does this test give an overall figure of intelligibility, but it can also highlight problems with particular types of sound.

The Mean Opinion Score (MOS) is commonly used for assessment of quality. Again, this is a subjective test and must be performed with a large number of listeners and speakers. Listeners are asked to assess quality on a scale of 0 to 4 or 1 to 5, where the grades correspond to

4 *or* 5 Excellent
3   4 Good
2   3 Fair
1   2 Poor
0   1 Bad

It is usual when carrying out these tests to include a reference codec, such as log-PCM, the performance of which is widely known. This can help when trying to compare results produced in different tests.

6.1.6 Channel Coding

An issue closely related to speech coding is the possible need for radio channel coding. Channel coding means that the digitally coded speech bits are divided into blocks and additional bits added to each block (according to some algorithm which uses the speech bits themselves to derive these additional bits) to provide a capability of detecting and correcting any errors in the received speech bits. In the more complex speech coding schemes such as LPC the bits have different importance and the more sensitive bits may need to be accorded better protection. In digital mobile radio systems the bits of the coded blocks are also normally interleaved. This has the effect that if the signal received by a rapidly moving mobile user experiences a fade, the fading dip will cause a few correctable errors in several blocks rather than concentrated uncorrectable errors in one block. The channel coding of the pan-European GSM cellular radio system is a good example of this approach.

For cordless telephone systems at present, interleaving such as just described offers little gain, since the system cannot afford the inherent large delay that would be needed to make it effective against the slow fading resulting from the very slow movement that is typical for a cordless handset. Instead antenna diversity is employed as a cheaper and more efficient counter-measure against slow fading, as mentioned previously in Chapter 2. Under these conditions error correction, which increases the required transmission bandwidth, is not considered useful either, provided the codec chosen does give more or less even weight to the coded speech bits.

Channel coding is not therefore currently envisaged for cordless telephones for the speech channel. It is, however, essential for the signalling and control data. The application of channel coding is discussed further in Chapter 7.

6.2 Voice Transmission Plan

The main difference between transmission plans for wired telephones and cordless telecommunications systems is the impact of specific speech codecs suitable for radio transmission and the extra delay introduced. This section emphasises the parameters in a transmission plan which are essential for the discussions on delay and echo control. For remaining parameters, often common with wired telephony specifications, as well as measuring methods, the reader is referred to the specifications for the various systems [14–17].

6.2.1 Definitions

Firstly, a number of basic definitions are needed. The main reference is the CCITT Red Book Volume III containing recommendations G.100–G.181 [18]. (This book is undergoing a revision and will reappear as G.100–G.181 in the Blue Book series. Another modern and very useful reference is [19].) Loudness ratings and similar terms referred to below are expressed in decibel attenuations. To assist in the understanding of the various definitions a number of figures are provided. The definitions in this section apply generally to a telephone system; extension to the cordless terminal is considered in the following section.

Sending Loudness Rating, SLR
Receiving Loudness Rating, RLR

Fig. 6.5 illustrates a terminal, e.g. an ordinary telephone, with a two-wire or four-wire interface to a PABX or PSTN extension. (The necessary filters and amplifiers are not shown in this general simplified diagram.) SLR and RLR express relations between sound pressure at the acoustic interface at the microphone and output transducer (M and T) of a terminal and the electrical signals in the network, e.g. at the extension interface (H) to a private or public switch. A two-wire interface is physically implemented by means of a hybrid, which permits signals to pass in both directions simultaneously. B is the Echo Balance Return Loss referred to the two-wire side of this hybrid (see below).

Echo Balance Return Loss, B

The Echo Balance Return Loss of the hybrid (B) refers to signals transformed to the two-wire side of the hybrid. For calculation of echoes B is defined as 11 ± 3 dB, the mean value of 11 dB generally being used ([18], Annex B/G.122 and Supplement No. 2 section 2).

Connection Loudness Rating, CLR

Fig. 6.6 illustrates end-to-end transmission in a simplified diagram. It is generalised for analogue and digital two- and four-wire transmission and mixtures thereof.

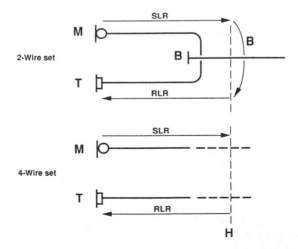

Fig. 6.5. Simple telephone terminal: definitions of SLR, RLR and B.

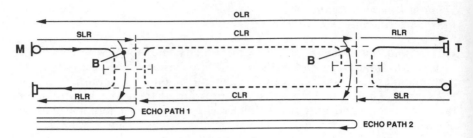

Fig. 6.6. Simplified end-to-end telephone circuit, showing echo paths.

The Connection Loudness Rating (CLR) is the loudness loss between two electrical interfaces – in this example between the extension line reference points close to the first switches. The CLR path can contain anything from a simple through-connection to a whole chain of PABX, national and international switches, satellite links, digital and analogue conversions, etc. If hybrids are contained in the transmission, echoes will occur, as indicated by the echo paths 1 and 2 in the diagram. Reference [18] uses the older expression Junction Loudness Rating (JLR) instead of CLR.

Overall Loudness Rating, OLR

The Overall Loudness Rating (OLR) defines the total transmission, sound pressure to sound pressure, from M to T, and is related to the previously defined terms by the equation:

$$OLR = SLR + CLR + RLR \qquad (6.2)$$

A value of OLR of 9 dB gives approximately the same sound pressure at T as at M. OLR is suggested to be 10 dB for digital networks. OLR for old analogue networks can vary significantly, e.g. from 4 to 30 dB, and is mostly larger than 10 dB.

Side Tone Masking Rating, STMR

The side tone is an electrical path from the microphone in a handset to the speaker device. Its purpose is to substitute for the sound that normally travels in the air from the mouth to the ear, but is blocked by the handset pressed to the ear. STMR expresses sound pressure to sound pressure, but is defined with a different frequency weighting function from that used for Loudness Rating (LR). For digital systems STMR is specified to 13 ± 5 dB. Taking the different weighting functions into account, an STMR of 13 dB approximately corresponds to the sound pressure obtained at the distant end speaker with an OLR of 10 dB. For analogue two-wire sets the STMR path is via the echo balance loss of the hybrid, path 1, and thus varies more than for (digital) four-wire sets.

The side tone is important not only for compensating for the blockage of the natural air acoustic path from the mouth to the ear but also because it has a subjective masking effect on echoes, as discussed later.

Telephone Acoustic Loss, TAL

Echoes may also be generated by another path, path 3 shown in Fig. 6.7, via the combined effect of the electrical and acoustic loss over the handset, TAL. (A new term, Terminal Coupling Loss (TCL), is also used.) TAL is defined at the same extension line reference point as SLR and RLR.

An earlier definition, which occurs in some references and specifications, here denoted TAL(0), is defined for the case RLR+SLR = 0. Thus

$$TAL=TAL(0)+SLR+RLR$$

TAL(0) is that part of the telephone acoustic loss that relates to the specific acoustic-mechanical design of a handset.

For digital transmission, CLR is 0 dB. Thus, since OLR = 10 dB (above), Equation (6.2) implies that SLR+RLR=10 dB. Hence

$$TAL=TAL(0)+10\,dB \tag{6.3}$$

For analogue connections where SLR+RLR is -1 dB, such as in Sweden or the UK, then

$$TAL=TAL(0)-1\,dB \tag{6.3a}$$

Overall Echo Loudness Rating, OELR

The OELR relates the sound pressure at the microphone (M) to the sound pressure of a returning echo at the speaker (T) of the same telephone. (Instead of OELR, the expression TELR, Talker Echo Loudness Rating, is also sometimes used. There is in fact a small difference, ~1 dB, between the two terms.)

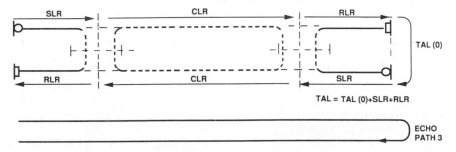

Fig. 6.7. Acoustic distant-end echo path.

For echo path 1 in Fig. 6.6 (short extension lines) OELR is given by

$$OELR = SLR + RLR + B \tag{6.4}$$

For echo path 2,

$$OELR = SLR + RLR + 2CLR + B \tag{6.5}$$

For echo path 3, Fig. 6.7,

$$OELR = SLR + RLR + 2CLR + TAL \tag{6.6}$$

or

$$OELR = 2OLR + TAL(0) \tag{6.7}$$

Note that Equation (6.4) has to be used with care for analogue transmission. If the extension line between the handset and the switch is long (>2 km) there will be attenuation on the line. $SLR + RLR$ defined close to the switch will differ from $SLR' + RLR'$ measured close to the terminal. In fact, for analogue transmission, since $SLR' + RLR'$ for path 1 will differ from $SLR + RLR$, the value for OELR is given by

$$OELR = SLR' + RLR' + B \tag{6.4a}$$

According to national specifications for analogue lines, the value of $SLR' + RLR'$ (attenuation) can nominally be as low as 10 dB below the value of $SLR + RLR$ for long extension lines. Thus the echo from path 1 can be larger at long extension lines than at short extension lines. Path 1 is the path that provides the side tone in analogue telephone sets.

6.2.2 Transmission Plan for a Digital Cordless Telephone System

The transmission diagrams discussed above can be extended to incorporate a digital cordless telephone, by replacing the fixed telephone part (Fig. 6.5) by the cordless equipment shown schematically in Fig. 6.8. The cordless link is shown separated into its two distinct parts: that comprising the cordless portable part (CPP, the handset), and that comprising the fixed part connected to the network infrastructure. (Different terms are used by different authors in discussing these different components of a cordless system; see the Glossary for other terms used.)

A number of specific interfaces shown in Fig. 6.8 are defined below (the notation adopted, A–H, does not follow a particular convention but is purely used for this example). Interfaces A–E relate to the handset and E–H to the fixed part. The fixed part includes base stations and central control and can range from a simple residential base station to a large cordless PABX connected to the public network. Thus the network interface H can represent not only extension lines but also trunk lines of a PABX, ISPABX, PSTN or ISDN. This transmission plan has been exemplified with the well-known CCITT G.721 32 kbit/s ADPCM codec for the radio transmission. Since the

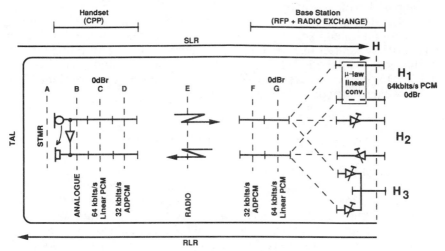

Fig. 6.8. Transmission diagram for a cordless telephone system.

measurements are made at 64 kbit/s reference, any codec fits into the transmission plan, provided requirements on quality and delay are met.

The interfaces A–H are defined as follows:

Interface A is the acoustic interface at M and T of the handset.

Interface B is the analogue electrical interface.

Interfaces C and G are the linear 0 dB 64 kbit/s PCM digital reference used in specifying digital telephones. Interface C never needs physically to exist; however, interface G must physically exist if digital 64 kbit/s PCM connection (e.g. ISDN) is to be supported. It is practical to include interfaces C and G in the diagrams since digital measurement methods refer to a 64 kbit/s PCM interface. There is a one-to-one relation between the digital signals of the 64 kbit/s PCM and the 32 kbit/s ADPCM. Thus under error-free radio transmission conditions the signals at C and G are equal.

Interfaces D and F are 32 kbit/s ADPCM G.721 interfaces. The diagram can easily be modified for another choice of codec.

Interface E is the radio interface carrying the 32 kbit/s ADPCM information.

Interface H is the interface to the trunk or extension line of a private or local switch. H_1 represents the case of digital transmission, 64 kbit/s μ-law PCM. For analogue transmission, analogue-to-digital and digital-to-analogue converters, filters and amplifiers have to be included in the cordless radio exchange or central part, and the attenuation has to be adjusted according to national requirements on SLR and RLR. H_2 represents analogue four-wire connection and H_3 analogue two-wire connection.

STMR indicates the side tone path of the handset. This does not necessarily have to be an analogue path, but the path must not contain substantial extra delay (<1 ms approximately).

Compared with a standard wired telephone, delay will be introduced, especially at interface E, but also in codecs and other digital processing. This is not indicated explicitly in Fig. 6.8, but is treated later in this chapter.

A cordless handset may be used as a loudspeaking set by placing it onto a table stand with built-in loudspeaker, microphone and voice-operated switch. This set has to have the voice-operated switch at the B or C interface, as for ordinary wired loudspeaking telephones.

6.2.3 Transmission Plans for Specific Systems

Having established a frame of reference, Table 6.2 lists the requirements which arise in respect of SLR, RLR, STMR and TAL for specific systems, taking as examples the CAI, the Swedish DCT and the emerging DECT cordless systems. All the tabulated values are presented in decibels.

For digital interfaces, H_1, SLR and RLR are defined by the NET33 standard and this is followed for DECT. For longer lines (>2 km) with analogue interfaces, H_2/H_3, the amplification has to be increased to compensate for extension line losses (see relevant specifications [14–17]).

An example of the application of a voice transmission plan using the H_3 interface, the CAI high level transmission plan, is included as Fig. A2.2 in Appendix 2.

6.3 Delay and Echo Control

It is important to distinguish between two effects of delay. One effect is the delay itself. One-way delays of up to about 100 ms result in no subjective interference to a telephone conversation. However, larger delays, e.g. a 260 ms one-way delay arising from a satellite link, is noticeable and inexperienced users may start to talk simultaneously or think that the other

Table 6.2. Example SLR, RLR, STMR and TAL requirements for specific systems

	SLR/RLR		STMR	TAL (SLR+RLR=10 dB)
	H_1	H_3 (short extension lines)		
CT2 CAI	7±3/3±3	3.3±4.2/−4.5±3.5	13±5	>25
DCT900	7±3/3±3	6.7±3.3/−6.3±3.3	13±5	>34
DECT	7±3/3±3	National Specification	13±5	>34[a]

[a]Proposed value at time of writing.

is slow responding. The effect of pure delay itself, however, is not very large if an extra small delay, e.g. 10–15 ms, introduced by a cordless telephone link, is added to existing delays.

The second effect is the introduction of delayed echoes, which are much more degrading to the perceived speech than the delay itself. Such degradation begins to occur for delays of a few milliseconds in the presence of very strong echoes. For long delays, weak echoes may also contribute a degradation to the link quality. Thus, imperfect means for echo control is more noticeable than direct effects of the delay itself.

When specifying allowable extra delay from a cordless telephone system the limitation is not the total delay itself. For example, adding 25 ms (10%) to the delay of a satellite link will not be noticeable. The reasonable limits for extra delay depend on its influence on echoes, on existing network echo control means, and, if needed, on the cost and complication of echo control means in the cordless system. Therefore the different possible echo paths have to be analysed, as do, in the case of satellite links, the requirements imposed by existing echo control means.

Three echo paths relevant for the cordless handset user have been indicated in Figs. 6.6 and 6.7. These are shown in Fig. 6.9 together with two more echo paths relevant to the distant-end user, paths 4 and 5.

In Fig. 6.9 the left-hand terminal is a cordless telecommunications system as in Fig. 6.8. T indicates the total extra one-way delay that is introduced compared with a wired telephone. EC indicates an echo control means that, for some cases, is needed on trunk or extension level at the linear interface G of Fig. 6.8. The right-hand terminal is normally a wired telephone, but could also be a cordless device.

6.3.1 Criteria for Acceptable Echoes

Echoes do not influence the subjective perception of speech if they are sufficiently attenuated. Such attenuation comes from line losses and the hybrid return loss or the telephone acoustic path loss, as exemplified in Equations (6.4)–(6.7).

The commonly used reference for minimum echo return loss as a function of the one-way delays from 10 to 300 ms is G.131 [18]. In [18] the echo return loss is expressed in Corrected Reference Equivalents (CRE), an older term; in Fig. 6.10 the corresponding Loudness Ratings (OLR) have been used, being 4 dB less than the CRE talker echo path. (OLR will be used in the new Blue Book version of [18]. As previously mentioned, TELR and OELR are closely related, with less than 1 dB difference between them. It should be noted, however, that new subjective tests have recently been carried out on TELR or OELR requirements under conditions relevant to modern telecommunications and these results may necessitate another revision of G.131 [18].)

The curves shown indicate the 1% and 10% probabilities for subjectively encountering an objectionable echo; the 1% curves are used as design

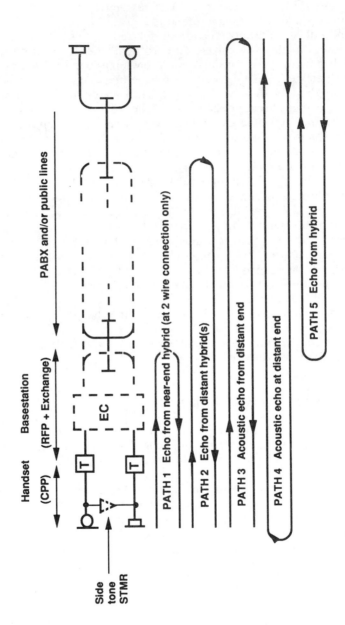

Fig. 6.9. Echo paths relevant for a cordless telephone system.

criteria ([18]: 2.3.1.1 Ideal rule – A/G.131). The dashed line is for digital transmission and the continuous lines refer to transmission over a chain of one to nine analogue four-wire circuits. The OELR has to be larger for larger numbers of analogue circuits in the chain, due to the increasing statistical spread of the line attenuations. For examples in this chapter we assume digital or a single four-wire analogue transmission link.

As an example of applying Fig. 6.10, we make an estimation of the maximum delay which can be accepted for a long distance call between two analogue wired telephones. In this case it is the path 2 (or 5) that causes the echo. The OELR for path 2 (see Fig. 6.6) is given by

$$OELR = SLR + RLR + 2CLR + B$$

or

$$OELR = 2OLR + B - (SLR + RLR) \qquad (6.8)$$

In order to evaluate this expression, we note from earlier the value of 11 dB for B. Also, from Table 6.2 we find that nominally $SLR + RLR = -1$ dB in the UK or Sweden for analogue trunks (H_3). If we assume OLR has a typical value of 10 dB, this gives an OELR of $2(10) + 11 - (-1)$ dB, i.e. 32 dB. Using Fig. 6.10, following the curve for a single analogue circuit, we see that this corresponds to a 20 ms one-way delay as the limit for 1% probability of encountering unacceptable echoes. Thus there is a CCITT rule ([18]: 2.3.3.2.3 Rule M/G.131) that echo control devices are required in the network if the one-way delay exceeds 25 ms, otherwise an unacceptably high line attenuation has to be used. This situation arises most commonly when a connection includes a satellite link.

Fig. 6.10 is useful for studying the echo paths 2–5, but not the echo path 1. Path 1 is not considered for a wired telephone, since it has no significant delay. This may not be the case, however, for a cordless device. For path 1 we refer to recent limited subjective tests in a report to CCITT [20]; more test results from other sources will eventually be available. Fig. 6.11 shows results in terms of Mean Opinion Scores (MOS). The tests were performed for 0, 2, 8 and 16 ms one-way delay and an OELR ranging from 0 to 30 dB, with a direct side tone masking (STMR) of 15 dB. (Note that an MOS of only 2 is obtained for the case of zero delay and an OELR of 0 dB. The reason for this is that the indirect side tone is heard as a very loud direct side tone. Such a situation occurs for an analogue telephone if $SLR' + RLR' = -11$ dB (long lines) and B=11 dB.)

An interpretation of Fig. 6.11 gives the approximate limits shown in Table 6.3 for path 1, if one half point of MOS degradation is allowed instead of 0 ms delay. A cross-check between the 8 ms one-way delay results from Table 6.3 and the 10 ms one-way delay result in Fig. 6.10 shows good correlation. Correction from 8 to 10 ms adds 2 dB to the 21 dB tabulated value, giving 23 dB; adding a few decibels for the side tone masking effect gives values close to the 25–26 dB of Fig. 6.11.

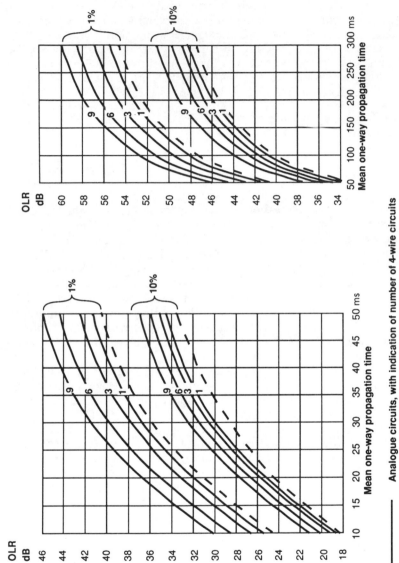

Fig. 6.10. Minimum allowable overall loudness rating of the echo path as a function of delay. (From [18], courtesy of CCITT.)

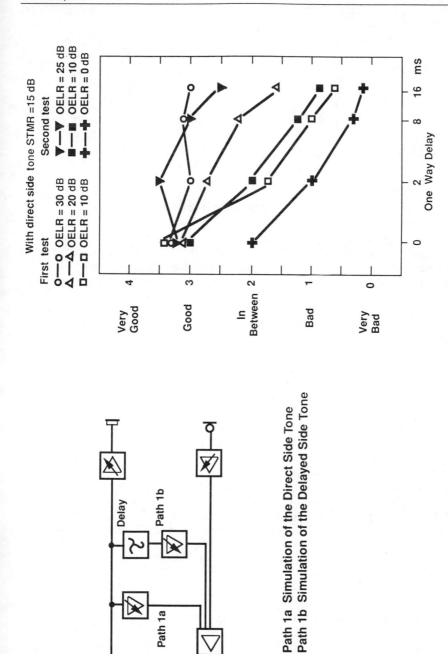

Path 1a Simulation of the Direct Side Tone
Path 1b Simulation of the Delayed Side Tone

Fig. 6.11. MOS test of delayed side tone with direct side tone.

Table 6.3. OELR values as a function of delay, for one half point MOS degradation

Delay, one-way (ms)	OELR (dB)	
	$\frac{1}{2}$ point degradation	No degradation
1	0	20
2	15	22
8	21	25
16	25	30

6.3.2 Echo Control at International Gateways

A single satellite link adds 260 ms one-way delay and about 0 dB transmission loss. The allowed national delay is a maximum of 12 ms; if, for example, 4 ms are needed for digital processing in the transmission chain, then the remaining 8 ms correspond to 2000 km transmission. As seen from Fig. 6.10, a total OELR of 55–60 dB is needed to suppress 300 ms delayed echoes. The OELR for the echo from the distant end hybrid is only 20–30 dB without extra echo control means. It is for this reason that, for satellite transmissions, echo control is always used at the international gateways (see Fig. 6.12 and [18]: G.131, G.164, and G.165).

Echo control can be performed either by an echo suppressor, which is a speech-controlled directional switch, or by an echo canceller, which by means of adaptive linear filters makes an estimate of the transfer function of the echo path and uses that information to subtract the echo in the return path.

An echo suppressor operates by connecting different losses in the receive and send paths. During one-way talk from the distant end the receive loss is 0 dB and the suppressor loss typically 50 dB; thus no echoes are allowed through independent of their delay. No delayed acoustic echoes are therefore heard at the distant end. The only requirement is that the further delayed acoustic echoes from a cordless telephone are attenuated sufficiently so as not to be interpreted as a break in speech signals which could switch the echo suppressor state. If TAL(0)>24 dB, as mentioned above, the acoustic echo will be low enough to meet this requirement.

During double talk, that is when speech signals are simultaneously present at both ends of the link, a fixed 6 dB attenuation is employed in each direction. This means that echoes are heard but are partly masked by the local speech. This state of operation represents a weakness in the behaviour of an echo suppressor. It should be noted, however, that the echoes from the normally present hybrids (which have nothing to do with the extra delay of a cordless system) dominate and mask the weaker, further delayed acoustic echoes by some 13 dB for the case of B=11 dB and TAL(0)>24 dB.

Echo suppressors often degrade speech due to the time constants needed in the switching. Therefore more complex echo cancellers are increasingly being used.

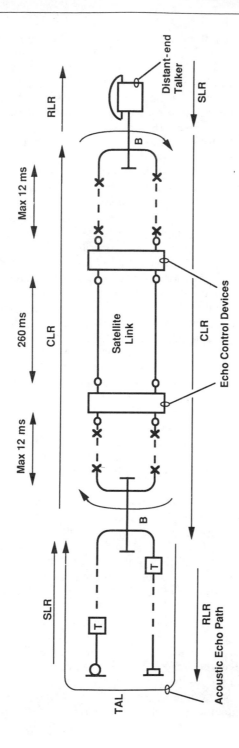

Fig. 6.12. Schematic diagram of satellite-linked connection.

The echo canceller employs adaptive processing to construct an estimate of the anticipated echo which it then subtracts from the returning signal. The normal echo canceller has a control range of 30 ms, i.e. it can cancel echoes over this spread of delay. The canceller comprises a linear canceller component, capable of echo subtraction down to 25–40 dB, and a non-linear processor that adds additional attenuation to a total of more than 65 dB. The latter acts like a centre clipper and cancels everything below its suppression threshold. In the idle condition the non-linear processor is switched off (i.e. transparent).

One great advantage of an echo canceller compared with an echo suppressor is that full echo control is possible during both one-way and double talk states. It is only the non-linear processors at the two sides of the link that are switched on and off between the two one-way talk states (one state for each direction). During double talk some echo cancellers have the non-linear processors active, others do not.

During one-way talk from the distant end all echoes are suppressed which are within the 30 ms control range of the canceller but, since the non-linear processor is active, all echoes that exceed the control range but are below the suppression threshold of the nonlinear processor are totally suppressed. If $TAL(0)>24$ dB, as mentioned above, the acoustic echo will be low enough, including an adequate safety margin, to be totally suppressed by the non-linear processor. The acoustic echo will also be well below the limit to be detected as a break in signal for going to the double talk state.

During double talk, if the non-linear processor is not active, acoustic echoes outside the control range of the canceller will not be attenuated. However, the level of these echoes will be more than 30 dB below the level of the interfering double talk, and will be masked by this.

Analysis of the situation of international gateway links [21] shows that for analogue near-end extensions the distant-end user is protected from echoes over the delayed acoustic path provided $TAL(0)>24$ dB for a cordless system. TAL must be >23 dB for an analogue two-wire interface $(SLR+RLR=-1$ dB). The digital case is more easily analysed, since the speech signal can never exceed $+3$ dBm, and the threshold for break-in signals is -31 dBm. This gives the requirement that $TAL>34$ dB for a digital interface $(SLR+RLR=10$ dB). Note that the TAL is limited by the physical properties of the cordless handset. For the same handset, TAL will automatically change 11 dB between analogue and digital interface application, following the amplifier settings for SLR and RLR in this example.

Note: The implementation of the non-linear processor is only given as an example in G.165 [18]. Thus, for the 4-wire interface H_z, the DECT specification recommends insertion of a switchable pseudo-hybrid echo (20 dB) to ensure that the echo canceller always has an in-range echo to operate on, and thus has its NLP active. The pseudo echo is only needed for international connections and for certain makes of echo cancellers. (It is also allowed to implement an NLP in the DECT fixed part.)

6.3.3 Echo Control for Non-international Circuits

Both the distant-end and near-end user can suffer echoes through the paths shown in Fig. 6.9. Having examined the requirements imposed upon a cordless system by the echo control at international gateways we now examine the constraints which arise when a cordless system is used within a simple PABX or local, national scenario where no echo control means is normally provided by the transmission chain. Examination of these constraints leads to a limit upon the maximum delay which can be tolerated from a cordless telephone system. It is also found that for cordless telephone systems which indeed introduce significant one-way delay (e.g. >3 ms approximately) a means of echo control must be incorporated within the cordless equipment. To establish these conclusions, we consider protection firstly of the distant-end user and then the local user.

The innocent distant-end user can get echoes through paths 4 and 5 of Fig. 6.9. Path 5 concerns echoes from hybrids equivalent to those present in ordinary analogue telephones and is thus not considered further. For the echo path 4 via the delayed acoustic path of the cordless system, we refer to Fig. 6.7. Applying Equation (6.7), assuming an ideal OLR for analogue and digital connections of 10 dB and a value of TAL(0)>24 dB, we can derive an OELR of >44 dB. Thus, from Fig. 6.10, we can conclude that the largest permissible one-way delay is ~70 ms. Thus if the wired network gives a maximum of 25 ms (the maximum for a network without echo control) then 45 ms remains for the cordless system. Allowing for the case of a cordless link at each end of the line places a maximum limit on the cordless system one-way delay, T, of 22 ms. (This maximum delay figure may be increased by incorporating a soft echo suppressor in the cordless handset to increase the OELR.)

As regards the near-end user, three cases must be considered: the case of four-wire connections end to end, and the cases of hybrids at the distant end and at the near end.

The first of these, path 3 only (Fig. 6.9), is usual for analogue or digital trunk interfaces for modern PABX and modern public networks with ISDN terminals. The general analysis is the same as above for echo path 4 with cordless handsets at both ends.

For four-wire connection at the near end, with a hybrid at the distant end, the hybrid echo of path 2 will always dominate over the acoustic echo of path 3. In this case the delay T of the cordless system will be added to the delay (<25 ms) of the network. The slope of Fig. 6.10, i.e. required OELR as a function of delay, over the interval of 10–25 ms is ~0.5 dB/ms. Thus, to maintain the subjective quality additional attenuation of this order must be added. (For T below 5 ms the difference is so small that no compensation is needed.) This extra attenuation can be introduced in the cordless system as a soft suppressor in the speaker line. In this way the distant-end talker or outgoing levels are not affected at all. This simple suppressor unit can be in the handset or on trunk level in the central part and is activated by near-end speech. Thus, for connections which contain distant-end hybrids (which most do), a soft suppressor with ~0.5T dB attenuation (where T is in ms) has to be employed in the speaker connection of the cordless system. The term "soft suppressor" is used to indicate that the speech in the suppressed direction is not completely suppressed – only some 6–18 dB of suppression occurs compared with the 50 dB associated with a normal suppressor. This imposes less stringent requirements on, for example, switching times.

For the case of connection with a hybrid at the near end, i.e. analogue two-wire connections, the echo corresponds to path 1 of Fig. 6.9. As explained earlier, for long extension lines SLR'+RLR' can be as low as −11 dB and thus, if B=11 dB, Equation (6.4a) implies that the OELR can be as low as 0 dB. In this case echo control within the cordless system needs to provide attenuation of as many decibels as indicated in Table 6.3 for half point degradation. For short extension lines, SLR'+RLR' may be around −1 dB, resulting in the extra echo control attenuation being ~10 dB less than the tabulated values. If the echo control is implemented with an echo canceller, only ~4 ms control range is needed, leading to a chip with less than 10 000 transistors.

The control range needs to be 10 ms if the connection is made via a digital PABX connected via a two-wire interface to the PSTN and if the internal PABX one-way delay is the maximum allowed 5 ms [19] (2 ms is more typical). This extra control range leads to a requirement for a more complex, 20 000-transistor integrated circuit.

The general requirement is thus for an echo canceller with 25 dB attenuation and 10 ms control range at trunk level in the cordless central part. If a soft suppressor also is used with, for example, 10 dB suppression, then the attenuation of the echo canceller can be decreased to 15 dB.

In many installations to PABXs an echo canceller may not in fact be needed, partly because the extension line will be short (e.g. SLR+RLR ~−3 dB) and partly because the balance of the hybrid is very well defined (e.g. B ~18 dB). Thus, for a digital PABX, or other PABXs with well-defined line impedances and four-wire connections to the PSTN, a simple soft suppressor (~10 dB) can provide the remaining attenuation needed.

For cases such as a domestic cordless telephone, the line impedance is not well controlled. However, in most cases B is in the order of 15–18 dB or more. Thus, either the general case (with 4 ms control range) can be applied using an echo canceller and a soft suppressor, or alternatively an adaptive soft suppressor can be used. The soft suppressor can be adapted in steps of 6, 12, 18 and 24 dB. In most cases settings of 6 or 12 dB will be used. Since this soft suppressor does not affect the distant-end user at all, but only the user of the cordless handset, the adaptation algorithm might be left as a manufacturer's proprietary feature.

6.3.4 Requirements and Solutions for Specific Systems

Having considered the principles relating to echoes and delay, we now briefly outline the ways in which these issues have been specified in particular cordless telephone systems in recent years.

The Common Air Interface, CAI

The CAI system has succeeded in avoiding the complexities of echo control by minimising system delays. CAI embodies Time Division Duplex (TDD) transmission, but not Time Division Multiple Access (TDMA), with the result that the one-way delay is sufficiently short that no soft suppressor is needed to compensate in echo path 2.

For echo path 4, when satellites are used, no specific requirements are set. Since the extra delay is so short, the statistical risk is low that the national delay budget of 12 ms will be exceeded.

The requirement on TAL is only 25 dB (with $SLR+RLR=10$ dB) and is not intended to help for cases when the delay budget is exceeded.

The hybrid echo at two-wire connection does not require any echo control means in spite of the risk of quality degradation. However, the value $B=11$ dB may be conservative. If instead 18 dB is used, degradation will only occur at long extension lines.

Swedish Digital Cordless Telephone

The Swedish DCT system is a TDMA scheme with concomitant system delays. The specification permits a one-way delay, T, of up to 20 ms, in line with the results above. A soft suppressor is required with an attenuation of $0.45T$ dB (T in ms).

When a near-end two-wire connection is used an extra echo canceller with $8+0.6T$ dB attenuation and 6 ms control range is required. TAL is required to be more than 34 dB ($SLR+RLR=10$ dB), or TAL(0) to be at least 24 dB, including variable speaker volume settings.

Digital European Cordless Telecommunications, DECT

The DECT system is not yet fully specified at the time of writing and the figures presented here represent anticipated values. Further results from recent subjective tests may lead to refinement of these values.

Like the Swedish system, DECT is also a TDMA scheme, and it is likely that a maximum one-way delay of ~14 ms will be specified. A soft suppressor of about 10 dB is likely to be required in the speaker line. TAL(0) is likely to be specified as 24 dB.

For two-wire connections the requirements will depend upon the application. An adaptive soft suppressor with steps 6, 12, 18 and 24 dB is likely, or else an extra echo canceller on the trunks in the central controller associated with the wire-less PABX will be needed. The extra echo attenuation of the echo canceller is likely to be 10–20 dB and the control range about 4 ms.

6.4 Voice Security and Speech Encryption

Normal wired telephones do not use speech encryption, neither do analogue mobile telephone nor mobile radio systems, although the latter systems can rather easily be listened to with a radio receiver. In the case of a cordless telephone, which will be used, for example, as the prime office telephone, it will be vital to provide speech security for the radio link. Since the transmissions are digital, they cannot be accessed by normal radios. However, special radios designed to receive the specific digital radio transmission of a cordless telephone could easily find their way onto the market. Digital transmission, however, does make it rather easy to implement speech encryption. Such encryption may be achieved simply by scrambling of the digitally encoded data according to some predefined encryption algorithm. This may be performed either in software or in an integrated circuit, possibly some additional gates on an existing speech coding chip. The key issue is in fact not the encryption process as such, but the distribution and security of the (individual) keys which tailor the encryption algorithm to the individual user or equipment.

Key distribution and security for a residential set or a closed PABX user group is rather uncomplicated. Both the user of the residential set and the communications manager at the office can, by simple instructions, program into the fixed system and the portable personal keys that need neither to be known by anyone else nor transferred.

It is not so easy to provide speech encryption for public Telepoint systems or for roamers in private PABX systems (in this context the term "roamer" means a user registered on a cordless PABX who is visiting another site where the cordless PABX is also linked in to the same private PABX network). In these cases the key has to be transferred via wire from the home location register (i.e. the control system at the "home" PABX) to the actual base station or system covering the area visited. This is both more complicated and less secure than for the closed user group with limited mobility. Another possibility would be for the base station to assign a temporary key to roamers. Transmitting the key over radio, however, would also appear to be insecure. A visitor at an office could perhaps have his temporary key transferred via a wired table stand in which the visitor's handset is inserted.

A reasonable level of security might be achieved by providing encryption for the frequent use at the home location (office and/or residence) while providing the roamer with less security – or high security at a premium, if available. CAI has no explicitly specified speech encryption in existing cordless systems, although encryption could be provided by the mechanism of defining a new codec type [14]. The Ericsson DCT900 system has encryption as a standard feature and DECT has it as an option.

6.5 Summary

In this chapter we have addressed the key audio processing requirements of cordless telephone systems. The relevant speech coding schemes were described – ADPCM, Delta Modulation and Linear Prediction – together with the difficulties associated with measurement of speech quality. The parameters associated with the voice transmission plan for a cordless system were defined and typical values presented. Working from these same definitions the significance of delay and echo control were explored, in order to explain how the limits on system parameters are derived. Echo control requirements for international and non-international links that involve cordless terminals were established. This permitted us to illustrate the way in which the complexity requirements for echo control devices for cordless systems are derived. Requirements for specific systems were given as examples. Finally, the issues of speech privacy and encryption were presented.

Acknowledgements The prior authorisation of the ITU, as copyright holder, to reproduce Fig. 6.10 is gratefully acknowledged. The choice of excerpts from G.131 is, however, the authors' own and the ITU has no responsibility for it. The full text of the various CCITT recommendations may be obtained from the ITU Sales Section, Place des Nations, Geneva, Switzerland.

References

1. BM Oliver, JR Pierce and CE Shannon, "The philosophy of PCM", Proceedings of the IRE, vol 36, pp 1324–1331, October 1948
2. B Smith, "Instantaneous companding of quantised signals", Bell System Technical Journal, pp 653–709, 1957
3. NS Jayant, "Digital coding of speech waveforms: PCM, DPCM and DM quantisers", Proceedings of the IEE, vol 62, pp 611–632, May 1974
4. RW Stroh, "Optimum and adaptive differential PCM", PhD dissertation, Polytechnic Institute of Brooklyn, Farmingdale NY, USA, 1970
5. P Cummiskey, "Adaptive differential PCM for speech processing", PhD dissertation, Newark College of Engineering, Newark NJ, USA, 1973
6. P Cummiskey, NS Jayant and JL Flanagan, "Adaptive quantisation in differential PCM coding of speech", Bell System Technical Journal, pp 1105–1118, September 1973

7. CCITT, "32 kbits/s adaptive differential pulse code modulation (ADPCM)", CCITT Red Book vol 3, fascicle III.3 – Rec. G.721, 1984
8. CCITT, "Pulse code modulation (PCM) for voice frequencies", CCITT red book vol 3, fascicle III.3 – Rec. G.711, 1984
9. A Tomozawa and H Kaneko, "Companded delta modulation for telephone transmission", IEEE Transactions on Communication Technology, vol COM-16, pp 149–157, February 1968
10. JE Abate, "Linear and adaptive delta modulation", Proceedings of the IEE, vol 55, pp 298–308, March 1967
11. JD Maskell and AH Gray, "Linear prediction of speech", Springer-Verlag, Berlin Heidelberg New York, 1976
12. OFTEL, "Provisional code of practice for the design of private telecommunication branch networks", Office of Telecommunications, London, UK, December 1986
13. ETSI, GSM Recommendation 06.10, annex 1, table 2, 1989
14. UK Department of Trade and Industry, "Common air interface specification to be used for the interworking between cordless telephone apparatus including public access services", MPT 1375, London, May 1989 (amended November 1989, February 1990)
15. Swedish Telecom, "Swedish telecom regulations on radio technical requirements on digital cordless telephones in the frequency band 862 to 864 MHz", Swedish Telecom Code of Statutes TVTFS 1989: 103, 1989
16. Swedish Telecom Specification, "Technical telephone requirements for a digital cordless telephone", 8211-A:130, 1989
17. ETSI RES-3, DECT reference document, RES 3(89) 42, 1989
18. CCITT, "General characteristics of international telephone connections and circuits", CCITT Red Book, vol 3, fascicle III.1 – Rec. G.101 – G.181, 1984–1985
19. ETSI, "Overall transmission plan aspects of a private branch network for voice connections with access to the public network", ETS T/TE 10–05, 6th edn, European Telecommunications Standards Institute, BP52, F-06561, Valbonne, Cedex, France
20. CCITT, "The effect of delayed side tone on the overall sound quality of the telephone connection", CCITT Com.XII-226, November 1987, CCITT, Place des Nations, CH-1211, Geneva 20, Switzerland
21. D Åkerberg, "On echo control when a BCT with T ms inherent one-way delay is connected via a satellite link", report TY87:2017, Ericsson Radio Systems AB, S-16480, Stockholm, Sweden

7 The Radio Channel

Bob Swain and Peter Hulbert

Cordless telecommunications is just another branch of radio communications.[1] Its development is rooted in the practical demonstration of mobility by Marconi but its commercial success is only achieved by using the results of the early pioneers, and the many who followed, to make products that the present-day market can accept in terms of applicability, user friendliness, quality, reliability, size, weight, appearance, flexibility, robustness, adaptability, supply, regulatory regime, cost and price. This list (and there are no prizes for adding to it) shows that the product purchasers and/or users are not interested in the radio channel technology. They will not marvel at the cleverness or originality of radio design, but they will expect it to do whatever they wish when they switch on, without having to undergo a training course, and without fail. Even the name cordless telecommunications eschews radio and the basis of product performance comparison will be the wired telephone or terminal with little, if any, licence given to the radio connection. This comparison is inevitable when cordless telecommunications is equated with communications in and around buildings, and not necessarily mobile in character.

In this context the radio engineer's objective must be to make the radio part of the design responsibility invisible, i.e. he must

- Aim for 100% radio coverage of the nominated communication area
- Aim for communication reliability, in its widest sense, akin to that expected of a wired telephone or terminal
- Aim for cordless apparatus that is no more complex to use than the wired equivalent
- Aim for physical characteristics that are suited for mobility, e.g. pocketability

---

[1] No doubt the telecommunications engineer would introduce his chapter "Cordless telecommunications is just another branch of telecommunications"!

- Aim for a radio system that encourages the widest application
- Aim for a standardised radio interface that allows interworking between different manufacturers' products but does not stifle proprietary innovation
- Aim for a radio design not constrained in its use by intellectual property rights (patents)
- Aim for a basic end-cost that will cause the various products to sell in numbers that will reap the full benefits of scale

In the following no radio issues will be addressed in the depths appropriate to detailed design. Instead attention will be given to those issues in which cordless telecommunications currently brings a somewhat different need, viewpoint or character. To the expert radio engineer the omissions may seem awesome; to such I apologise in advance and recommend reference to their favourite collection of text books, or to references [1,2]. To those others looking for a broader perception of cordlessness, "Welcome aboard". I trust we can be of some service.

7.1 Spectrum Choice

Classically, the electromagnetic spectrum extends from d.c. to light and beyond, but internationally the radio spectrum is considered to range from 9 kHz to 275 GHz. This radio resource may seem enormous in extent yet only the bottom 60 GHz or so is commercially usable at present. Indeed, to achieve radio equipment costs appropriate to the mass consumer market the exploitable spectrum is currently limited to below 2 GHz. The consequence is a multi-dimensional conflict of interests over the use of the prime radio spectrum allocations at national and international levels.

The 9 kHz to 275 GHz range has been allocated to many users under the auspices of the International Telecommunications Union (ITU), with international agreement being achieved through calling at intervals a World Administrative Radio Conference (WARC) at which changes and additions to the table of allocations can be made. This table is then administered by the International Frequency Registration Board (IFRB) of the ITU. (This regulatory framework is discussed in greater detail in Chapter 3.)

Under these international agreements and recommendations each national administration allocates spectrum to appropriately licensed and controlled users, service providers, researchers, etc. Some countries, for example the UK, operate a policy whereby some low radiated-power devices operating in certain bands do not require a licence. These devices include radio-controlled toys, alarms and cordless apparatus. Consequently, such products benefit from not having a licence procedure involved in the mass market sales process.

In Europe the Conference of European Posts and Telecommunications Administrations (CEPT), through a sub-body known as the Comité Radio

(CR), seeks to coordinate European-wide policy towards the identification, allocation and timely provision of spectrum for apparatus expected to be standardised by ETSI for wide use and sale throughout western Europe (generally the EEC and EFTA countries). The CEPT also coordinates the European response to World Administrative Radio Conferences, for example the coming WARC in 1992.

The range of services recognised by this regulatory process encompasses terrestrial and satellite point-to-point and point-to-multipoint (broadcast) systems, radar, navigation, astronomy, emergency services, radio and TV broadcasting and of course mobile services. The mobile services include communications for vehicle fleet operators, paging and cellular radiophone as well as cordless communications. The distribution of these services with respect to frequency does vary and furthermore in most nominated bands of frequencies more than one service is identified.

Unacceptable mutual interference between sharing services is often possible, with the result that one of the services is given primary status. This in practice means the secondary services cannot expect protection from interference from the primary service, nor must they cause unacceptable interference to the primary service. It can be readily appreciated, therefore, that if the mobile service is accorded secondary status in a particular frequency band already used by the primary service in a particular area, then the use of the band for mobile services is virtually excluded if the above interference criteria are to be met. Such conflicts occur, for example, in those bands allocated on a primary basis to TV broadcasting (470 MHz to 862 MHz) or to terrestrial point-to-point and point-to-multipoint micro-wave links (e.g. 1.7 GHz to 2.3 GHz). In the face of the current burgeoning demand for radio spectrum for mobile services the radio frequency regulatory authorities, at national and international level, have the very difficult task of judging the relative merits of one service with respect to another within the constraints of political and socio-economic policies and the perceived needs and preferences of the public at large.

To exemplify the problem, we consider the question "Should 50 MHz of prime broadcast TV spectrum be vacated and transferred to serve the needs of mobile services?" These services are, after all, serving business both large and small and making significant inroads into the consumer market. Indeed projections for the year 2005 suggest that 50% of all telephone calls will involve a mobile link. Thus mobility will provide employment as well as facilities important to a country's well-being. However, broadcast TV offers hours of entertainment and edification per person per day at a minimal price to the viewer. A government that proposed such a swap policy would scarcely be popular. The now classical response to this problem is to recommend the transfer of broadcast services onto multi-channel, multi-choice, coaxial or optical-fibre networks feeding each home. Yet doing so in a densely populated country can cost billions and far outweigh the economic benefits of an increase in mobile services and opportunities. The question of who pays also arises. Should the money come from the tax payer or a levy on the mobile service users? In resolving such issues of choice the frequency regulator should not be envied, nor castigated.

The mobile service provider could avoid these problems by identifying and requesting to occupy unused spectrum but, in the interests of European standardisation, such spectrum should be available throughout western Europe. This is a difficult task to achieve below about 30 GHz and almost certainly impossible below 10 GHz without major changes in present spectrum allocations. So, what is the optimum frequency band for present cordless technology?

Cordless apparatus is very sensitive to component costs. The relative lack of success of the analogue CEPT CT1 cordless telephone can be attributed to its near to 5 : 1 mature cost differential compared with the more freely available and lesser technology solutions, of which UK CT1 and the illegal imports in other countries are prime examples. For cordless products to succeed in the mass consumer and small business markets fundamental component technology must be mature and basic component production costs must have the potential to be reduced to levels competitive with existing products. The ability to exploit existing high-volume component technology developed for other mobile services in the region of 1 GHz would assist cordless products in this regard. Other factors point to about 1 GHz being a favourable choice of frequency.

Man-made noise is one such factor. The unintentionally-radiated radio frequency noise produced by electrical equipment raises the effective receiver noise level well above that expected from consideration of thermal noise alone. Sources of this noise are electric motors, car ignition, radio frequency heaters and domestic appliances. From this abbreviated list it would be expected that the level of noise will be a function of urban population density and many researchers have confirmed this (see [1] for a comprehensive list). Thus no precise statistical definition can be given to the quantity but, as Fig. 7.1 indicates, the importance of man-made noise significantly diminishes for radio equipment operating in the 1 GHz to 2 GHz range. This tendency for man-made noise to push the desirable choice of frequency upwards is offset by the fact that free-space transmission loss increases in proportion to the square of the frequency. Thus, a frequency increase from 200 MHz to 2 GHz produces a hundredfold increase (20 dB) in transmission path loss for a given range. In the range 1 GHz to 2 GHz these two factors tend to balance each other.

Component cost, man-made noise and the fundamental law of transmission loss all point to an optimum choice of cordless telecommunications band between 1 GHz and 2 GHz, with 1 GHz being preferred for cost reasons. After extensive deliberations involving all the above factors and a consideration of the ease with which existing users of the band can be re-accommodated, the CEPT recommended an allocation for the Digital European Cordless Telecommunications standard (DECT) in the region of 1.9 GHz. In making this decision the CEPT recognised that by the turn of the century Europe will probably have standardised a further generation of mobile equipment and it would seem pragmatic to focus these potential

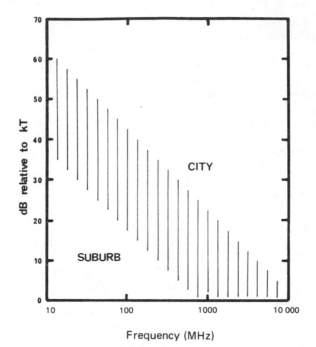

Frequency (MHz)

Fig. 7.1. The variation of man-made noise with frequency. k, Boltzmann's constant; T, 290 K.

developments in the same range of frequencies. Consequently, there is now in prospect the possibility that the band 1.7 GHz to 2.1 GHz could be identified with mobile communications on a primary basis throughout western Europe and, through due process of international agreement, perhaps the world.

7.2 Spectrum Requirements

Cordless telecommunications no longer means a simple cordless telephone [3]. It spans a diversity of applications and uses, up to high-capacity high-density cordless business communication systems designed for speech and data communications. The corresponding spectrum requirement is equally wide ranging for it is a function of traffic density.

Traffic density is generally expressed in terms of erlangs per square kilometre (E/km^2), for low-density housing or, ideally, erlangs per cubic kilometre (or alternatively erlangs per km^2·floor) for high-rise office blocks. Typical traffic densities are given below [4] for the busiest period of the day (the "busy hour"):

Residential suburban $= 150$ E/km^2
Office (localised peak) $= 10\ 000$ E/km^2·floor

A cordless penetration factor for residential situations of 30% and for the office of 100% has been assumed in these figures.

Clearly the office requirement dominates the spectrum requirement and, since a single Cordless Business Communication System (CBCS) could service the requirement, then it is clear there is no scope for allocating radio spectrum based on growth of mean wide-area traffic densities. The full allocated spectrum must be available from the day of service launch, even if there is only one CBCS in operation.

Traditionally spectrum would be allocated on the basis of one radio carrier per user and an assumption that carrier frequency re-use range is greater than that determined from transmitter power and receiver noise sensitivity. Extrapolating this approach to the office environment referred to above would for, say, 100 kHz effective bandwidth per two-way channel, require 1 GHz of spectrum allocation per floor – a requirement impossible to serve in the band below 2 GHz!

If cordless technology is to meet the requirements posed by high-rise office blocks then it must adopt cellular-frequency re-use techniques akin to mobile telephone systems. Importing these techniques into a building results in many small-radius cells per office floor, cells perhaps as small as 10 m in radius. Naturally, a multi-storey building extends the cellular concept into a three-dimensional system, with cells and corresponding transmitters located on every floor and forming part of a unified building CBCS. To distinguish these cells from the relatively very large mobile telephone cells of radius 1 km or more, they have been termed "picocells". Cellular techniques allow frequency re-use because care is taken to ensure that the distance between base station transmitters using the same carrier frequency is not less than that required to achieve a given co-channel carrier to interference ratio. Consequently in a cellular system, the operational range of a radio link is limited by co-channel interference rather than by receiver sensitivity as in the earlier spectrum-greedy example.

The situation of co-channel interference-limited operation is illustrated in Fig. 7.2. For a handset H to communicate successfully with base station T on frequency f the wanted signal power (C) from T and the interference power (I) from T_1 must be such that their ratio (C/I) exceeds a minimum value appropriate to the system technology used and the quality of transmission required. For 32 kbit/s ADPCM speech encoding to the CCITT G.721 standard, the threshold probability of bit-error (P_e) allowable is 10^{-3}. Assuming the use of Gaussian filtered minimum shift keying modulation (GMSK) with a bandwidth symbol period product (BT) of 0.5 and the use of coherent detection, such a $P_e = 10^{-3}$ threshold requires $C/I = 11$ dB, after taking into account a reasonable engineering implementation margin.

Unfortunately the wanted signal also suffers from Rayleigh fading (a narrow-band system assumed), a consequence of the multiple transmission path environment encountered in mobile communications ("multipath").

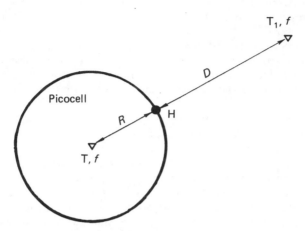

Fig. 7.2. Frequency re-use: the co-channel interference-limited scenario. D, re-use distance; H, handset; R, maximum handset range; T, base station.

Consequently the threshold will be breached for about 65% of the time unless a fade margin is allowed for. Fig. 7.3 shows that, for Rayleigh fading, a 20 dB fade margin without diversity results in the received signal level staying above threshold for 99% of the time. Naturally the interference signal also suffers from Rayleigh fading but the acceptably small divergence between the mean and median probabilities of Rayleigh fading allows the

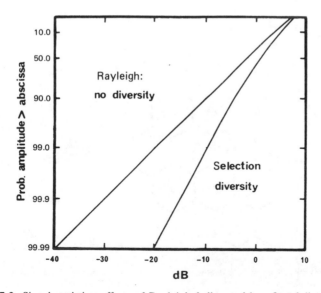

Fig. 7.3. Signal statistics: effects of Rayleigh fading and benefits of diversity.

statistics of interference to be equated to Gaussian amplitude distributed noise. Allowing for such a fade margin implies the need for a carrier to interference ratio, C/I, of 31 dB.

The interference levels within a given cordless system will be a function of the physical distributions of base stations and active handsets as well as the choice of channel for every call. In an ideal conventional cellular mobile radio approach, base stations are considered to be deployed on a hexagonal grid; the spectrum is divided amongst these base stations to provide non-interfering channel assignments according to a pre-planned spatial re-use pattern. For reasons discussed in Section 7.5, this approach is not proposed for any business cordless telephone systems, current or future. The approach is rather to employ Dynamic Channel Assignment (DCA), algorithms which seek to select the optimum channel from all (or a large subset) of those available. (This approach is described in Section 7.6.3.) Nevertheless the pre-planned cellular grid approximation is, to a first order, a relatively simple-to-analyse representation and the results of such an analysis can provide a useful yardstick. Thus we now examine the CBCS according to such an approximation in order to obtain an estimate of the spectrum requirement. In Section 7.5 we discuss a computer simulation approach which more fully models the effects of DCA and irregular base station deployment.

For current purposes we assume that a handset experiences interference arising from, on average, six first-order interferers disposed in a hexagonal pattern, as shown in Fig. 7.4. In this scenario the distance between co-channel base stations and the reference handset is the re-use distance (D). The area within which all channels can be used, but not re-used, is given by:

$$A = \frac{\sqrt{3}}{2} D^2 \qquad\qquad\qquad\qquad (7.1)$$

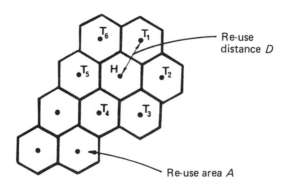

Fig. 7.4. Hexagonal cell deployment, showing interference scenario. H, handset; T_1–T_6, base stations, all of frequency f.

Assuming the wanted and interfering signals decay as the mth power of distance, then the carrier to interference ratio becomes:

$$\frac{C}{I} = 10 \log_{10} \frac{1}{6} \left(\frac{D}{R}\right)^m \tag{7.2}$$

With a net busy-hour traffic density of T E/km²·floor, the traffic offered in area A is:

$$E_a = T \cdot A \tag{7.3}$$

Combining all three equations generates:

$$E_a = \frac{\sqrt{3}}{2} \, 6^{\frac{2}{m}} \, T \cdot R^2 \, 10^{\frac{2C/I}{10m}} \tag{7.4}$$

which is the traffic per re-use area per floor. The three-dimensional characteristic of the cells is introduced by a vertical re-use factor F, usually defined as the number of floors an interfering signal must penetrate before the resulting signal strength becomes of the order of or less than the horizontal components of interference. F depends on the floor penetration loss, which has been shown to be a wide-ranging variable dependent on such factors as building construction, the opportunity for signals to propagate along stairways, etc. Excess loss values for floor penetration ranging from 6 to 15 dB have been quoted [5,6], suggesting that the vertical re-use distance, in terms of number of floors (F), should range between $F=5$ and $F=2$ respectively to cover the extreme cases. Applying this factor to Equation (7.4) generates the traffic per re-use volume:

$$E_r = \frac{\sqrt{3}}{2} \, 6^{\frac{2}{m}} \, F \cdot T \cdot R^2 \, 10^{\frac{2C/I}{10m}} \tag{7.5}$$

By the use of erlang-B tables, E_r can be converted to the number of channels, N, that a system has to offer to satisfy the demand for a required probability of successful call set-up. Typically this probability is 99%. The product of N and the specific bandwidth per channel (B_S) then produces the required estimate of spectrum requirement, B.

From the foregoing, it can be shown with a reasonable degree of accuracy that:

$$B \propto F \cdot T \cdot R^2 \, 10^{\frac{C/I}{20}} \tag{7.6}$$

In deriving this equation we have assumed a value of $m=4$. From this expression the sensitivity of spectrum requirement to changes in parameters can be gauged. For example:

1. Doubling the vertical re-use factor doubles spectrum requirement
2. Doubling offered traffic density doubles spectrum requirement
3. Raising operational cell radius range from 10 m to 32 m increases spectrum requirement tenfold
4. Reducing C/I threshold value from 31 dB to 21 dB reduces spectrum requirement by 3.2 times

These examples show that the required spectrum allocation demanded of spectrum regulators is very susceptible to changes in quality of communication and extent of service coverage per base station.

Conversely, for an externally regulated and fixed bandwidth B, and hence fixed N, the proportionality of Equation (7.6) has implicit dangers for system installers. When installing a system a trade-off must be made between offered traffic, T, and cell operating radius, R, i.e. base station layout. In making this trade-off a margin must be allowed in T to suit the customer's likely communications growth demands; otherwise, for a fixed layout, growth will erode the C/I margin above the system performance threshold with a consequent reduction in quality of communication. For example, if growth in T disturbs the equality of Equation (7.5) by a factor of 2 then the compensatory change in C/I is 3 dB, equivalent to a doubling in probability of exceeding threshold performance or indeed a doubling in outage probability.

By application of Equation (7.5) the spectrum requirement to service a given set of assumptions can be determined; one example is shown in Fig. 7.5. This result shows that of the order of 70 MHz is required to service an office offering 10 000 E/km²·floor with 4-floor re-use. The requirement can be reduced by decreasing operating range in classical cellular fashion, but there is also scope for improvement through the introduction of diversity. Fig. 7.3 shows that switched diversity reduces the C/I requirement by 10 dB for a 1% outage probability. Item 4 above indicates that this improvement

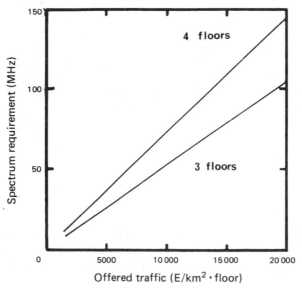

Fig. 7.5. Example of spectrum requirement vs. offered traffic. Cell radius, 15 m; propagation law 4; bandwidth per channel, 100 kHz; C/I, 31 dB; no diversity; gos, grade of service, 1%.

reduces spectrum demand by a factor of 3.2. Whether this significant reduction can be achieved in practice, however, depends on the extent to which frequency selective fading is a significant factor resulting from the multipath radio environment typical of cordless telecommunications.

7.3 Radio Coverage in Buildings

The most challenging application of cordless telecommunications is the cordless business communication system. Before investing any capital in a CBCS a telecommunications manager would want to be assured that a usable radio signal exists in his nominated CBCS coverage area. If replacing, say, more than 30% of wired PABX terminals with cordless equivalents were being considered then the manager could rightly demand that the usable radio signal strength must occur for more than 99% of the nominated area. This is a reasonable objective, for users of normal, wired terminals have come to expect probabilities of call blockage (grade of service) of less than 0.5%. As far as the handset user is concerned call blockage, whether arising from traffic congestion in the switch or from poor radio signal coverage, is unacceptable; the user is not likely to give much free licence in this respect in return for cordless mobility.

From the installer's point of view the objective is to provide the necessary standard of radio signal coverage first time every time but, to be competitive with the wired alternative, highly skilled, highly paid radio engineers versed in the art of radio propagation cannot be used to achieve this. Thus there is a requirement for simple-to-use tools that can predict accurately transmission path loss, taking into account visible structural details of the building in question, preparatory to determining the positions of the fixed base station transceivers. These simple planning tools are expected to involve the use of a personal computer operated by, at most, semi-skilled operatives.

There are two techniques available that potentially provide good quality radio coverage. The first uses small antennas distributed around the customer's premises, each antenna effectively providing a three-dimensional coverage volume – a picocell. The alternative is to radiate the signal from relatively poorly screened coaxial cables, known as "leaky feeders", laid along corridors or around corners; this enables the coverage to be tailored to meet specific, perhaps otherwise impossible requirements. In both cases the requirement is for an expression that relates transmission path loss to distance between base station and mobile terminal. Such a relationship for mobile systems can be expressed as [6]:

$$\overline{P}_r = P_t - \overline{L} - 10n \log_{10} d \qquad (7.7)$$

where $\overline{P}_r$ = mean received power (dBm)
P_t = transmitted power (dBm)
$\overline{L}$ = path loss at $d = 1$ m (dB)

d = direct distance between transmitter and receiver, and

n = signal decay exponent

P_r is subject to rapid Rayleigh distributed amplitude fading due to the multipath environment typical of mobile transmission. The transmission path loss, L_p (dB), is the difference between P_t and $\overline{P_r}$ and hence:

$$L_p = \overline{L} + 10n \log_{10} d \tag{7.8}$$

Much propagation measurement effort has been expended worldwide to obtain parameters for equations of the form above that accommodate a range of building layouts and construction techniques. In the remainder of this section we discuss reported results which attempt to express in such a form in-building propagation using antennas and leaky feeders.

An example of propagation measurement is shown in Fig. 7.6 for a reinforced concrete building with internal metal partitions. The hatched area represents the extent of usable radio signal coverage from the central receiver. Allowing for the fact that the experimental receiver is near the outside wall of the building it clearly shows that coverage tends naturally to be cellular in a building of reasonably consistent structure. The received signal figures refer to the room-average value and the histogram to the variability around that value.

Plotting the room-average signal strengths against distance produces Fig. 7.7, to which has been added the best-fit line computed to minimise the mean square error of the data. Relating this result to Equation (7.8), the gradient of the line identifies the signal decay exponent (n), which in this example is 5.7. Unfortunately this is not a generally applicable result, for reference [7] reports signal decay exponents for fourteen buildings of concrete or brick or plaster-board construction that range between $n=1.2$ and $n=6.5$. The highest values tend to be associated with buildings using metal-faced partitions that impede transmission, whereas the lowest value occurred in a hangar-like workshop that appears to have acted like a waveguide [7]. Nevertheless there is no sufficiently consistent picture from which widely applicable conclusions can be drawn, and no ready explanation for the variability of n.

It has been postulated that for distances greater than, say, 40 m in a building the radio signal that has penetrated the internal clutter may often be exceeded by a signal that has taken a more indirect reflection route, perhaps by reflection from an adjacent building. The converse has also been suggested. In the latter case it is argued that the short-range results are dominated by localised reflections while the longer ranges are subject to relatively high clutter loss. Such a model based on classical two-path ray theory [8] would predict $n=2$ at short range increasing to $n \geqslant 4$ at longer ranges. Certainly mixed models of this type have been used to explain mobile transmission phenomena with some success, for example in Fig. 7.8 and [9]. Either possibility is very dependent on the detailed layout and construction of the building and in many cases the true picture could be a combination of both.

The work reported in [6] sets out to investigate whether or not in-building

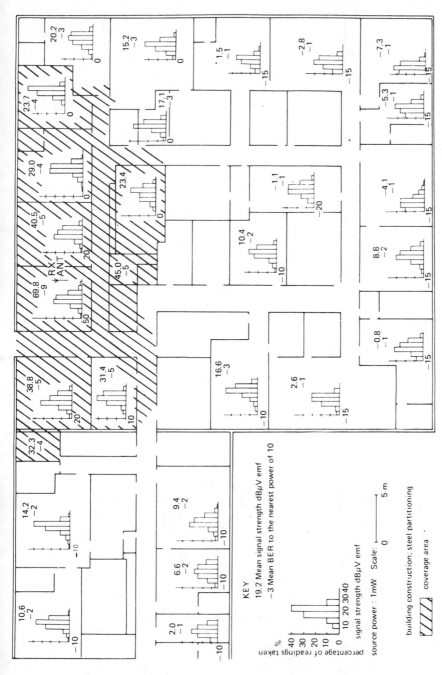

Fig. 7.6. Example of propagation measurement for a reinforced concrete building.

KEY

19.2 Mean signal strength dBµV emf
–3 Mean BER to the nearest power of 10

percentage of readings taken %

signal strength dBµV emf

source power : 1 mW   Scale: 0 —— 5 m

building construction : steel partitioning

coverage area

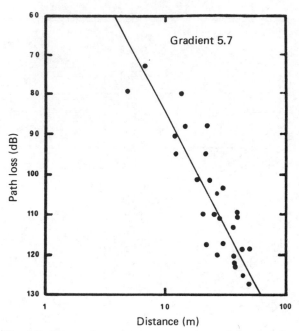

Fig. 7.7. Propagation measurement results: path loss vs. distance.

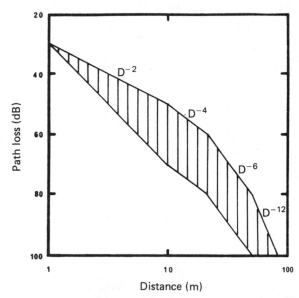

Fig. 7.8. Classical ray theory mixed model for in-building propagation. Propagation law as indicated: D^{-2}, D^{-4}, D^{-6}, etc. (Adapted from [9].)

data for ranges less than 40 m can be treated to produce a more generally applicable solution for path loss. The distance limitation was not considered overly restrictive since the picocell radius in most high-capacity CBCSs is expected to be considerably less than 40 m.

The approach taken was to apply Equation (7.8) to the situation modelled in Fig. 7.9. The need to penetrate (or bypass) walls and floors must be taken into account in predicting the path loss at 1 m, noting that it will vary widely from one receiver position to another for the value of $\overline{L}$ reflects the mean clutter loss. To obtain a practical expression for path loss, therefore, the value of $\overline{L}$ must be related to structural features of the building. Even this degree of relative sophistication will still leave some variability in L due to furniture and people moving around. In [6] it has been shown that the variability can be described by a log-normal distribution with variance v and mean $\overline{L}$. Hence

$$L_p = \overline{L} + 10n \log_{10}d + L(v) \tag{7.9}$$

In Fig. 7.10 a typical set of results is shown for path loss related to distance for two frequencies (864 MHz, appropriate to CT2/CAI, and 1728 MHz, which is close to the DECT frequency). These results relate to a multi-storey office block with reinforced concrete shell and plaster board internal office walls; each floor was 50 m long and 15 m wide with a central corridor. Each point on the graph refers to the room-average path loss obtained by automatically recording a multitude of measurements through the office. In [6] the results were processed to obtain the best-fit line and, by comparison with Equation (7.9), values for $\overline{L}$ and n were obtained; these are recorded in Table 7.1.

The high value for mean square error in Table 7.1 gives little confidence in the broad application of the results, but the signal decay exponent at least indicates that an assumption of $n=4$ is reasonable for both frequencies.

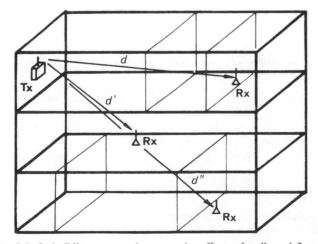

Fig. 7.9. In-building propagation scenario: effects of walls and floors.

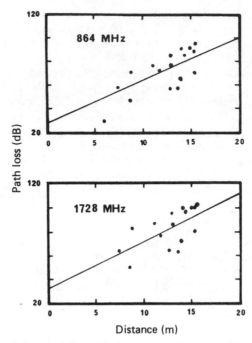

Fig. 7.10. Typical path loss variation with distance at 864 MHz and 1728 MHz for in-building propagation.

Table 7.1. Best-fit propagation parameters

Frequency (MHz)	$\overline{L}$ (dB)	n	Mean square error (dB)
864	27.5	3.6	133
1728	32.0	3.9	185

Indeed the slight difference in value of n accounts for the difference in $\overline{L}$, being less than the 6 dB that theory would predict for a doubling in frequency. Closer analysis of the results was reported to show that similar but parallel regression lines could be obtained for each set of points associated with each floor. Consequently the path loss expression was modified to:

$$L_p = \overline{L} + 40 \log_{10}d + kf + L(v) \tag{7.10}$$

where k = number of floors traversed
f = floor attenuation factor (dB), and
n = 4.

To obtain the best-fit regression line f was varied to minimise the mean square error of the data, with the results shown in Table 7.2. These results present a significant improvement in terms of mean square error, reduction in clutter loss $(\overline{L})$ and difference in $\overline{L} = 6$ dB, as would be expected from theory. Accordingly they indicate that it should be possible to characterise a range of building types in terms of a mean residual clutter loss $(\overline{L})$ and a floor attenuation factor (f), and to apply these to an equation of the form of Equation (7.10).

By applying Equation (7.10) to each floor-corrected data point, the range residual clutter loss values (L) were obtained. Their distribution showed a log-normal characteristic from which the standard deviation $(v^{\frac{1}{2}})$ was determined. For the office block, standard deviations of 3 dB and 4.2 dB were obtained for 864 and 1728 MHz respectively.

In practice the transmission path loss between dipoles spaced 1 m apart is 32 and 38 dB for 864 and 1728 MHz respectively, with an initial decay exponent of $n=2$ because the line-of-sight path is dominant at small values of d.

Accordingly the transmission path loss can be written as:

$$L_p = 38 + 20 \log_{10}d$$

or

$$L_p = \overline{L} + 40 \log_{10}d + kf + L(v) \tag{7.11}$$

whichever solution is the greater for 1728 MHz. This leads to a path loss curve of the form of Fig. 7.11. Clearly to apply these expressions to a range of buildings requires a knowledge of $\overline{L}$ and f as a function of building type and construction. Present results suggest 10 dB$<\overline{L}<25$ dB and 5.5 dB$<f<15$ dB for a range of buildings at 864 MHz. At 1728 MHz $\overline{L}$ is 6 dB greater than for the corresponding 864 MHz result; likewise the floor attenuation factor at 1728 MHz is 3 dB greater.

Radio coverage from a radiating coaxial cable is shown in Fig. 7.12 and can be expressed by an equation similar in form to that for antennas, as follows:

$$\overline{P}_r = P_t - \overline{L}_c - L(v) - 10n\log_{10}d - kf - XA \tag{7.12}$$

where A = attenuation per metre of the cable
X = distance from the nearest point of the cable to the base station termination
$\overline{L}_c$ = cable coupling loss referenced to a 1 m radial distance from the cable

Table 7.2. Revised best-fit propagation parameters

Frequency (MHz)	$\overline{L}$ (dB)	n	Mean square error (dB)
864	10	−4	15
1728	16	−4	22

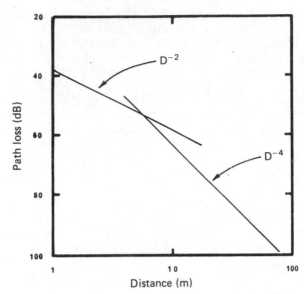

Fig. 7.11. Path loss curve of the form of Equation (7.11). Propagation law as indicated: D^{-2}, D^{-4}.

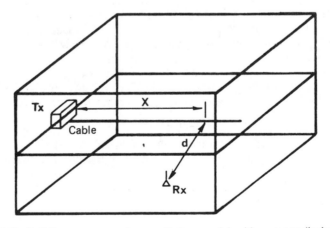

Fig. 7.12. Building coverage using a radiating coaxial cable antenna (leaky feeder).

To evaluate the various parameters, a 900 MHz coaxial cable laid in the corridor of the building used for the antenna experiments was studied [5]. The measured signal levels along the cable are shown in Fig. 7.13, and demonstrate good agreement between the best-fit line and the specified cable attenuation factor. The undulation in the results is a standing-wave effect caused by interaction between the internal and surface cable propagation modes. Plotting the signal decay in a direction radial to the

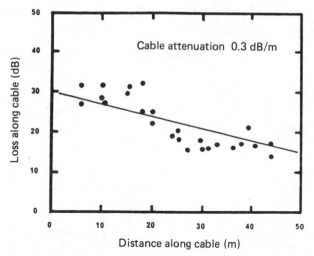

Fig. 7.13. Signal level longitudinal variations for a leaky feeder antenna.

cable produced Fig. 7.14, in which cable attenuation and floor factor (f) have been corrected for. As indicated, the signal decay exponent (n) is 3 and the mean coupling loss ($\overline{L_c}$) at 1 m is 60 dB. Using a technique similar to that for antenna calculations the variation in $\overline{L_c}$ due to building proximity effects was found to be log-normal with a standard deviation of 3 dB. Accordingly, for the selected cable at 900 MHz, the path loss relationship is given by:

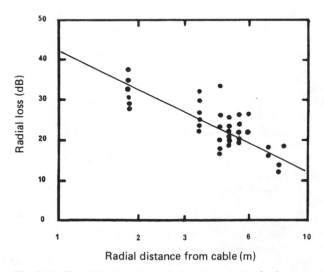

Fig. 7.14. Signal level radial variations for a leaky feeder antenna.

$$\overline{P}_r \text{ (Rayleigh)} = P_t - 60 - L \text{ (log normal}, v)$$

$$- 30 \log_{10} d - kf - 0.3X \qquad\qquad (7.13)$$

where both k and f have the same meaning as adopted for the antenna results.

7.4 The Dispersive Channel

In the previous section the underlying concern was that the received signal strength should be sufficient to maintain acceptable communication quality for better than 99% of the time in the nominated coverage area in the presence of noise and co-channel interference. The fundamental asumption, however, was that the modulated carrier signal could be reasonably equated to an unmodulated carrier signal. This assumption is reasonable for the early analogue modulated cordless telephone equipments but questionable for the more modern digitally modulated cordless systems which have relatively large modulated-carrier bandwidths. For these systems the dispersive nature of multipath radio transmission may well be significant.

Mobile radio transmission channels are dispersive in both time and frequency. Time dispersion is the result of the received signal having been propagated over many different paths of different length and hence suffering different transmission delays and different attenuations. The end result is that the received signal is a summation of many copies of the original transmitted signal with a spread of delays and amplitudes. Frequency dispersion, however, is caused either by movement of the receiver relative to the transmitter because one or other is in motion, or by the signal reflecting surfaces themselves moving with respect to the receiver or transmitter even though these themselves may be stationary.

Frequency dispersion appears as a variable Doppler shift of the transmitted signal components which can cause rapid changes in their instantaneous phase thereby creating problems for coherent signal-detection techniques and post-detection noise in non-coherent detection, e.g. discriminators. Fortunately for cordless telecommunications most apparent motion is somewhat pedestrian! For example, Doppler shift of a 1 GHz carrier frequency is less than ± 6 Hz for a healthy walking speed of 6 km/h and consequently the problem generally can be ignored. Exceptions to the rule may well occur when cordless equipment is operated in high-speed vehicles, for example trains, with reflections from passing buildings, or near to fast-moving traffic.

Let us return to time dispersion. The signal distorting effects can be represented in the three dimensions of space, frequency and time. Remembering that the received signal is a summation of many independent copies of the transmitted signal, each relatively delayed in time and suffering differing attenuation, then at a given point, or position, for a particular frequency component of the modulated signal the copies will add vectorially. Any movement of the receiver (or transmitter or reflecting surfaces) will disturb this vector summation. The resulting signal level is shown in Fig. 7.15a. Note that this figure indicates the way antenna (space) diversity can be effective. For conditions of no movement any change in frequency will equally disturb received signal vector conditions because of phase changes, giving rise to Fig. 7.15b. This shows the channel response to a swept frequency source and the frequency-selective nature of multipath propagation with respect to an assumed system bandwidth. Fig. 7.15c is representative of the same phenomenon in the time domain; many relatively delayed copies of the signal cause a spread of signals. If there is a direct line-of-sight component to the received signal then this shows as the largest component near the origin.

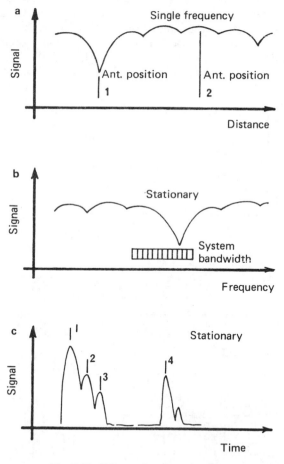

Fig. 7.15. Effects of a dispersive channel.

Fig. 7.15c is perhaps most useful in describing the effect of such transmission on the received signal. If the spread of delay is of the order of 0.3 of a transmitted symbol period then significant signal degradation occurs, as Fig. 7.16 shows diagrammatically. It is clear from this simple demonstration that the signal can be corrupted very considerably due to the delayed symbols interfering with each other, causing what is known as intersymbol interference. Furthermore this is a result for a static transmission condition; in practice the amplitude and phase of each of many delayed components of the received signal will undergo independent random variation. This results in a system performance having an irreducible mean bit-error ratio. The significance of this effect on signal reception has been found to depend on the delay spread of the received components, their relative amplitude and the period of the transmitted symbol. Generally delay spread and relative amplitude are linked by calculating the root-mean-square (RMS) value of the power-delay profile, for it has been found that the resulting irreducible mean bit-error ratios (expressed logarithmically) are broadly proportional to the square of the normalised RMS delay spread (normalised to the symbol period) [10]. It is of course possible for widely varying power-delay profiles to produce similar RMS delay values, so variability of receiver system performance about the mean must be expected,

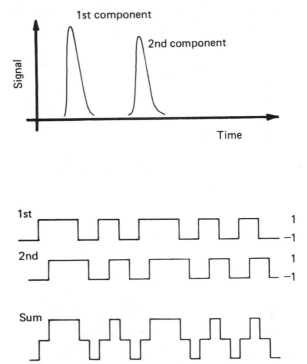

Fig. 7.16. Intersymbol interference caused by delay spread.

particularly when one multipath component may have significant amplitude and relatively long delay with respect to all others.

Several studies [e.g. 11,12] have shown clearly that the RMS delay spread is a function of the environment in which the measurements were taken. Delay spreads in the range 50 ns (corresponding to measurements in the inner offices of large buildings) to 300 ns (inside-to-outside office and residential buildings and Telepoint situations) have been recorded. The significance of such RMS delay spreads (t) to system bit-error ratio performance can only be judged when they are normalised to the symbol period (T). It has been shown that for GMSK modulation the mean irreducible bit-error ratio will exceed 10^{-3} for a normalised delay spread $t/T = 0.05$, which corresponds to 50 ns delay spread for a 1 Mbit/s symbol rate [10]. However, at this normalised delay the application of antenna spatial diversity (antenna spacing in the region of a wavelength for the enclosed environments of, say, an office block) would be expected to reduce the bit-error ratio to insignificance. The effectiveness of diversity, however, is rapidly lost as the normalised delay spread increases, and becomes of little residual value at $t/T = 0.3$ – a value of 300 ns in this example. This loss of performance results from the frequency-selective fading nature of the phenomenon having a correlation bandwidth (which is proportional to the inverse of RMS delay spread) of the order of the system's occupied bandwidth.

To recover system performance out of this situation requires the application of time-dispersion equalisation techniques. Unfortunately the need for this solution tends to be application specific because of the relationship between delay spread and environment. Consequently careful consideration must be given to the application and services to be operated with respect to the desired quality of reception when designing cordless terminal equipment. Such equalisation techniques have not been employed in conventional cordless telephones to date, nor are they yet envisaged for most common applications, save those involving open area Telepoint-like evolutionary applications.

7.5 System Modelling Techniques

The previous section described an approach to determining the requirements for achieving adequate coverage for individual communication links. The purpose of this was stated as being to provide the installer with a simple portable computer-based tool for planning the installation. For installing large indoor cordless communications systems another issue arises, namely that of planning the sizes of the picocells in order to ensure adequate handling for the traffic densities predicted for that particular installation. This has already been covered empirically for the pre-planned re-use approximation described in Section 7.2. However, as we shall see, in all current and projected high-density systems re-use is not pre-planned but automated. Once such automatic channel assignment is considered in a cordless system, its operation becomes too complex for empirical evaluation and computer-based models come into their own. The rationale for the adoption of such strategies is initially outlined below, followed by a description of a common approach to the problem of modelling.

As discussed in Section 7.2, the provision of cordless communications in buildings requires the use of cellular re-use strategies in order to satisfy the call traffic demands without excessive spectrum requirements. Moreover, multi-storey buildings will need to establish three-dimensional re-use patterns to ensure acceptable interference levels from all directions. The number of degrees of freedom which this affords is potentially an embarrassment, yielding great potential for efficiency through optimisation but only at the expense of considerable effort. This is best illustrated with reference to consideration of interference between floors. As mentioned in Section 7.2, the re-use factor for floors is estimated to range between 2 and 5. Interference between floors is a complex phenomenon. Optimum re-use is obtained through staggering the positions of the co-channel users on different floors. Depending on the areas of the picocells and the two-dimensional re-use pattern employed, it is feasible that base station position staggering could permit some co-channel re-use on adjacent floors. The level of potential planning difficulties should not be underestimated. Indeed they could be greatly exacerbated where an installer needs to deploy a new CBCS in a shared office block which already has some systems operational. Clearly it would be impracticable to replan the existing systems to accommodate the new one.

It is in part considerations such as these that have led to the adoption of fully self-organising anarchic approaches. In these approaches, all base stations may choose from all channels. Optimal (or sub-optimal) channels are chosen on the basis of carrier-to-interference ratio, i.e. Dynamic Channel Assignment (DCA); this theme is expanded in Section 7.6 on usage of the radio channel.

The benefits of such an approach are considerable. Firstly, it is unnecessary to perform detailed measurements to assess the propagation characteristics of a building to plan re-use. Secondly, the existing system will automatically and immediately adapt to the incorporation of new base stations or of a new adjacent system.

The problem of installation amounts to one of economics, i.e. deploying the minimum density of base stations necessary to support the predicted traffic levels (with an appropriate allowance for growth). For a given base station density the supportable traffic will depend upon the propagation characteristics of the building. For the somewhat amorphous channel re-use which arises with fully adaptive systems there are no break points (i.e. the cellular re-use patterns do not change in discrete numbers) so there is, on average, a smooth monotonic relationship between the attenuation law and the supportable traffic density.

Recent modelling studies [13] have shown that the number of base stations required exhibits a very strong dependency on the propagation model, in particular the standard deviation of the path loss at any given range. Indoor propagation can be very different from that outdoors insofar as partitions can introduce sharp propagation thresholds. In particular, the standard deviation of interfering signal levels can be quite small due to guaranteed screening effects. The implication of this is that in practice fewer base stations may be required than might otherwise be expected.

In considering computer modelling, we now outline a commonly adopted approach. Firstly, the area/volume to be modelled is determined. Towards the centre of an office floor the cordless links may be subject to interference from any direction. Near the external walls, however, interference can only come from directions over an approximately 180° span. Thus a simple model will be subject to noticeable edge effects, i.e. blocking will be less significant near the edges. Because the requirements for a cordless system will generally be determined by the worst case conditions, the results relating to equipments operating near the edge will need to be ignored. Edge effects tend to decay only gradually with increasing distance from the boundary, so quite large floors need to be modelled in order to obtain useful results from a significant proportion of their area.

In one modelling approach [14] this problem has been tackled by the use of an abstraction which eliminates edges altogether! The concept is to cause each boundary of the model to wrap around to its opposite boundary. This is achieved simply by causing distance parameters to be measured modulo d, where d is the deployment width distance parameter. Surprisingly, this approach is appropriate for hexagonal as well as rectangular deployments. The effect is akin to that observed on some video games where an object may disappear off one edge of the screen and re-appear on the opposite side. The approach may also be used in three-dimensional office blocks, with each floor wrapping independently. This method allows accurate modelling to be performed with relatively modest floor areas; results can be taken from the entire area.

Once the modelling area/volume has been determined it is necessary to decide on the appropriate propagation model to be used. In early research into cordless systems some attempts were made to create models of office buildings, including partitions of specific materials in specific locations. Propagation was modelled use ray tracing, scattering and diffraction techniques. It quickly became apparent that not only would the results so obtained be very particular to the office modelled but also the computational burden of the approach would prevent usefully large models (in terms of numbers of links and operating time) to be considered. Accordingly, almost all modelling in recent years has taken a model for propagation based upon the averaged results of a large number of measurements, as described in Section 7.3. Given such a propagation characteristic, the attenuation over paths between base stations and handsets may be modelled.

Let us now consider the overall system model. The usual approach is to generate, in numeric form, a representation of a cordless system with base stations deployed in some defined manner and handsets distributed across the deployment. This representation is then set to operate for a period of time, with calls generated at random times and from random sites. At the end of the model run, various statistics can be derived such as the proportion of call attempts which succeeded, the proportion which were blocked and the proportion which were prematurely curtailed. Other parameters of interest include the average carrier-to-interference ratio and the average utilisation of base station channels.

A useful method of modelling for this type of system is discrete event simulation. In this approach, model time is stepped forward in non-uniform increments determined by the time at which each event should take place. Future events are stored in time order in a list, along with the event times, thus forming an event queue. The model operates by successively removing, reading and executing the event at the head of the queue.

New calls are generated according to a Poisson process (i.e. they start at random time) and have durations which may be fixed at a median value or are random according to some appropriate probability distribution. A common approach is to start every new call by placing a new handset at a randomly determined new location. It is then possible to calculate its distance from all other active base stations to determine the interference levels on all channels. The handset then selects a channel according to the DCA algorithm and attempts to set up a call. Once the call has been set up the effect of interference from this new call needs to be evaluated on all other links.

It is not difficult to appreciate that a significant amount of computational effort is commonly required for the above type of model. The statistical nature of the answers required often dictates the need for a large set of results in order to obtain reliable values. This is particularly true of blocking probabilities, where figures of the order of 0.5% are commonly of interest. Obtaining a reliable figure could require some 20 000 calls to be modelled!

The value of modelling can be seen by reference to an illustration. In a recent model an examination of blocking was done comparing interference in a one-storey building with that in the centre floor of a three-storey building for a 16-channel system. The excess floor attenuation was taken as 10 dB and 21 dB was assumed for the minimum required C/I (i.e. two-branch diversity was assumed). The ratio of traffic capacity between the two deployments was found to be approximately 1.6, rather than the figure of about 2 which Section 7.3 would predict. This illustrates both the power of DCA in assigning frequencies at separated locations on adjacent floors and also the benefit of modelling to take account of the specific case where only three floors need be considered (a relatively common requirement).

7.6 Usage of the Radio Channel

In mobile radio communications, and particularly cordless applications, there is a basic need to set up many independent communication links between mobile terminal and fixed base in a confined volume – confined in the sense that all these independent links, in attempting to use the same spectrum allocation, would interfere with, and potentially destroy each other unless appropriate avoidance measures were taken. The problem is to ensure that multiple communication links can gain access to the available spectrum resources in an orderly manner which avoids the worst effects of mutual interference and yet achieves optimally efficient spectrum use. The process of doing this is known as multiple access and, taken in its widest sense, it also includes duplex (two-way) transmission.

7.6.1 Duplex Transmission

Conversation between people is (generally) two-way across a common, literal air interface from mouth to ear. The imposition of a radio link between them then raises the problem of providing a concurrent two-way link in a manner that ensures conversation is uninterrupted by artificial restraints – for example one person only being allowed to talk at any one time (simplex).

Conventionally in many radio transmission applications two separate links are created on separate carrier frequencies for each direction of transmission. This is known as frequency division duplex. The present CEPT CT1 analogue system is an example that uses the two frequency bands of 914–915 MHz and 959–960 MHz in this way to support forty duplex channels. One of these bands is used for transmission from the handset and one for transmission from the base station, the spacing between the bands being necessary to permit adequate filtering within the equipments for simultaneous transmission and reception in the two bands.

Discussions with the UK frequency regulatory authorities during 1981 for the nascent digital CT2 standard soon demonstrated that a two-frequency allocation in the 800–900 MHz region was not possible, although a single contiguous band was potentially available. Consideration of how to exploit this opportunity resulted in the adoption of time division duplex transmission (TDD). In this technique a single carrier frequency is used to provide two-way communication (handset to base and base to handset) by dividing the transmission time into two equal parts each supporting unidirectional transmission of a digitised sample of speech (say 2 ms) that is compressed by bit-rate doubling into half the sample period (1 ms) before transmission. The intervening gap is filled by the return transmission using the same technique. After reception the compressed sample is expanded back to its normal period and then decoded. Of course this technique can also be used in multi-burst time division multiple access systems, and is employed too in DECT for voice links.

The use of TDD has a number of advantages:

1. The transmission path characteristics are identical in each direction because the same carrier frequency is used. Thus the received

communication quality is closely similar to that transmitted, enabling in-built transmission quality monitoring

2. Antenna diversity at the base station will optimise both directions of transmission

3. Terminal and base units have identical radio frequency circuit and component requirements

4. Cordless telecommunications systems that use TDD do not compete with conventional cellular mobile radio systems for scarce paired-band spectrum resources

7.6.2 Multiple Access

There are three basic forms of multiple access technique:

1. Frequency Division Multiple Access (FDMA)
2. Time Division Multiple Access (TDMA)
3. Code Division Multiple Access (CDMA)

These are reviewed below from the point of view of cordless telecommunications.

FDMA

FDMA is the access technique in which the available spectrum resource of P MHz is subdivided into n discrete channels each of bandwidth P/n MHz (see Fig. 7.17). In operating this multiple access technique the associated radio transmission and receiving equipment must ensure that the signal occupying, say, channel $(n-2)$ does not spread unduly into the adjacent

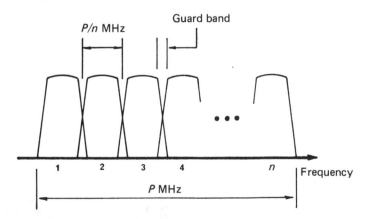

Fig. 7.17. Frequency division multiple access scheme.

channels. Equally channel $(n-2)$ expects equivalent protection from channels $(n-3)$ and $(n-1)$. This mutual protection is provided by a guard band between channels, by appropriate modulation techniques and by the use of filters that attenuate signals that otherwise would fall outside the allocated channel. Nevertheless, because of spectrum economy, filter characteristics and technical prudence this isolation is not perfect and some energy leaks from one channel to the next. A compromise between the various factors is of course indicated, but the guard band in practice constitutes a spectrum overhead and in the interests of spectrum efficiency it is desirable to minimise it.

The transmission capacity $(b_r$ bit/s) of each channel determines the necessary modulation bandwidth (B), but the need for a guard band results in $B < P/n$ and hence capacity falls below the maximum attainable, assuming a given modulation technique.

Consequently the effective spectrum efficiency becomes n/P traffic channels per MHz. Typical examples for European FDMA cordless systems are 20 channels/MHz (CEPT CT1, analogue transmission, frequency division duplex operation) and 10 channels/MHz for digital CT2 CAI. As noted elsewhere this apparent discrepancy in spectrum efficiency is more than compensated for by digital transmission's greater robustness to co-channel interference [3].

From an implementation point of view FDMA has the disadvantage that each radio frequency carrier only conveys one erlang of traffic, with the result that base stations needing to offer E erlangs of capacity require E radio transceivers per base station. The radio frequency combining of such channels is also a requirement, but for cordless equipment with its low radiated power of 10 mW this is not a technical or cost problem. Indeed, combining can be achieved using multi-element antenna designs. On the other hand the radio channels so created can be considered to be narrowband, and hence insensitive to time dispersive propagation appropriate to cordless use, have a peak to mean radiated power ratio of 2 : 1 (time division duplex assumed) and introduce negligible processing time delay that might otherwise raise implications for overall speech transmission with regard to echo delay (see Chapter 6).

TDMA

In contrast to FDMA, which offers the user access to a fraction of the available spectrum for 100% of the time, TDMA allows each user to access the full spectrum allocation for a fraction of the time. TDMA is a technique in which the available spectrum resource of P MHz is occupied by one modulated carrier and each of n channels (of traffic signal bit rate b_r bit/s) gains access to that carrier for $1/n$ of the time in an ordered sequence. The process is shown diagrammatically in Fig. 7.18, where n channels are serially and synchronously combined onto a single carrier, after compressing each

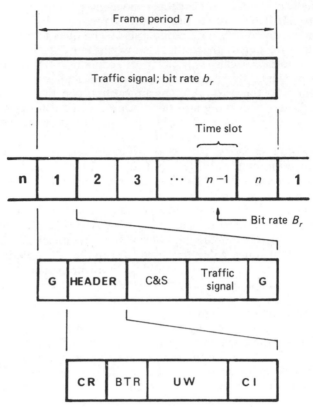

Fig. 7.18. Time division multiple access scheme. CR, carrier recovery; BTR, bit timing recovery; UW, unique word; CI, channel identity; C&S, control and signalling; G, guard space.

T seconds of traffic signal (speech or data) into a period approximately $1/n$ of the time.

In a TDMA system serving multiple independent users it is wise to leave a guard space (G) between individual time slots, thereby easing the requirements for perfect instantaneous synchronisation and allowing a buffer for a modicum of timing drift between independent terminal equipments. In addition the guard space will cater for differential absolute transmission path delay for different terminal to base station ranges. The guard space is generally identified as being equivalent to a number of bit periods.

Fig. 7.18, however, shows the inherent need in TDMA systems to have a header sequence. The header sequence ensures faithful recovery of the traffic signal by the receiver through the provision of carrier recovery (CR) and bit timing recovery (BTR) sequences to aid synchronisation of the receiver's carrier and bit timing clocks. These are followed by unique identification of, and synchronisation to, the traffic signal by means of a unique word (UW) and channel identity (CI) sequences. The example illustrated is classical in showing the individual header functions, but in practice some of them are merged into one sequence (e.g. CR and BTR), sometimes omitted (no CI), or perhaps distributed over several frames in the case of distributed frame synchronisation words.

As a result of these transmission overhead bits the transmission bit rate B_r is greater than that demanded by the traffic signal (nb_r) and in order to maintain acceptable spectrum efficiency care is exercised in deciding the size of the guard space and the need for, form of and integrity of the header functions. In this context integrity refers to the ability of the unique word and channel identifier to resist being mimicked in the traffic signal sequence or to avoid not being recognised because of transmission errors within them. Robustness against these effects is generally determined by sequence length – the longer the better.

An alternative to reducing, and perhaps weakening, the header sequence is to increase the frame period T, thus associating more traffic signal bits with each header sequence and significantly raising the traffic-to-header ratio. This is an effective measure to restore spectrum efficiency (in terms of channels per MHz) but the penalty is an increased one-way processing delay of T seconds. As discussed in Chapter 6, excessive processing delays have implications for the quality of speech transmission in respect of speech echo performance, with the possible need for echo control devices in both terminal and base station equipment. Hence a trade-off between complexity and performance against TDMA frame period results.

The modulation bit rate for a TDMA system is much greater than the inherent traffic signal bit rate per channel and typical cordless TDMA systems have transmission symbol rates in excess of 1 Mbit/s (time division duplex assumed) with attendant wide transmission bandwidth of about 1.25 MHz. Consequently under certain operating conditions cordless TDMA systems may suffer from the effects of transmission path time dispersion common to all so-called wideband systems (see Section 7.4). The wide transmission bandwidth also requires a peak-to-mean radiated power ratio of $2n : 1$ to maintain a given performance under thermal-noise-limited conditions.

The prime advantage of a TDMA system clearly resides in its ability to transmit n channels, or offer n erlangs of traffic capacity, from one base station transceiver. The implication for base station equipment cost in a high-density business communications system is significant, and the full potential will be retained through careful matching of traffic density requirements and base station location within a business entity. TDMA also offers a means of providing dynamic capacity allocation in which more than one time slot can be concatenated. The transmission capacity offered to a single terminal can, therefore, range from one to n time slots to form higher-capacity links for specific applications, of which data transmission would be an important case.

CDMA

CDMA is often cited as an appropriate multiple access technique for communications systems subject to high interference levels and multipath fading. It is natural, therefore, for CDMA to be considered for cordless applications.

In this technique, born out of anti-jamming system requirements, the traffic signal of bit rate b_r bit/s is multiplied by a much faster pseudo-random (spreading) sequence such that the final modulated symbol rate is mb_r bit/s, where typically $m>10^3$. The resulting wanted signal, post modulation, is spread across a bandwidth m times larger than the inherent requirement of the traffic signal. This bandwidth is also much wider than the likely coherence bandwidth of any multipath fading, hence averaging out the frequency selective and signal strength variations in the fading signal. The multiple access feature of CDMA arises through the use of a different spreading sequence for each traffic signal; hence n channels require a set of n spreading sequences with very low cross-correlation properties.

At the receiver the wanted signal is de-spread by mixing the incoming sequence with a synchronised, locally generated version of the original spreading sequence, with the result that the receiver outputs the wanted traffic signal. This de-spreading process, however, re-spreads any non-synchronous, different sequence interference (including very strong unmodulated carrier wave signals). The end result is that the C/I power ratio is effectively enhanced by a factor of m times. If $m=10^3$, the enhancement is 30 dB for a single co-channel co-system interferer. If there were ten interferers, however, the enhancement would fall to 20 dB, or could alternatively be restored to 30 dB by raising m to 10^4, with a consequent tenfold increase in bandwidth spread.

Clearly CDMA has much potential but has not yet been widely exploited in the commercial cordless field. Three important factors arise in this context:

1. The wide spectrum requirement needed ranges from 10 to 100 MHz according to application. In principle, this spectrum could be shared with other, perhaps totally different, service operators, given their agreement and that of spectrum regulators.

2. A need would exist to provide some regulation and control of the spreading codes to ensure acceptable cross-correlation properties.

3. The detection enhancement can be significantly eroded by nearby interfering sources that tend to swamp a wanted signal coming from a greater range (the so-called near–far effect). To overcome this effect radiated power control according to range is necessary to ensure stable performance. This may be difficult to implement in a multi-user, multi-system, liberalised environment.

All these factors tend to cast doubts over the suitability of CDMA (and the similar frequency-hopping multiple access system), but further purpose orientated development may mitigate them; CDMA systems are being trialled in the USA. For further in-depth study the reader is referred to [15].

The choice between multiple access schemes is a complex function of equipment complexity, regulatory situation, fixed network requirements, system robustness, interference susceptibility, spectrum need and cost of implementation. Since no one solution meets all the criteria it is perhaps not surprising that hybrid solutions have been adopted. The case in point is the multiple access process adopted for the Digital European Cordless Telecommunications (DECT) equipment. This seeks an optimum solution to needs and requirements by using time division duplex transmission with a combination of 12 time slots per carrier TDMA and 10 carriers per 20 MHz of spectrum FDMA. Thus DECT is a 120-channel system in 20 MHz with a spectrum efficiency of 6 channels per MHz. DECT is a TDD/TDMA/FDMA system; through such combinations and compromises are successful products born.

7.6.3 Dynamic Channel Assignment, DCA

To achieve high orders of traffic capacity with good spectrum efficiency, cordless equipment must be able to seize any available channel when establishing a communication link. For TDMA this means any free time slot and for FDMA any free radio frequency channel. With this requirement cordless telecommunications realises the full advantage of trunking, the process familiar to fixed telecommunications networks. Its use ensures that all available channels are assignable to any user, thereby maximising the use of spectrum and maximising the probability of a call being established. Cordless systems are expected to be operated under co-channel interference-limited conditions and in this regard DCA, through the use of appropriate channel selection methods, can be used to select the channel with the least, or an acceptable level of, interference [16]. Thus again channel usage and call success probability are maximised.

Since there is no central control of channel selection in cordless equipment the DCA process is autonomous to the terminal equipment in residential, business and Telepoint applications. Clearly some standardisation of the DCA procedure is necessary to avoid mutually destructive interactions between independent equipments while at the same time maintaining the advantages of DCA. Bearing in mind that the destructive effects of co-channel interference depend upon the C/I power ratio, rather than the absolute interference power, then channel selection procedures tend to select the channel with the least interference coupled with some measure of channel quality indicative of C/I power ratio – for example error detection measurement of a regular (known) link sequence. It is also wise to adopt random channel search techniques, although this requirement may be modified if paging techniques are used to identify calling channels.

7.7 Modulation

Traditionally, modulation has been analogue, and commonly FM, as for the first generation analogue cordless telephones. In more recent years there has been a growth in the use of digital modulation for voice communications, and cordless systems are no exception to this trend. The reasons for this are many, but the following are the more important ones:

- The development of low rate (i.e. less than 64 kbit/s) toll quality voice coders. This improves the spectral efficiency of the transmission
- The emergence of spectrally efficient digital modulation formats. These new formats permit the necessary transmission rates to be accommodated within modest bandwidth channels
- The enhanced tolerance of digital format transmissions to co-channel interference

Together, the above can result in a spectral efficiency for digital transmission which exceeds that for analogue in spite of the generally wider minimum channel spacing for digital systems. In addition the following advantages arise:

- The flexibility of digital modulation formats in permitting time division multiplexing and/or duplexing
- The ease of switching channels in digital format
- The ease of multiplexing signalling data onto the transmission
- The inherent voice privacy and potential for security
- The flexibility and efficiency for adding data services (potential for ISDN compatibility)

Finally, the availability of the technology in the form of high-performance silicon and of the relevant tools to develop digital systems has made them technically feasible and economically viable. In reviewing modulation for cordless operation, therefore, we will consider only the digital formats.

7.7.1 Requirements of Digital Modulation

The desirable elements for digital modulation may be summarised as follows:

- Spectral compactness (to maximise the number of channels per MHz for a given adjacent channel rejection performance)
- Good error performance in noise (for range capability)
- Good error performance against co-channel interference (for channel re-use)
- Low power consumption
- Ease of implementation

The last of these has several implications for the choice of modulation.

Digital modulation formats can be divided into those which have a constant transmitted envelope and those which do not. Constant envelope modulation permits transmitter amplifiers to operate in a non-linear Class C mode, permitting high efficiencies and simple implementation. Those modulation types which require some variation in the transmitted envelope need a linear transmitter amplifier with its attendant cost in terms of power and complexity. Those modulations requiring high transmitter linearity can sometimes yield particularly good spectral efficiency. This may justify the additional cost/complexity for some systems, but for a cordless system where cost is vital this is not yet the case. The emergence of new techniques for power amplifier linearisation (Cartesian and Polar loop schemes: [17]) may bring about a change in the situation, but this is still some way off.

We focus, therefore, on the constant envelope class of modulation formats. For this class it is, of necessity, the phase angle of the transmitted signal which is varied. In the same way as for the case of analogue modulation, we can modulate either the phase or the frequency of the output. We initially consider phase modulation.

7.7.2 Phase Shift Keying

The simplest and most common form of digital modulation is Phase Shift Keying (PSK). A PSK modulator is very straightforward and consists of a simple mixer in the transmitted path of the carrier, as illustrated in Fig. 7.19.

Demodulation is achieved in the receiver by performing the same process. In order to do this it is necessary to produce a replica of the transmitted carrier in the demodulator. This may be done by phase locking a local oscillator to phase information derived from the received signal. The need for carrier estimation implies that PSK must be demodulated coherently. In general, coherent modulation schemes provide better performance in Additive White Gaussian Noise (AWGN) than do non-coherent. They are, however, usually more complex.

The amplitude spectrum of unfiltered PSK is rather wide and decays very slowly with offset from the centre frequency, having a sinc function shape.

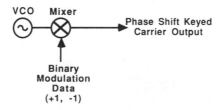

Fig. 7.19. PSK modulator block diagram.

Simple filtering of the modulated signal can greatly improve its spectral containment without compromising power efficiency but results in a nonconstant amplitude signal waveform. For this reason, PSK has not been proposed for any of the digital cordless systems.

7.7.3 Frequency Shift Keying

By contrast, Frequency Shift Keying (FSK) is in use with current digital cordless systems. With FSK the frequency is varied in sympathy with the baseband waveform, as illustrated in Fig. 7.20.

All frequency modulation systems are characterised by their modulation index, this being defined as the ratio of the peak frequency deviation to the highest frequency component in the modulating signal. For digital systems the highest modulating frequency is one half of the bit rate. In order to shape the transmitted spectrum a filter is commonly placed between the modulation sequence source and the VCO input. This greatly improves the shape of the spectrum and, in this case, does not result in any envelope modulation. Such filtered FSK modulation is employed in CAI, with a modulation index being specified as between 0.4 and 0.7.

It is possible to demodulate FSK with a simple limiter discriminator as used for conventional analogue FM signals. This is not always used, however. There is a class of FSK-type modulation schemes which can benefit from coherent demodulation. This class is generically known as Continuous Phase FSK (CPFSK). The best known in this family is Gaussian Filtered Minimum Shift Keying (GMSK). (MSK modulation may also be viewed as a special case of the summation of two filtered PSK signals: see [18].) This modulation has been adopted for the DCT900 cordless system and also for the GSM cellular radiotelephone system. It is therefore appropriate to give some attention to this type of modulation. First we will examine the simpler, unfiltered modulation: MSK.

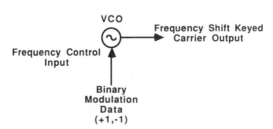

Fig. 7.20. FSK modulator block diagram.

7.7.4 Minimum Shift Keying

MSK may be viewed as FSK with a modulation index of one half. Thus, for example, a 32 kbit/s MSK modulator would have a peak deviation of ± 8 kHz. This choice of modulation index for MSK is significant because it implies that the accumulated phase change over a single bit period is $90°$. It follows that for every bit period the phase either progresses or regresses by this amount. This leads to the result that the carrier phase on alternate bit periods is either varying between $0°$ and $180°$ or between $90°$ and $270°$. Thus it is possible to demodulate the data by examining the sense of the phase and quadrature components of the carrier. A carrier recovery circuit is required to generate a phase reference for demodulation in this way. Of course, the MSK waveform can be demodulated using a simple limiter discriminator, as for other types of FSK. Such coherent demodulation yields a theoretical 3 dB performance advantage over simple limiter discriminator detection in AWGN however.

An important feature of the above properties of MSK is the fact that the phase and quadrature components of the carrier are only varying at one half of the bit rate. It is therefore possible to apply narrow bandwidth filtering to the modulating signal without loss of performance. Moreover, it follows that the transmitted spectrum may also be filtered in this way.

7.7.5 Gaussian Filtered MSK

In GMSK the baseband modulating signal is filtered to restrict its transmitted spectrum. For relatively modest filtering the MSK demodulation technique can be applied in unmodified form. However, heavy filtering (Bandwidth-Time (BT) products[2] less than 0.5) results in intersymbol interference. The effects of this can actually be exploited to provide improved performance in noise, but only at the expense of increased complexity in the demodulator. If the demodulator is not adapted to operate with the heavy filtering a significant degradation of Bit Error Rate (BER) performance in noise will result.

In general, the standards for cordless telephony have been generated with a view to placing the minimum of unnecessary constraints on manufacturers. A choice of heavy filtering (e.g. BT<0.4) would necessitate the use of coherent demodulation for acceptable noise performance. For this reason, a figure of 0.5 is more common. This permits the use of non-coherent demodulation, albeit with slightly poorer performance than can be achieved with coherent demodulation.

The coherent demodulation of GMSK relies upon the modulation index

[2] The bandwidth of a bit shaping filter is usually defined in terms of the bandwidth-time product, BT. The bandwidth is that of the filter and the time is a symbol period. Thus for BT = 0.5, the 3 dB filter bandwidth is equal to the frequency corresponding to the highest bit rate.

being essentially exactly equal to 0.5. For the simple FSK modulator shown in Fig. 7.20 this will not generally be the case, since the circuit will be subject to design tolerances leading to errors in modulation index of anything up to ±10%. (To implement GMSK modulation requires a more complex circuit – for example a vector modulator, as discussed in Chapter 9.) On the other hand, limiter discriminator demodulation places no such constraint upon the modulator, even poorer tolerances being acceptable. This potentially creates something of a difficulty in attempting to generate common standards for cordless telephony. One manufacturer could decide to use a fully coherent system requiring a complex modulator circuit whereas another might choose to use simple limiter discriminator detection and so be able to use the simple modulator configuration of Fig. 7.20. Both could be compliant with the specification and coexistence would be guaranteed. However, the transmitters of the second manufacturer's scheme could not be received by receivers of the first manufacturer's approach. Such a problem is amenable to solution, but should not be overlooked.

The above factor, taken together with the very limited improvement in range offered by coherent modulation (because of the fourth power range law for the in-building environment) and considerations of implementation complexity, perhaps explains why some standards makers have appeared to date to favour simple filtered FSK modulation for cordless telephone applications.

7.8 Error Control

Cordless communications are moving from the use of analogue to digital transmission; this allows the support of digitised voice along with any data services provided. Analogue voice transmissions are subject to perturbations from noise from the receiver and/or from the radio propagation environment. For digital voice transmission the effect of noise is manifested in data errors. These, in turn, cause degradation to the quality of the voice signal when converted back to analogue form. For a data service errors may be even more serious, with the potential to corrupt totally the sense of a message.

Error control is a generic term for all the procedures which may be employed to ensure that the data errors or the effects of data errors experienced by the user/system are kept to an acceptable level for any error rates likely to be produced by the raw communications link under normal operating conditions. Moreover error control serves to prevent unpredictable system operation whenever error rates exceed those which can be handled as part of an active communications process.

There are two basic strategies for error control, namely error detection and correction. The former ensures that the occurrence of data errors is recognised in order that some other appropriate action may be taken; the latter actually corrects data errors (up to a certain limit, determined by the capabilities of the error correcting code employed). Both techniques involve sending error control data bits in addition to those data bits required for the transmission of the raw information.

Error detection results in a relatively modest coding overhead, in terms of error control bits. In this case information is transmitted with a small number of error detection bits appended (commonly referred to as a checksum). When used in conjunction with a communications feedback protocol such as Automatic Repeat Request (ARQ), error detection can result in a very effective means of error control. If detected without errors the communication has been successful and the recipient can confirm this by transmitting an acknowledgement message. If not, no acknowledgement will be sent and the transmission source will try again until an acknowledgement is received. Such an approach is attractive in that it adapts automatically to the prevailing channel conditions. It is, however, appropriate only for the transmission of non-voice data (system signalling and data communication services) since it is subject to variable user-to-user transmission delays. Typically, a checksum approach is used for signalling in a cordless system. Telepoint CAI, for example, uses block transmissions with 48 data bits and a 16 bit checkfield (15 bit cyclic redundancy checksum plus 1 bit parity). In a signalling scheme the acknowledgement generally takes the form of a transmission embodying a response to the command in the original message. The principle, however, is fundamentally the same as ARQ.

For voice transmission, error control, if employed, would need to be implemented using forward error correction. In this case the coding overhead is significant (commonly 100%, since, typically, half-rate coding schemes are employed). Such an approach is used within the GSM cellular radio system, although in that case such protection is only afforded to the more sensitive of the (parametrically coded) speech bits. The benefit of such an error correction approach is that a significant proportion of transmitted errors (either in the information or in the redundancy bits) can be corrected. For the normal digital cordless telephone application employing waveform coding such as ADPCM and where rapid radio channel fluctuations are reasonably limited, error coding is not normally employed.

7.9 Protocols

"Terms of a treaty agreed to in conference – a formal statement of transaction" – thus does the *Concise Oxford Dictionary* define a protocol. In human terms a protocol is a means of formalising and standardising communication, and its meaning, across what otherwise would be a barrier to the full and free flow of information and understanding. Perhaps it is a prophetic sign of the increasing power of computers to usurp mankind that computer communication experts were compelled to produce communication protocols. On the other hand there are those computers who would argue that the imposition of protocols is mankind's last resort in maintaining a semblance of understanding and control of what is going on in those ubiquitous intercommunications boxes!

Whenever information must be passed across an interface between otherwise independent, perhaps different in kind, communicating entities, clear unambiguous understanding demands the use of protocols. This is true for modern communications networks of all forms including cordless telecommunications networks, particularly when they act as multi-service channels between users (e.g. a computer to its terminal, an ISDN to a telephone handset). The creation of a protocol hierarchy (or architecture) is the essential element to the logical partitioning of processing and communication resources between networks and/or users in the establishment of a communication service.

In endeavouring to formalise such matters the Open Systems Interconnection (OSI) reference model was established, which proposed a layered structure approach to protocol specification. The use of such a structure has several benefits:

1.   The overall problem of logical communication definition is thereby divided into smaller, more manageable units.
2.   Each layer has a homogeneity of purpose and procedure, permitting layer-to-layer logical communication and independent modification.
3.   Each layer, therefore, has independence of function except for the need to interact with adjacent layers.

The standard OSI reference model has seven layers as tabulated and defined below:

Layer	Description
7	Application layer
6	Presentation layer
5	Session layer
4	Transport layer
3	Network layer
2	Data link layer
1	Physical layer

Relating this to cordless telecommunications, the lowest three levels can be defined as below:

Physical layer: identifies the radio methods, radio channel allocation, performance monitoring, fault detection, channel shaping and coding and other functions and procedures necessary to create, maintain and release the radio channel. To layer 2 it provides a service of transparent bit transfer.

Data link layer: possesses the means to create, maintain and release the logical (data) link. It provides framing and synchronisation (hence data transparency), sequencing of bits and sequences, error detection and correction, and offers these facilities to layer 3.

Network layer: furnishes the means to create, maintain and release the network path/connections between the terminating users/networks. Terminal-to-terminal signalling and control, data flow control, priority control belong to this layer. It offers these facilities to layer 4.

Protocol layers 1, 2 and 3 serve to support the creation of a functional data link through the cordless network whereas layers 4, 5, 6 and 7 are concerned with supporting communication between the end users/networks. Thus the cordless link provides them with transparent, non-interventionist layer-to-layer communication.

Essentially the OSI structure is a user–network interface architecture that does not preclude modified structures being used within the cordless network. In fact this occurs in DECT where layers 1, 2 and 3 have been rationalised as:

1. The Physical Layer (PHL) and the Medium Access Control Layer (MAC), a mix of OSI layers 1 and 2;
2. The Data Link Control Layer (DLC) and Network Layer (NWL) formed from OSI equivalents 2 and 3.

This application is shown structurally in Fig. 7.21 and described further in Appendix 3, where the DECT specification itself is outlined.

7.10 Summary

The early part of this chapter described the issues relating to spectrum requirements for cordless telecommunication systems and the characteristics

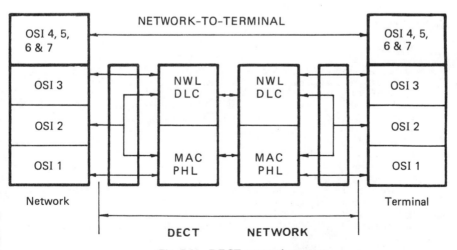

Fig. 7.21. DECT protocol structure.

of in-building propagation and the dispersive nature of the radio channel. After examining the fundamental constraints upon spectrum choice, an approximate theory was introduced to derive some "rules of thumb" in terms of interrelationships between spectrum requirement and, for a given grade of service, a range of parameters – traffic density, cell size, range propagation law, floor attenuation (for multi-storey buildings) and required C/I ratio. Detailed propagation studies were then described, which have led in recent years to new propagation models for the in-building environment. Such models will be necessary in the development of effective system installation procedures. The ways in which the performance of high-density cordless office installations can be predicted by the use of computer simulations were then described.

In the latter parts of the chapter the issues relating to the choice of parameters for the radio system needed to match the radio channel were described. This included a review of the usage of the radio channel, introducing the concepts of duplex transmission, multiple access schemes and dynamic channel assignment. This was followed by a look at various relevant digital modulation schemes: PSK, FSK, MSK and GMSK. The issue of error control was then briefly discussed. Finally, the concepts of communication protocols were introduced and the application of the ISO OSI model to cordless telecommunications described.

Overall, this chapter has attempted to survey the very broad issues of the characteristics and usage of the radio channel, drawing out in particular those aspects peculiar to the cordless telephone application. The basics of radio communication technique have also been presented for those readers less familiar with these and a range of references has been provided for the interested reader to pursue.

References

1. WC Jakes (ed), "Microwave mobile communications", John Wiley, Chichester, 1974
2. K Feher (ed), "Advanced digital communications, systems and signal processing techniques", Prentice-Hall, Englewood Cliffs NJ, 1987
3. RS Swain, "Cordless telecommunications in the UK", Proceedings of the National Communications Forum 1984, Chicago, September 1984, pp 163–168
4. ETSI-RES 3, "DECT reference document", Sophia-Antipolis, Nice, France
5. AJ Motley and AJ Martin, "Radio coverage in buildings", Proceedings of the National Communications Forum 1988, Chicago, October 1988, pp 1722–1730
6. JM Keenan and AJ Motley, "Radio coverage in buildings", British Telecom Technology Journal, vol 8, no. 1, January 1990
7. SE Alexander, "Characteristics for building propagation at 900 MHz", Electronic Letters, vol 19, no. 20, p 860, September 1983
8. DMJ Devasirvatham, "Radio propagation studies in a small city for universal portable communications". IEEE Vehicular Technology Conference 1988, pp 100–104, Philadelphia PA, June 1988
9. D Akerberg, ECTEL/ESPA Working Group document no. BCT 18/87, "Additional

simulations of the traffic in the TCS/BCT test installation", 1987 (Ericsson radio document no. TY 87:2062)

10. JCI Chuang, "The effects of time delay spread on portable radio communications channels with digital modulation", IEEE Journal on Selected Areas in Comm, SAC-5, pp 879–889, June 1987

11. DMJ Devasirvatham, "Multipath time delay spread in the digital portable radio environment", IEE Communications Magazine, vol 25, pp 13–21, June 1987

12. DMJ Devasirvatham, "Delay spread and signal level measurements of 850 MHz radio waves in building environments", IEEE Transactions on Antennas and Propagation, AP-34, pp 1300–1305, November 1986

13. RC Bernhardt, "The effect of path loss models on the simulated performance of portable radio systems", IEEE Global Communications Conference, Dallas, USA, 1989

14. AP Croft, S McCann and WHW Tuttlebee, "Digital European cordless telecommunications system simulation performance results", IEE Mobile Radio and Personal Communications Conference, Warwick, UK, December 1989

15. RC Dixon, "Spread spectrum systems", 2nd edn, John Wiley (Wiley-Interscience Publication), New York, 1976

16. F Al-Salihi and LP Straus, "Simulation of cordless communications systems", Electronic Letters, vol 24, no 12, pp 742–743, June 1988

17. A Bateman and RJ Wilkinson, "Linearisation of class C amplifiers using Cartesian feedback", IEEE Workshop on Mobile and Cordless Telephone Communications, London, September 1989

18. S Pasupathy, "Minimum shift keying: a spectrally efficient modulation", IEEE Communications Magazine, pp 14–22, July 1979

8 Cordless Data Communications

Frank Owen

Integrated communication systems in the commercial environment are becoming increasingly important to the modern business. The consequent reduction in expensive, incompatible systems with their associated service contracts and skilled staff, and the benefits of increased economies of scale, promote the integrated solution. With the advent of products based on Integrated Services Digital Network (ISDN) technology this trend is likely to continue.

For an integrated business communication system to be successful it is essential that it is as versatile and future-proof as possible. The requirement for cordless voice communications in offices and factories has been presented in previous chapters. This chapter will show that a number of digital data services will similarly benefit from being attached to a cordless local area network (cordless LAN). The implications of providing these services on a cordless connection will be discussed and methods of service implementation will be presented. It will be explained how data communications are an integral part of the facilities to be provided by DECT and the ability of the existing CAI standard to support data services is briefly discussed.

8.1 Cordless Data Services and Their Applications

All existing commercial or domestic data equipment that requires a communication link could, in principle, implement this as a cordless link. However data services vary in their connection requirements and certain services are more suited to cordless transmission than others. Table 8.1 considers a number of currently available data services together with those communication link attributes which are necessary to support them and which affect the design of any cordless network connection. These requirements are approximate and illustrate the differences between services rather than providing accurate values.

Voice

Digitised voice can be considered a data service in an integrated services system, requiring a constant information transfer rate and a constant, low delay. With high bit rate digital speech encoders, as initially envisaged for cordless telephony systems, a large bit error rate over a voice link can be tolerated due to the high redundancy in speech. Voice is likely to be one of the most mobile of the cordless services provided and is expected to make up a high proportion of all cordless terminals.

Facsimile

A number of standards exist today for facsimile transmission and it is likely that there will be continued growth of this service. The latest facsimile standard for digital networks defined by the CCITT is known as Group 4. Facsimile has an almost constant data rate but, in common with a large number of other data services, has a greater information flow in one direction of the link than the other. Delay is not as critical as with other services and a high link error rate can be tolerated for short periods. Retransmissions providing error correction add a small amount to the delay.

Table 8.1. Potential cordless data services

Service	Information rate (bit/s)	Packet size (bits)	Delay limit (s)	Integrity (bit error rate)
Voice	8–64 k	Continuous	0.01	10^{-2}
Digital facsimile	64 k	10–50 k	10–1000	[a]10^{-2}
Keyboard	1–10	10	0.5–2	10^{-4}
VDU screen	10–20 k	0.1–1 k	1–10	10^{-6}
Video telephony	64 k–2 M	Continuous	0.1	[a]10^{-2}
Computer file	64 k–10 M	0.1–2 M	1–1000	10^{-11}
CAD graphics	64 k–10 M	1 k–2 M	1–1000	10^{-11}

[a]Before error correction.

VDU and Keyboard Terminal

The conventional computer terminal has significantly different communications requirements in each link direction. Keyboard entry produces a low data rate but requires minimum delay (tens of milliseconds with distant-end character echo). VDU bit rate is very low or zero until a screen refresh is required, when a large communications bandwidth is required for a short period.

Wideband Services

Examples of wideband services requiring data rates greater than 64 kbit/s include:

Video telephony. Desirable where the visual information in a conversation plays an important part. Video telephony may be point-to-point, point-to-multipoint (e.g. video conference), or simply unidirectional (e.g. video surveillance).

High-speed computer file transfer. In a large networked computer system there is often a requirement for large quantities of computer data or programs to be moved around the network – for instance from a central storage device. This function may typically be provided by a wired LAN, such as Ethernet, operating at up to 10 Mbit/s.

CAD/CAM graphics. In the modern factory design environment there is a significant requirement for high-speed graphical presentation of designs. Often a dedicated link or very high speed LAN (hundreds of Mbit/s) is used to minimise VDU screen refresh time.

8.1.1 ISDN Connections

It is likely that much of the equipment supporting the data services described will, in future, be ISDN compatible. ISDN specifies many wired bearer interfaces which are unsuitable for translation to the wire-less spectrum without significant modification. In order to provide a transparent ISDN connection to the terminal endpoints of a connection, a protocol converter will be required between the fixed, wired network and the cordless network. This converter would be present at both the mobile terminal and the fixed end. It is essential that a cordless network faithfully reproduces the ISDN features so that the fixed and mobile endpoints perceive a transparent ISDN connection. This does not mean that a cordless link with bearer capacity equal to the wired ISDN link has to be provided continuously at all times, e.g. a 144 kbit/s 2B+D connection (the B channel being a dedicated 64 kbit/s information channel and the D channel a 16 kbit/s control and information channel). It is important in cordless communications that sufficient bearer capacity is provided only on demand, as is discussed in Section 8.2 Further details on the ISDN and how it interfaces to various data services can be found in [1].

8.1.2 Benefits of the Cordless Connection

Cordless connections have many advantages over fixed, wired links [2,3]. The following additional features are available to data services with a cordless communications link:

Mobility. A prime benefit, where both voice and data terminals are no longer constrained by their communications link to a specific geographical location.

Flexible terminal layout. Layout need no longer be based around interconnection requirements and can be modified both quickly and simply.

Reduced installation costs. A significant proportion of a data terminal's cost can be its installation into a network. In the case of voice terminals it is as high as 60% of the total cost [4]. Subsequent reorganisation costs, whether the move is temporary or permanent, are also reduced.

Removal of unsightly cabling links. An active office with a large quantity of equipment that relies on networked communications may not have the space for large amounts of cabling. This is a particular problem in buildings that were erected a decade or so ago and did not have saturation wiring technology built into them at construction.

Communications in hostile environments. There are applications in industry where it is undesirable or expensive to install wired links because of the nature of the environment involved (see e.g. [5]).

8.1.3 The Cordless Office

One of the principal application areas for cordless data services is in the commercial office environment. All the services discussed previously may be present in the office and a cordless communication system can link these together and also connect them to the outside world. The literature on this subject often refers to the cordless LAN in more specific terms such as a Radio Area Network or Wireless Area Network. Usually there is a specific reason, but for the purposes of this book the general term "cordless LAN" is used. Several cordless connection scenarios can be envisaged for the office [6,7] including:

Cordless Extension to a Backbone LAN or PABX

Fig. 8.1a illustrates a fixed, wired network linking floors and offices, onto which terminals are directly connected. Equipments which would benefit

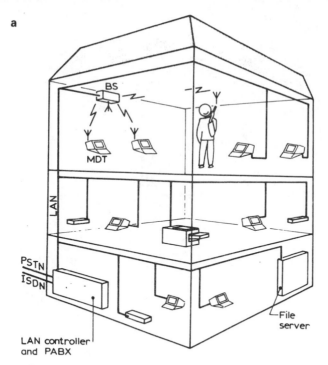

Fig. 8.1.a **a** Cordless extension to a fixed LAN. BS, base station; MDT, mobile data terminal; CDC, cordless data controller.

from mobility or from a flexible network connection communicate on a cordless extension to the central wired network. A cordless base station taps into the wired network as a conventional fixed terminal. It intercepts data destined for the cordless equipment and then relays this data over the cordless network. This scenario is suitable where a fixed network may already exist and the degree of mobility and flexibility required is limited.

Distributed Control Cordless LAN

With this scenario, illustrated in Fig. 8.1b, the cordless network control is distributed throughout the terminals present in the network. All terminals share responsibility for routing, media access and other control functions. Connections are established by direct terminal-to-terminal communications, possibly via a repeater to extend coverage, rather than through wired base stations. Specific terminals are present to provide an interface to external networks, such as the ISDN or the PSTN. The distributed control cordless network is not currently being considered for cordless telephony systems in Europe although a great deal of attention is being paid to this form of network in the USA [8,9].

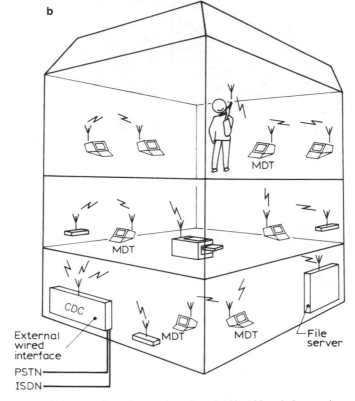

Fig. 8.1.b Distributed control cordless LAN. Abbreviations as in **a**.

Cellular Cordless LAN and PABX

An example of the system architecture necessary for a cellular cordless network is shown in Fig. 8.1c. All connections for both voice and data terminals are cordless and a fixed network for direct terminal connection now no longer exists. It is likely that in order to meet the traffic capacity demands the cordless system will be based on a cellular structure and the wired hardware will then be limited to the infrastructure required to support the cellular system. A central controller is present for system coordination and all connections are routed via the fixed base station network. This system may be more desirable where a large degree of mobility and flexibility is required and where there is no existing wired communications network. The cellular cordless network will be more expensive than cordless extensions alone, but will provide greater functionality and be of lower cost than the combined fixed LAN and cordless extension network. Although DECT will be capable of supporting the scenario illustrated in Fig. 8.1a, it is primarily being designed as a complete cellular cordless PABX and LAN as illustrated in Fig. 8.1c.

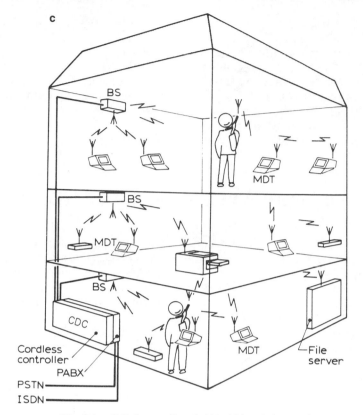

Fig. 8.1.c Cellular cordless LAN. Abbreviations as in **a**.

8.1.4 Factory Management

The scenarios described above for the office are also applicable to a factory environment, where mobile terminals will additionally include robots and transport systems. Cordless connection provides the benefit of flexible equipment reconfiguration which permits a production line to adapt to changes in product demand. Wholesale and retail businesses also require systems to monitor the inventory of large amounts of stock. They are discovering the benefits of using cordless data connections rather than wired links to connect information processing and storage hardware to their warehouse or counter data terminals [10]. This application is likely to grow with the availability of more sophisticated integrated systems.

8.1.5 Home Information Services

Cordless data connections in the home have been available for many years (e.g. television remote control), but always in limited applications. An integrated cordless system could allow many home control functions to be contained in a domestic cordless telephone handset. These could include domestic appliance control and security systems [11]. The second generation of Telepoint networks, conforming to both DECT and UK CAI, is being evaluated to determine its suitability for supporting home information services as well as road traffic or emergency services data. The pan-European ESPRIT and DRIVE programmes, promoted by the Commission of the European Communities, are performing these studies in an effort to integrate communications technology throughout Europe.

8.2 The Cordless Interface and Bearer Access

The second part of this chapter concentrates on the cordless medium and potential access methods. Three example systems are discussed. The first is a proprietary cordless LAN which is capable of supporting a number of non-voice services within a cordless office. The second is a proprietary radio cordless LAN for voice and data with distributed control. Finally, suitable access methods are discussed for the DECT interface which is being designed to support both voice and data services, including ISDN.

There are many different cordless media that can be considered for short-range voice and data communications, the principal ones being:

V/UHF radio	<1 GHz
Microwave radio	>1 GHz
Millimetric radio	>30 GHz
Infrared optical	850–950 nm

All of these media have specific characteristics that make them more suited for use in some applications and environments than others. UHF radio and the low microwave spectrum provide good area coverage at reasonable transmitter power levels and at a cost which is acceptable to the mass market. As radio frequencies increase, the radio component technology cost rises rapidly but additional system advantages appear, including greater availability of bandwidth, better defined coverage areas through the use of directive antennas, and a potentially higher degree of frequency re-use (e.g. carriers in the 60 GHz oxygen absorption band [12]). Diffuse infrared is a suitable medium for cordless communications. Bandwidth is limited but the technology is not expensive and a great deal of remote control equipment already uses the technology.

Whatever the cordless medium the communications channel will have different characteristics from that of a wired link. There will be physical limits on the maximum bandwidth of the channel, the reliability in terms of errors and the distribution of those errors in time. The methods by which the channels must be accessed and maintained are specific to the medium.

These points lead to the use of different communications protocols for cordless media compared with those that exist on fixed, wired networks.

A cordless medium, whether it is V/UHF radio, microwave or infrared, is generally a broadcast transmission medium unless a specific effort is made to constrain the direction of transmission. For the majority of application areas considered above this directivity is not feasible with the carrier frequencies and coverage areas currently being considered for cordless telephony systems. The cordless interface can therefore be said to be analogous to a broadcast Ethernet LAN rather than to a dedicated line for an individual connection. It is essential when accessing a broadcast cordless medium that the minimum possible bearer capacity is used for the communication. This is because the amount of bandwidth available to a cordless service is limited compared with that for a wired link, where the available bandwidth and re-use factor of that bandwidth may (by laying a second cable) be far greater. Cellular coverage is particularly suitable for an integrated services system as the gain in bandwidth efficiency from frequency re-use is extremely beneficial. Efficient use of the cordless bearer maintains the maximum information transfer and ensures that the highest number of user connection requests are satisfied. As the attributes of individual services are so diverse a single, fixed-capacity bearer interface does not provide sufficient efficiency and the cordless interface must therefore adapt the cordless bearer to a particular service or combination of services. There is also a trade-off between the product's protocol complexity and the need for efficient use of the cordless spectrum.

An example of the need for the medium to adapt to the service being supported is the comparison between voice and computer file transfer. Voice communications require a continuous, fixed information rate, duplex channel, whilst computer data is often largely unidirectional and requires varying information rates depending on the individual service transmission needs. Voice lends itself to circuit-switched logical connections whilst computer data is often better transferred using a mixture of circuit-switched and packet-switched techniques [13]. Any efficient cordless interface specification designed for integrated services must support both circuit-switched and packet-switched logical connections.

8.2.1 Diffuse Infrared Cordless LAN Extension

Developed at Philips Research Laboratories in 1986, this distributed control LAN was designed to investigate a cordless extension to a fixed LAN. The cordless medium chosen was free space infrared, rather than microwave or radio, as only short-range communication within a single office was required. Several authors have reported on the use of diffuse infrared for short-range communications [14,15]. Diffuse infrared technology requires no licensing and can provide free-space ranges up to 50 m. Coverage is limited by opaque surfaces and bit rate by multipath dispersion.

The network configuration is that of Fig. 8.1a. Individual nodes on the cordless network can communicate directly with any other within their local group or via a LAN gateway to wired terminals in different parts of the office. A photograph of the prototype hardware for a cordless node together with the attached terminal is shown in Fig. 8.2.

Data packets are transmitted using a Synchronous Data Link Control (SDLC) based protocol on a single wideband channel. Access to the shared infrared medium is controlled by a Carrier Sense Multiple Access/Collision Avoidance (CSMA/CA) discipline, which is similar to that described in [16]. CSMA has been extensively researched and, with the enhancement of packet collision detection, forms the basis of the IEEE 802.3 Ethernet Layer 1 specification. CSMA performance degrades under heavy load and the use of packet reservation requests enhances its performance under such conditions. A standard tutorial on random access techniques and CSMA in particular can be found in [13].

The transmitted burst format for a data packet is shown in Fig. 8.3. An acknowledgement, control or reservation request packet is similar but without the data field. Data packet length varies between 50 and 400 bytes depending on packet throughput success. If packets are being received error free at their destination then the packet length is increased. Low throughput may be due to a poor infrared channel or to the occurrence of excessive

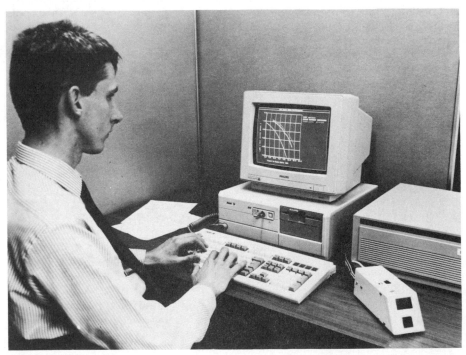

Fig. 8.2. Data terminal and cordless infrared node. (Courtesy of Philips Research Laboratories.)

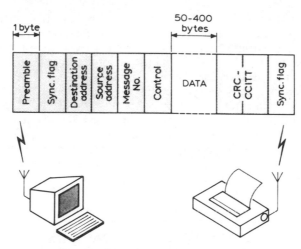

Fig. 8.3. Cordless LAN extension packet format.

collisions in a heavy load situation. Care has to be taken to ensure that the correct cause is identified, as the solution is to decrease packet size for a poor channel or to increase packet size for an excess of collisions.

Considering Fig. 8.3, a preamble byte permits demodulator and clock synchronisation. A synchronisation flag byte provides byte synchronisation and indicates the start of a packet. This flag byte is not permitted to occur in the data field of the packet and is prevented by zero insertion in the data field. The link endpoints' source and destination addresses follow. These allow a terminal to be addressed and to know the source of the transmission. A block or message number then follows which identifies the data in the data field for acknowledgement and possible retransmission purposes. The control field includes miscellaneous flow control and error management information. Following the data field a 16-bit CCITT Frame Check Sequence (FCS) provides an error detection capability at the receiver which is valid over the whole packet excluding the preamble. Finally a closing synchronisation flag is transmitted.

All cordless data terminals (nodes) monitor the wideband infrared channel and check the destination address field of every packet to determine whether the value in this field matches their own address. Transmissions are ignored unless the addresses match, in which case a link is set up between the two nodes and data is transferred. An Automatic Repeat Request (ARQ) protocol combined with the FCS information provides error control. All packets are acknowledged by an acknowledgement packet. In the prototype system positive acknowledgements only were returned to the source node and timeouts were used to retransmit unacknowledged packets.

CSMA with collision detection is not normally possible when using a cordless bearer because it requires the node transmitter and receiver to work simultaneously on the same channel. A further method of maintaining the efficiency and stability of CSMA under heavy load is to include a very short transmission reservation request packet. This is particularly suitable for the cordless environment and has become known in some quarters as Reservation Request CSMA (RRCSMA). The request is transmitted by the source node when it requires to send a data packet. If the request is successfully acknowledged by the destination node then a free time period is guaranteed; no other nodes will transmit as all nodes will have heard the reservation request and acknowledgement. This technique ensures that generally only short reservation packets of a few bytes in length are subject to collision whilst larger data packets, which take longer to transmit, will not collide as the preceding request will have reserved transmission time. RRCSMA can lead to efficiencies of greater than 80% which remain high and stable even under very heavy load.

8.2.2 Distributed Control Radio Area Network

A distributed control cordless LAN demonstrator with contention based channel access control was designed and built in 1986 by Plessey Research [3]. The LAN was designed to carry speech and data simultaneously and to be medium-independent. The initial experimental bearer medium was a UHF radio link. A serial bit stream between 100 kbit/s and 500 kbit/s was modulated using Continuous Phase Frequency Shift Keying modulation (CPFSK) onto a 450 MHz carrier with a transmitted power level of 10 mW.

Medium access control hardware implemented a CSMA, Ethernet-type protocol using an Intel 82586 dedicated communications integrated circuit. Control of the network was distributed equally amongst the nodes so that the breakdown of any single piece of equipment would not cause total network failure. Link quality was managed using an ARQ retransmission and acknowledgement protocol.

Digital speech transmission has not been implemented on the demonstrator but it is envisaged that it could be added. The CSMA contention based protocol would permit access for data connections, whilst a TDMA multiplex would be used for speech calls. The network would dynamically switch between CSMA and TDMA access techniques as the speech and data traffic levels varied.

8.2.3 Integrated Service Protocols For DECT

DECT is intended to provide both voice and data communications services in Telepoint, business and domestic environments. Existing cordless telephony systems provide for domestic, Telepoint and limited business usage but are not suitable for the capacity, or the multiple services, required in a high-density office environment. DECT is being specified to support integrated telecommunications applications including those summarised below:

Voice
Business PABX, single and multi cell
Residential telephony with intercom facility
Public Telepoint services

Data
ISDN services including:
  Telefax
  Teletex
  Videophone
Computer file transfer
VDU and terminal service
Real time file access

To support these applications, defined in [17] and explored in more detail in [18], the air interface has to use the available spectrum efficiently and be flexible enough to provide a high grade of service to all users.

The principles of voice communications on a cordless TDMA TDD interface are presented elsewhere in this book. This section describes DECT data services and gives examples of the kinds of communication protocols necessary for efficient radio connections on a TDMA TDD radio interface and how these are developed [19]. It does not specifically describe the procedures that will eventually be used in DECT, although the concepts and general principles will still apply.

DECT is a cellular based system and a typical office configuration is likely to be similar to the scenario illustrated in Fig. 8.1c. An ADPCM voice connection on DECT requires a pair of 32 kbit/s TDD physical channels, whilst data services require various bandwidths. Data connections for those services with data rates greater than 32 kbit/s duplex are provided by using multiple duplex channels. Those requiring less are served by intermittent packet access of a single physical channel. Data links are established between the Cordless Data Controller (CDC) and the Mobile Data Terminal (MDT). End-to-end data is transferred in numbered packets with a packet structure such as that shown in Fig. 8.4. Base stations may just pass on the information data to the MDT or CDC for them to provide error management, and to

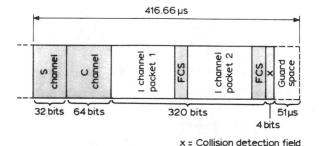

x = Collision detection field

Fig. 8.4. Example of DECT packet format.

resequence the data to ensure it is correctly presented for that service. As a base station does not alter the information data, wideband multiple channel calls may use several base stations.

As mentioned earlier, data connections are rarely symmetrical in their information transfer rate at any given moment. If this asymmetry is not considered then allocated channels may be under-utilised, with a resulting decrease in spectral efficiency. One answer is for an MDT or base station (whichever is sending more data) to transmit in both halves of the frame in one direction rather than to allow one frame half for the duplex reply as happens in voice connections. This maintains a paired slot structure to all users but allows considerable asymmetric data transfer without allocating underused duplex bandwidth. The alteration in transmission direction is indicated by a higher level protocol. These concepts can be better appreciated by examining Fig. 8.5, which illustrates the basic frame structure envisaged for DECT, showing the 12 TDMA full time slots, paired across the two halves of the frame.

With data communications on a cordless interface it is necessary to be able to allocate a variable number of physical channels to a connection, dependent on the required data rate, and to provide asymmetric radio channels to maintain spectral efficiency. During a call the number of physical channels required and the level of asymmetry may vary due to changes in network demand or radio link quality.

Low bit rate services are serviced efficiently by packet access and by making use of any half slot provision wherever available. Full and half rate slots can exist in the same system without reducing performance. The use of such half slots is envisaged, for example, within DECT (see Appendix 3).

The Medium Access Control Protocol Layer

The Medium Access Control (MAC) protocol layer performs physical channel and error management functions. These include the creation, maintenance and release of physical channels. Channel management considers

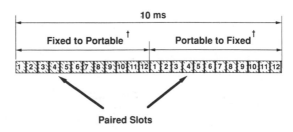

Fig. 8.5. TDD paired slot structure in DECT. †Paired slots may be used in the same direction for data communication.

variations in the required bearer bandwidth during a connection, as well as the need to modify physical resources as a result of unacceptable channel quality. A key parameter affecting the protocol design is the radio link set-up time. Many data services are sensitive to the latent time between the request for a service and the allocation of the radio link. Error management in the MAC layer provides error control for the radio link signalling, for the MAC channel management, for the Data Link Control layer and for data in the information field.

Of great importance is that the MAC protocol is capable of supporting both voice and data services together rather than only being able to support certain combinations of services at one time. For this reason the MAC procedures for a voice connection are a subset of those required for a circuit-switched data connection.

Initial Link Set-Up

Fig. 8.6 illustrates the exchanges between the mobile data terminal (MDT) and CDC for an initial physical channel set-up for a call originated by an MDT. These set-up procedures are as follows:

1. An *outgoing call request* is transmitted by the MDT on a physical channel which has been judged to be free or to have the lowest interferer signal strength. The transmission includes a field indicating the number of physical channels, in half slot multiples, that the MDT envisages the connection will require.
2. If the base station receives this request on a suitable channel and at

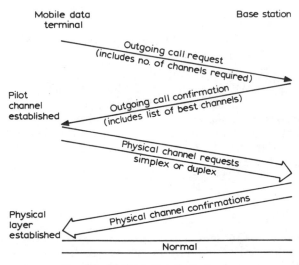

Fig. 8.6. DECT initial channel set-up.

sufficient signal strength then half a frame later the base transmits an *outgoing call confirmation* message. A "pilot" link, which may occupy either a half or full rate physical channel, is now established between the MDT and the base station. For voice communications this pilot link is of itself sufficient for the traffic. The pilot link is always duplex regardless of whether it is used for voice or data communications. It can be used to establish further physical channels if these are necessary to support higher data rate services. If further physical channels are to be activated then the base will transmit a list of its available channels to the MDT. This list of channels may be transmitted in an extended control field multiplex making use of the free information channel capacity at call set-up.

3.   The MDT may access further physical channels, with a high probability of them being successfully confirmed, by combining into a channel map the base station's available channel information and the MDT's own signal strength measurements. Using this map the MDT will transmit *physical channel request* packets on sufficient channels to satisfy the required link capacity. These requests include information on whether the channels requested will be simplex or duplex and full or half rate.

   Simplex: Transmissions in a simplex channel are from the same link endpoint in both the up- and downlink sections of the frame (e.g. MDT to base station). When assigning multiple physical channels for a high data rate asymmetric connection the ability to assign simplex physical channels permits efficient spectrum allocation.

   Duplex: Channels are used in the duplex form for voice transmissions, and both up- and downlink are used for MDT to base station and base station to MDT transmissions respectively.

4.   The base transmits *physical channel confirmations* on all channels on which it received requests and that are acceptable to the base. Network originated calls, routed via the base station, are set up with similar exchanges but with the addition of an initial paging transmission to alert the MDT that a connection is required.

Following the above procedure a suitable initial "bit pipe" for the connection between the base and MDT may be established. It is likely that during the connection the bearer capacity requirement will change and that some of the existing physical channels initially set up will become unusable due to MDT movement or to interference. Techniques to maintain the cordless bearer capacity at the level necessary to support the connection and no higher are detailed below.

Link Maintenance

In order to maintain throughput, to minimise delay and to preserve the connection's spectral efficiency, link maintenance algorithms are needed to monitor the physical channel allocation. Link maintenance considers the changing radio environment and adapts the links in a connection accordingly whilst ensuring minimum interference to other users. An increase in interference or reduction in signal strength on a particular physical channel will require another channel to be established and the existing, poor channel to be cleared down. Variations in the required data rate at either end of the data link may require additional physical channels to be requested, or existing channels to be released. This may be done in response to a higher layer request indicating a change in the required data rate.

The first maintenance procedure performed by the MAC when an existing channel deteriorates is to make use of any available spatial microdiversity. Microdiversity may be implemented at the base station by switching between two or more antennas spaced approximately one quarter wavelength apart. If the microdiversity switch is unsuccessful then alternative channels, possibly at new base stations, will have to be established.

Additional Channel Set-Ups

Additional capacity may be required in either the MDT to base station direction or vice versa, in order to replace channels cleared down or to provide greater bearer capacity. Fig. 8.7 illustrates the MAC procedures,

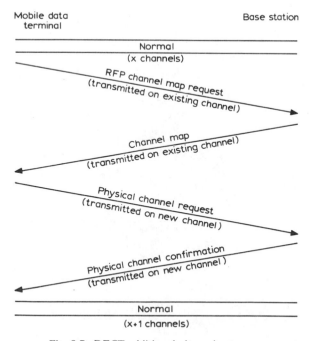

Fig. 8.7. DECT additional channel set-up.

described below, for establishing further physical channels in the MDT to base direction:

1. To obtain the list of free channels available at the base station the MDT may send a *base channel map request* on one of the existing physical channels allocated to the call.
2. The base will then transmit its current available channel list and the MDT will construct a map of channels which are suitable at both ends of the link.
3. Using the channel map, the MDT identifies a channel that has a high probability of providing a connection of sufficient quality for the service and transmits a *physical channel request* on the new channel.
4. The base station to which the physical channel request is addressed will transmit a *physical channel confirmation* to the MDT on the new channel if it is acceptable. An additional physical channel, which may be simplex or duplex has now been allocated to the connection.

Network originated, additional channel set-up is similar except that the initial physical channel request is sent by the base station on an existing, allocated physical channel. The MDT will then transmit a physical channel request to a base station on a new channel.

Channel Clear Down

Physical channels are cleared down when the complete connection is terminated, the bearer capacity is reduced or when the quality of that physical channel no longer meets that required by higher protocol layers. The clear down procedure as initiated by the MDT is illustrated in Fig. 8.8. On the channel that is to be cleared down a *physical channel clear down* message is transmitted. Higher layer information included in this message will indicate whether the complete connection is to be terminated or just this physical channel. An acknowledgement of the clear down from the base

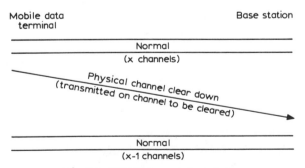

Fig. 8.8. DECT channel clear down.

station is not required as timeouts built into the algorithm will deal with MAC message corruption.

Physical channel handover during a data connection is a specific case of channel set-up and clear down. Handover requires no specific MAC procedures as those necessary can be constructed from the primitive procedures described above.

To prevent wideband data calls using up a significant proportion of a base station's capacity, resulting in an unacceptable blocking performance for voice traffic, it may be necessary to give voice a higher priority than data. High data rate calls would be slowed down by clearing down all but the last slot of a multiple-slot data call if new voice calls require these channels. When the channels once again become available they can be reallocated to the high data rate connection. Constraints on the set-up and clear down rates of links will be needed to present a stable interference environment to other users.

Burst Structure and Error Management

The CDC or MDT assembles the application data into fixed-length packets and arranges for them to be transmitted in the information (I) channel of the basic slot structure. Fig. 8.4 illustrates a possible TDM slot structure for use in data connections. In this example two data packets are contained in the full rate slot. Also contained in the I channel are the necessary 16-bit Frame Check Sequences (FCS) for error management.

The error control mechanism can be provided by an FCS and ARQ protocol. Acknowledgements and negative acknowledgements are returned to the transmission source which will then retransmit those packets which are in error or are uncorrectable. Selective retransmission is used rather than a "go back n" protocol as window size may be large and a frame may contain many packets. Error management in the I channel is controlled by the data handset and CDC link endpoints. Sequencing of packets, data error detection, correction and requests for retransmission are performed at both link endpoints. Depending on implementation, base stations may not process the I channel information data but pass it transparently to the endpoints.

Errors can be detected and, with more complex algorithms, corrected, using the 16-bit FCS attached to each data packet. If a corrupted packet cannot be corrected then a retransmission is requested by returning a negative acknowledgement (NACK) together with the packet number. Once the NACK has been received, or a timeout in the source node has expired, then the packet will be retransmitted promptly on another physical channel allocated to the connection. Each physical channel exhibits a changing bit error rate performance with time and therefore selecting another physical channel for retransmission is likely to result in greater throughput. If after three retransmissions the packet has still not been correctly received at the destination then bit by bit majority voting can be performed and the composite packet and FCS checked. If the majority voted packet is still corrupt then three new transmissions are sent in quick succession in order to minimise delay. To permit quicker retransmission of corrupt packets, negative acknowledgements are returned with a higher priority than are acknowledgements. Several types of acknowledgements can be envisaged including "acknowledge correct receipt of packet N" or "acknowledge correct receipt of all packets up to and including packet N".

The packet numbering window size is important. It must not be unnecessarily large as transmission efficiency will then decrease, nor so small that insufficient unacknowledged packets are permitted at any one time for a specific connection. The smaller the window size the higher the probability of delay and the greater the buffer requirement at the link endpoints.

Base stations will forward I channel data (correct or in error) to the endpoints only if the radio link handshake code is correct. This provides protection against an interferer stealing the existing channel and still generating valid FCSs and valid packet numbers. Apart from the error correction capacity of the FCS, more powerful Forward Error Correction (FEC) is less suited to the cordless telephony air interface as any particular code is only optimum for a small bit error rate range and thus, in the mobile radio environment, over a very small C/I or C/N range of a few decibels. As each physical channel has differing C/I, each would require a different coding scheme adapted to the prevalent conditions on that channel. Complex algorithms would be required to implement these schemes and the additional benefit over retransmissions and majority voting is questionable. It should be noted that retransmissions and packet majority voting provide error control that is adaptive to the conditions on any channel.

8.3 Existing Cordless Data Systems

CT2 CAI is capable of providing data connections but does not have the potential to provide the full variety of services that DECT will be able to offer when introduced, due to its lower bit rate. With CAI, low bit rate services up to 2400 bit/s can be provided through a conventional telephone data modem connected to the speech coder. The G.721 speech codec specified by the CCITT and used in CAI is audio transparent up to this bit rate. G.721 can accommodate higher rate services, up to 4800 bit/s, using conventional modems at slightly increased bit error rates and higher rates using specialised modems. The CAI also supports 16 kbit/s data services, using the MUX 2 multiplex. Higher data rates, up to 32 kbit/s, are in principle possible by transferring the data directly over the air interface and bypassing the speech coder. This option is not implicit within MPT 1375 and is currently under review. The CAI is constrained to 72 kbit/s half duplex communications regardless of service and therefore no adaptation is possible to the conditions on the radio channel or to the data service itself. Also, multiple channel configurations are technically possible.

Although many different cordless voice and data networks have been designed and prototyped in the laboratory, [3,20,21,22], very few systems are available in the marketplace. One of the reasons for the slow commercial availability is the lack of suitable licensed radio spectrum. Motorola petitioned the US Federal Communications Commission in 1985 for a 10 MHz allocation of radio spectrum at 1700 MHz for radio LANs [23,24], but ran into opposition from the US Meteorological Office. It is for such reasons that some manufacturers have explored the suitability of the spread spectrum concept for such applications, since low-power spread spectrum systems are capable of "peaceful coexistence" in the same radio spectrum. An example of this approach is a radio data network called ARLAN, marketed by Telesystems of Ontario, Canada. This network is capable of supporting a number of cordless RS232 data connections, operating a CSMA/CA packet switched protocol in the 900 MHz UHF radio band.

Another significant constraint currently hindering commercial products is the additional cost of the cordless solution over the wired LAN. Volume production of cordless equipment and acceptance in a market with ever-increasing data processing requirements will eventually reduce the costs to an economic level.

8.4 Summary

This chapter has explored the issues concerning data services on cordless telecommunication networks. It has discussed:

- Data services and their transmission requirements, the advantages of a cordless connection and application scenarios in which the services may be used
- The technical characteristics of cordless media and the important differences between cordless and wired interfaces
- Three example cordless networks that differ in the services they provide, the media they use and their system design philosophy
- Existing cordless data systems and the issues confronting further product introduction

Acknowledgements. The author wishes to thank the Institution of Electrical Engineers for permission to publish extracts from the paper "DECT – Integrated Services for Cordless Telecommunications", presented at the IEE Mobile Radio and Personal Communications conference in December 1989, and the management of Philips Research Laboratories and Philips Radio Communications Systems for permission to publish this chapter.

References

1. W Stallings, ISDN – An introduction, Macmillan Publishing, 1989
2. K Pahlavan, "Wireless intraoffice networks", ACM Transactions on Office Information Systems, vol 6, no. 3, pp 272–302, July 1988
3. JD Exley, "Cordless local area networks", IEE Colloquium on Packet Switching of Digital Speech and Data in Radio Systems (Digest no. 97), pp 7.1–5
4. M Hart, "Cordless in business communications as added value to the PABX", COMMED Cordless Conference, Meridian Hotel, London, May 1989
5. R Volpicelli, "Interactive water monitoring system accessible by cordless telephone", Rev Sci Instrum, vol 56(12), December 1985
6. FG Bullock and AR Urie, "Feasibility of microwave wireless office communications", IEEE GLOBECOM 1987, pp 1905–1908
7. DC Cox, "Universal digital portable radio communications", IEEE Proceedings, vol 75, no. 4, April 1987
8. DJ Goodman, "Indoor digital radio networks", 13th Biennial Symposium on Communications, Queens University, Kingston, Canada, June 1987
9. HP Stern, "Design and performance analysis of an integrated voice/data mobile radio system", IEEE/Rutgers University Wireless Information Networks Workshop, NJ, June 1989
10. "Easter tracks inventory with radio", Chain Store Age Executive, pp 242–245, May 1989
11. JL Ryan, "Home automation", IEE Review, October 1988
12. AJ Richardson and PA Watson, "Use of the 55 GHz–65 GHz oxygen absorption band for private local radio networks", IEE Millimetre Wave and IR Applications, Devices and Propagation Colloquium, May 1987
13. PE Green (ed), Computer network architectures and protocols, Plenum Press, New York, 1982
14. FR Gfeller and UR Bapst, "Wireless in house data communication via diffuse infra red radiation", IEEE Proceedings, vol 67, no. 11, November 1979
15. Y Nakata, J Kashio and T Noguchi, "In-house wireless communications system using infra red radiation", The New World of the Information Society, pp 333–339, ICCC, 1985
16. HT Smith, WJ Armitage and RJ Duckworth, "Using the Macintosh on a unix network", Byte, July 1987
17. ECTEL/TCS ETSI RES-3, "Digital European cordless telecommunications – reference document", ETSI, 1989
18. A Bud, "Data services in DECT", IEE Mobile Radio and Personal Communications Conference, December 1989
19. FC Owen and CD Pudney, "DECT – integrated services for cordless telecommunications", IEE Mobile Radio and Personal Communications Conference, December 1989
20. SD Dietrich, "The data link device", Wescon 87, Conference Record SS5, pp 1–5
21. P Freret, "Wireless terminal communications using spread spectrum radio", IEEE COMPCOM 1980, pp 244–248
22. L Golding and A Livne, "RALAN – a radio local area network for voice and data communications", IEEE GLOBECOM 1987, pp 1900–1904
23. C Gower-Rees, "Building LANs without cables", Canadian Data Systems, pp 65–66, May 1986
24. T Hartmann, "Wireless computers", Popular Computing, pp 64–70, February 1984

9 Implementation Technology

Brian Bidwell

Any cordless telephone system comprises a transceiver handset and a base station; both parts must be carefully designed for a successful product. Without any intention of underestimating the importance of the base station, it is generally accepted that the design of the portable transceiver presents both the main challenge to the designer and the toughest demands on the implementation technology. Since there is also considerable commonality between the radio parts of the portable transceivers and simple base stations, this chapter concentrates on the implementation technology of the portable transceiver, beginning with an introduction of the basic architecture options. We follow this by reviewing firstly the technology applied to the analogue low band and CEPT CT1 products and then to the first generation digital systems. Technology for DECT is then considered, with the chapter closing with an examination of future trends.

The overall architecture for a portable transceiver can be represented by the simplified block schematic diagram shown in Fig. 9.1. This is a very

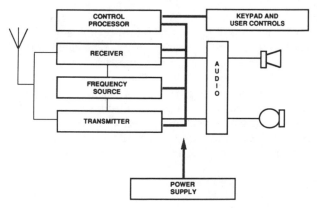

Fig. 9.1. Simplified block schematic of a cordless telephone.

general representation with the separate receiver and transmitter sections sharing a common aerial and frequency source which will vary from a simple single channel design to a full high-performance synthesiser. The audio section contains all the low-frequency circuitry necessary to meet the usually exacting requirements of the transmission specification for the send and receive paths, and in a base station would be the line interface. Dialling and other user input controls are shown as being handled by a control processor which also controls the radio transmitter and receiver operation, together with any radio link management functions.

Rechargeable batteries are the most common power source used, although some designs have offered primary cell options. This is an area of considerable research activity, spurred on by the obvious large commercial rewards awaiting the manufacturer of high energy-to-volume ratio battery technology.

Before considering the electronic design in more detail, the importance of the mechanical and acoustic design must be recognised. Like any portable products, cordless telephones are subjected to a large amount of physical abuse which they will be expected to withstand both cosmetically and functionally over their lifetime of over 5 years. The ability to withstand drop tests from heights of around 2m onto a concrete floor poses real problems for the designer when attempting to produce a small, lightweight, attractive product. In recent years the advances in material technology have helped considerably in this task, with polycarbonate becoming more popular than some of the older plastics such as ABS. Keypad and other user controls must be user friendly, attractive, reliable and low cost, and here the use of membrane switches can be of considerable help, although lacking any tactile feedback.

It is dangerously easy to overlook the interaction of the mechanical and acoustic designs in the belief that the electronic circuitry can always be tailored to the specification requirements. Acoustic tranducers, like many other components, require impedance matching – not just electrical but to their mounting cavities and the outside air path – putting clear demands on the mechanical design and styling. Delay is the other important parameter; this is expressed as a loop time from the mouth reference point to the microphone, over the radio link to the line interface and back again to the receiver earpiece and the ear reference point. The distinction between the reference points and the transducers becomes more significant as designers work towards smaller products. A typical maximum allowable delay is 5ms and the speed of sound is approximately 30cm/ms; the nodal distance between the mouth and ear is outside the designer's freedoms! This chapter does not attempt to give detailed insight into the very specialist subject of acoustic design, but the requirements, particularly delay, must not be ignored and will be referenced later when considering product evolutions.

9.1 Basic Transceiver Architecture and Design

This section reviews the basic options available for implementing the cordless transceiver. It should be noted that there is no obvious "right" architectural solution for a cordless telephone and this is reflected in the fact that different manufacturers have implemented different approaches for existing products and no doubt will continue to do so in the future. The receiver and transmitter sections can and will be treated separately, but the choice for one has implications for the other and this will be drawn out in the discussion. We consider first the receiver.

The classic implementation for receivers is the superheterodyne architecture illustrated in Fig. 9.2.

The principle of operation of the superheterodyne concept is that the local oscillator frequency is chosen to mix with the received radio frequency (RF) spectrum, thereby translating the wanted signal to the intermediate frequency (IF). Tuning is accomplished by varying the local oscillator to mix different input frequencies into the IF passband. The mixing process generates both the sum and difference frequency products. Thus, there is an input frequency other than the desired which can also mix to produce an output at the IF. This is known as the image and is one of the classic problems with the superheterodyne. The image response can be reduced by the use of RF filtering prior to the mixer input. The required selectivity for this filter and the choice of frequency for the IF represent a very important trade-off. The RF filter circuitry is simplified by the fact that the fractional bandwidth for any of the bands for cordless telephony is very small; this means that the RF filter can be fixed tuned.

It is, in principle, possible for the IF frequency of a superheterodyne receiver to be higher than the RF tuned frequency. However, for the frequencies applicable to European cordless telephones this would be inappropriate. The choice of high IF increases the separation of the image from the wanted frequency thereby simplifying the task of rejecting it in the RF filter. On the other hand it is usually more difficult to obtain the necessary channel selectivity, gain and demodulation processing within an acceptable power budget if the IF frequency becomes very high. The choice of frequency for the IF is also influenced by the technology available in

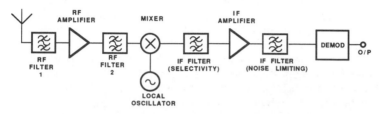

Fig. 9.2. Conventional superheterodyne receiver architecture.

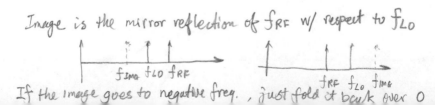

relation to the modulation and signal bandwidth of the applicable transmission standard. For example, the DECT standard involves a very wideband spectrum (> 1MHz) for which Surface Acoustic Wave (SAW) filters could perhaps be used. This would permit operation with a much higher IF than would be possible using a conventional crystal filter. Moreover, the wider bandwidth for DECT implies lower sensitivity and thus a requirement for less gain, again resulting in an easing in the IF circuitry requirements. The bandwidth for CT2, on the other hand, is only ~70kHz, for which SAWs might be less practicable. However, the operating RF frequency for CT2 is about half that for DECT so a lower IF could be countenanced.

One way of overcoming the limitations of the superheterodyne is to introduce a second frequency conversion. In this case gain is divided between the first and second IFs, easing the problems of stability. The selectivity of the first IF filter needs to be good if the first IF amplifier is to have a significant amount of gain, otherwise there exists a risk of high-level signals that fall within the band of the first IF but outside the second IF, causing limiting prior to the second stage filtering. If there is need to use only restricted selectivity in the first IF this must be at least good enough to provide adequate rejection of the image frequency of the second conversion. In this case, the gain in the first IF must be kept to the minimum necessary to ensure acceptable overall noise performance.

At this point it is worth noting the very significant advances in IF filter technology over recent years. The old concept of the IF filtering requirements being provided by interstage coupled tuned circuits disappeared in the sixties with the arrival of filter modules, but these were just a miniature pre-packed realisation of the same technology. Crystal filters are of course admirably suited to the IF function but their cost is a major obstacle to their use in a cordless telephone application and they are really confined to the high-cost professional communications market. This is where the ceramic filter technology comes in. From the first offerings which were hungrily snapped up for home entertainment transistor radios, a whole technology has been built up and at present has the dominant position in cheap IF filtering applications. Indeed the available performance possible from a ceramic filter is a prime input considered by those committees charged with the task of producing type-approval specifications such as BS 6833.

The reader will observe in Fig. 9.2 that a second RF filter is shown interposed between the RF amplifier and the mixer. The purpose of this filter is to prevent noise generated in the RF amplifier at the image frequency from being mixed into the IF bandwidth and desensitising the receiver. This second filter is not required, nor indeed is any filtering for the sake of image rejection, in the direct conversion (zero IF) architecture which we consider next (Fig. 9.3).

The direct conversion receiver operates on a similar principle to the superheterodyne except that now the IF is nominally at zero frequency, hence the term zero IF. The effect of this is effectively to fold the spectrum about zero frequency, which results in the signal occupying only one half the bandwidth. Because of this effect it is necessary for a pair of such zero

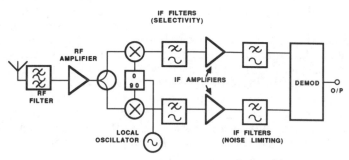

Fig. 9.3. Direct conversion (zero IF) receiver architecture.

IFs to be generated by mixing the incoming signal with in-phase (I) and quadrature (Q) components of the local oscillator. This process may be understood simplistically as a way of resolving the ambiguity in the instantaneous frequency of the received signal – if the quadrature component leads the in-phase signal the frequency is positive, if it lags the frequency is negative. A more rigorous explanation is to say that the in-phase and quadrature components represent the real and imaginary parts of the complex envelope of the signal (1). Another helpful way of looking at the problem is to view the two IF components as providing the X and Y coordinates of the tip of the vector in the signal phasor diagram.

The zero IF architecture possesses several advantages over the normal superheterodyne approach. Firstly, because the IF is at zero frequency the image response frequency is coincident with the wanted signal frequency. This results in the selectivity requirement for the RF filter being greatly eased, (except obviously for an FDD system where a diplexer requirement arises). Secondly, the choice of zero frequency means that the bandwidth for the IF paths is only half the wanted signal bandwidth. Thirdly, the channel selectivity filtering can be performed using simply a pair of low-bandwidth low-pass filters. These can be implemented using one of many available low-cost, low-complexity technologies, based on active filter concepts. With modern silicon technology it is quite practicable to implement entire active filters, including capacitors, on silicon, the main candidate circuit approaches being switched capacitor filters and gyrator filters.

Although the superheterodyne and the zero IF approaches have been presented as separate it is possible to combine them in a double conversion receiver where the first frequency conversion is to a high-frequency IF and the second to zero IF. This approach can be attractive under some circumstances.

Having introduced the normal receiver architectures we now briefly consider how other issues may impinge upon the choice of architecture. Firstly we consider demodulation; this is described in more detail in Chapter 5. Until now the demodulator has been shown as an undefined functional block for both architectures. The modulation formats employed or proposed for current and emerging cordless systems are constant envelope schemes, namely FM, FSK and GMSK. Given this fact it might be supposed that the IF chain of a receiver could be allowed to hard limit, since there is no amplitude information in the transmission which would be lost. For non-coherent demodulation this is indeed the case and the superheterodyne architecture of Fig. 9.2 may be used with a limiting IF amplifier. No Automatic Gain Control (AGC) is needed. The addition of receiver noise to the received signal, however, results in an apparent modulation of the signal envelope.

In a coherent demodulator all information in the phase and amplitude of the signal plus noise is exploited, so this amplitude modulation must be preserved. Thus, in a superheterodyne receiver designed for coherent demodulation it would be necessary to apply AGC to the IF. To some extent this argument, at present, is somewhat academic, in that the sensitivity improvement offered by coherent reception is at most a few decibels which, because of the near fourth-order propagation law over the radio path, translates into a very small improvement in operating range. Such a small improvement does not justify the increased power consumption currently needed to implement a coherent receiver. As technology develops over the next decade, though, it is possible that this situation may change and that coherent demodulation may begin to be utilised.

Coherent detection of FM digital signals invariably requires I–Q demodulation, so a superheterodyne implementation of a coherent receiver would look like the double conversion receiver with a final conversion to zero IF described earlier. It is a moot point whether such an architecture is a double conversion receiver or a single conversion receiver followed by a demodulator which happened to contain a frequency conversion. Generally, if most of the gain and all of the AGC circuitry and selectivity resided in the first IF, then the latter view would apply. On the other hand if a significant proportion of the gain, selectivity and AGC circuitry occupied the second IF then the receiver would be viewed as a double conversion circuit.

For the twin IF chains of a direct conversion receiver AGC is always required. This need arises because although the IFs, when combined, compose the complex envelope of a constant envelope signal, individually the amplitude of the I and Q IF components varies between zero and the envelope peak at rates much lower than the highest signal bandwidth frequency. The additional complexity of this AGC is a disadvantage for zero IF with non-coherent demodulation compared with a superheterodyne which requires no AGC.

An additional requirement of the newer systems is that for a Received Signal Strength Indication (RSSI) signal to permit the cordless handset to measure the signal or interference level on any given channel. In an architecture embodying AGC, an RSSI signal is essentially implicit in the AGC signal, although the linearity requirements of AGC are in fact usually less stringent that those for RSSI. Compensation for such non-linearity may under some circumstances be undertaken in software however, since the RSSI signal is used by the controller within the transceiver to choose a quiet channel to set up a new call. In a superheterodyne receiver, where AGC is not a requirement of the fundamental architecture, separate RSSI circuitry must be provided. Such circuitry is indeed incorporated in some superheterodyne receiver chips now on the market.

The components industry has for many years provided a wide range of catalogue integrated circuits for the superheterodyne architecture and it is hard to justify a costly and lengthy full custom design for these functions, but the zero IF architecture is slightly different. The first commercially successful application of a zero IF design in consumer products was that in the STC VHF wide area radio pager launched in 1979. This was a fully custom STC designed integrated circuit using the Plessey Semiconductors high-frequency bipolar 3 process, and triggered immediate interest in the architecture. From this start the semiconductor industry now produces catalogue parts for zero IF receivers, with Plessey Semiconductors not surprisingly having some very useful offerings.

We now move on to consider the transmitter architecture. The task of generating an RF signal is generally much simpler than that of receiving one. A transmitter fundamentally consists of the three main components: a final frequency carrier generator, a modulator and a power amplifier. These components may sometimes be combined into common circuits, e.g. a frequency sythesiser with an inbuilt modulator. However, initially we shall examine them separately.

The problem of generating a carrier at a high frequency is largely one of frequency control, since devices offering useful gain at all frequencies currently considered for cordless communications are readily available. The main approaches for providing an accurately defined output freqency are direct generation from a crystal reference or frequency synthesis, conventionally employing a Phase Lock Loop (PLL).

The crystal oscillator approach has some fundamental limitations. Firstly, it is in essence a single, fixed, frequency technique and can support a maximum output frequency of not higher than around 300 MHz, limited by the availability of suitable crystals. Also, the frequency accuracy of a crystal oscillator tends to be poor. The fact that the frequency is not easily changed is particularly unfortunate for superheterodyne receivers since a separate oscillator will generally be required for receive and transmit – except for FDD systems where an IF could be chosen at the difference frequency between receive and transmit. The upper limit on frequency is traditionally overcome by the use of harmonic frequency multipliers. These circuits produce all the harmonics up to and beyond the wanted frequency, with the wanted frequency being selected by a bandpass filter. A fairly exacting specification has to be placed upon the filter in order to restrict the levels of the unwanted harmonics.

Whilst acceptable for some of the early analogue cordless telephones, for second generation digital systems single frequency operation would represent an unacceptable restriction. Frequency sythesis is therefore employed in these systems. Fig. 9.4 shows a simple phase locked synthesiser loop.

An ouput from a voltage controlled oscillator (VCO) running at the final

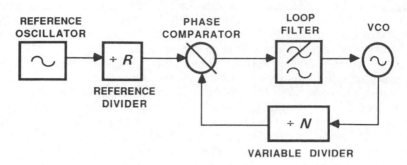

Fig. 9.4. Typical phase locked synthesiser.

frequency is divided by a counter circuit to a frequency suitable for comparison with a reference source. These two signals are fed to a phase comparator which produces an output proportional to their phase difference. This output is passed through a low-pass loop filter to provide a d.c. control signal for the VCO. This feedback system operates to minimise the loop phase error, thereby phase locking the output VCO frequency at the desired multiple of the comparison frequency. The comparison frequency is often selected to be equal to the channel spacing with the effect that adjacent values of N, the division ratio, specify adjacent channels at the output frequency. By switching the division ratio the output frequency can thus be made to switch between channels. Because the comparison frequency is low it is possible to choose the reference oscillator frequency as appropriate to provide good frequency stability. A typical figure is 5 MHz.

The requirements of CT2 (for free channel search) and of DECT (for frequency switching between time slots at a base station) impose a requirement for rapid switching between channels, more so potentially for DECT than for CT2. The switching time of a PLL synthesiser is inversely proportional to the bandwidth of the loop; thus one might expect a wide loop bandwidth to be employed. A frequency synthesiser will, however, generate not only the desired frequency but also unwanted spurii, notably reference frequency sidebands. These arise from modulation of the VCO by any reference frequency components from the phase comparator which remain after the loop filter. A wide loop bandwidth results in poor attenuation of these components and hence a higher level of unwanted spurii. Thus the issue of synthesiser design is complicated for the newer systems and certain refinements and subtleties must be employed to achieve the twin requirements of rapid switching and spurious-free signal generation. Further discussion of frequency synthesis techniques may be found in [2,3].

Until recently, the maximum input frequency of the variable divider limited the output frequency of this type of synthesiser to a few hundred megahertz. However, advances in technology have made final frequency synthesis practicable right up to 10 GHz[4].

We now turn our attention to the modulator. As mentioned earlier, CT2 and DECT both employ constant envelope modulation schemes. If only non-coherent demodulation is to be supported then the modulation can be achieved by directly modulating the synthesiser VCO. The lower frequency components of the modulation will be stripped off by the operation of the PLL but, provided the loop bandwidth is not too great, this will represent only a small proportion of the signal energy. This effect can be ameliorated by phase or frequency modulating the synthesiser reference by an amount scaled by the division ratio – a technique known as two point modulation [5].

Depending upon the tightness of the phase accuracy specification of a cordless telephone system it may be necessary to apply tight control to the modulation index to ensure that the phase path of the signal remains tied to 90° increments. This is difficult to achieve for the conventional PLL frequency synthesis approach. A more common approach in this situation is to use I–Q vector modulation, either at the final frequency or at a lower frequency which is then upconverted to the final RF (see Fig. 9.5).

The DSP processor drives two digital-to-analogue converters, each producing a baseband signal representing the in-phase and quadrature components of the desired signal. After low-pass filtering these signals are upconverted with in-phase and quadrature signals from an RF frequency oscillator, comprising a PLL synthesiser. These upconverted signals, when combined, generate the desired constant envelope modulated signal. Power consumption of such DSP implementations is discussed later in the chapter.

The power amplifier stage of a cordless terminal is relatively straightforward, the required power being modest and the tuned band being small. The output stage would be expected to operate in Class C (non-linear switching mode) to provide high efficiency. A particular requirement for any TDMA or TDD system such as CT2, Swedish DCT or DECT is the ability to achieve smooth gating of the transmitted carrier output to restrict the adjacent channel interference. This can be achieved by the use of control of the d.c. bias of the output stage(s).

Having considered the basic transceiver architecture and design, the next sections attempt to show the interrelationship of the product design with specification requirements and technology developments for a number of phases of product evolution.

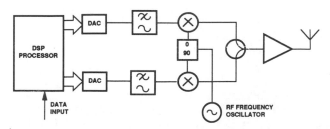

Fig. 9.5. Digitally implemented I–Q vector modulator.

9.2 Technology for Analogue Low Band and CEPT/CT1

The first successful cordless telephones were analogue low band designs which in the UK were produced to the requirements of British Telecom Technical Guide 47. A large part of this specification is devoted to the detailed requirements for the telephony performance to maintain the operational quality of the wired network. It also reflected the need for the radio parts to be realisable in a simple cost-effective manner. Thus, in line with radio spectrum availability at the time, the portable transceiver had a VHF low band, single channel transmitter in the 47 MHz range and an MF receiver in the 1.7 MHz range. This meant that products could use the techniques of contemporary radio systems, such as radio control for model aircraft, to achieve a low cost, low power consumption, robust design which did not stretch the basic technology or require costly pioneering development work.

The British Telecom "Freeway" is a good example of the typical design of UK CT1 produced to BT Technical Guide 47. Here the circuit architecture of the 47 MHz FM transmitter is conventional in using a 16 MHz oscillator which is frequency modulated followed by a tripler, filtering and a power amplifier. The 1.7 MHz FM receiver is of the traditional superheterodyne type. Realisation of both transmitter and receiver is in standard miniature discrete components with one integrated circuit and a ceramic IF filter. There are numerous variable resistors, capacitors and inductors typical of Far East sourced radios of the period. The basic assembly is on a printed circuit board produced to good but not limit standards. This is clearly in keeping with the objective of a cost-effective robust product that is not demanding of advanced techniques and materials.

Simplicity is the key theme of the UK CT1 products. The specification of a fixed factory-set channel (one of eight) with analogue FM in the 1.7 MHz and 47 MHz bands achieved its purpose of enabling low-cost products to become quickly available, but this very success is also the root cause of the commercial limitations of the product range. Call blocking, interference, lack of privacy and short operating range all result from the specification and can be only marginally improved by the use of advanced implementation technology. It was against this background that the specification for the CEPT CT1 was produced. This has achieved success in parts of Europe, notably Germany and Switzerland, even though the demands on the implementation technology are much more severe than those of the low band designs.

It often happens in life that the response to a condition is an over-reaction, with the pendulum swinging in the opposite direction. This is arguably the case for the CEPT CT1, where the prime objective of making the maximum possible use of the limited frequency spectrum availability resulted in a specification which can only be met by complex designs and higher cost realisations. The CT1+ specification defines operation on 80 paired duplex channels in the 900 MHz band with analogue FM. Channel bandwidth is 25 kHz with a 45 MHz duplex separation between transmit and receive channels. This frequency allocation is combined with tight requirements on receiver sensitivity, spurious response rejection and intermodulation rejection to permit operation on adjacent channels with transceivers in close proximity, to achieve the required high user density figures. The complexity required to meet these stringent specifications is ably illustrated by the block schematic of the Ascom product, illustrated in Fig. 9.6.

Referring to this block schematic, a key feature is the need for three crystal oscillators. The high stability frequency synthesiser has to be very agile to scan all 80 channels in a reasonable time period and still has to achieve a stability of ±5 kHz in set-up mode and ±2.5 kHz (2.5 ppm) in operating mode. Full analogue duplex operation means that a duplex filter is obviously required, but additional filters are also used in the separate transmit and receive channels to achieve the required specification performance. The transmitter design is required to achieve very low adjacent channel power – a maximum of 10 nW (−50 dBm) under normal conditions – which affects the design of the modulator and mixer as well as placing further demands on the frequency synthesiser. Receiver performance specification is also extremely tight, with the very high adjacent channel performance requirement of 53 dB placing exacting demands upon the IF filter performance.

Generally, the design is much closer to that of professional communications equipment and expensive cellular radio hand portables than the UK first generation cordless telephones and it is a very creditable reflection on both the design development and the manufacturing that a commercial product has been achieved. Once again, emerging improvements in technology can

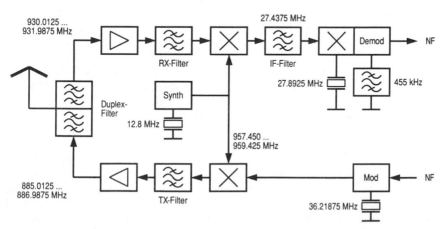

Fig. 9.6. RF block schematic of Ascom CT1+ handset. (By courtesy of Ascom.)

only result in relatively minor "fine tuning" of the design to achieve cost reductions. It is the regulatory specification which dictates the basic product cost range and this created the situation for the new generation of digital designs to exploit.

9.3 Technology for First Generation Digital Systems in the UK and Sweden

Before the specification of the newer digital systems, there was extensive consideration of the existing analogue products and of the opportunities which the emerging technologies afforded for a product to satisfy the proven market demand.

This time coincided with a major change in manufacturing technology with the emergence of leadless and chip components designed for surface mounting on the printed circuit boards. The components industry had served the designer well with an ever-increasing range and reducing size of the normal wire ended and leaded components, with automatic insertion machinery being developed for them by manufacturing plant industry. Indeed, the use of these components with automated assembly is still a very attractive proposition for products where space is not a first order consideration. However, during the eighties the cost of chip capacitors and resistors continued to fall and dropped below that of some leaded offerings, giving the business planning manager a new factor to consider. The chip components certainly enable a much tighter component packing density on the printed circuit board but this places tighter demands on board accuracy, and the layout designers needed to learn a new variant of their art. Both of these factors increased the cost of the development if not of the final product. Manufacturing plant was a different matter, however, with no option but to capitalise with expensive new machinery to perform the automated component placement function. This also involved a rethink of quality standards and manufacturing qualification which all took time to mature.

High product volumes are clearly required to justify the investment and it was in radio paging that some of the first products to use surface mount technology (SMT) emerged. The later versions of the CT1 equipments mentioned earlier also began to use the technology, which was firmly established by the time of the digital cordless telephone revolution. With ceramic substrate hybrid circuits still remaining somewhat fragile and expensive, there was really no design alternative but to base the new designs on the use of chip components.

In considering first generation digital systems, it was recognised that there was a prime need to increase the user density capability and also the user perceived operating quality, notably in operating range and speech quality. There is no substitute for spectrum allocation as a means of providing user density, but since spectrum is a finite limited resource, the demand on the technology is to achieve efficient use of allocations in competition with other services. At that time the 900 MHz band was being developed, and in the UK and Sweden attention focussed on an allocation for cordless telephone applications. RF technology and semiconductor processes were continuing to improve, giving confidence that the 900 MHz band would be usable, but it was the more fundamental swing from analogue to digital techniques for the speech channel which dramatically changed the specifications. It is not proposed to attempt to detail here the protracted discussions on the relative merits of Frequency Division Multiple Access (FDMA) and Time Division Multiple Access (TDMA), but rather to show the demands on the implementation technology of the different approaches.

A starting point must be a clear understanding of the objective of the product which the specification is defining and it is important to recognise that "cordless telephone" is too general for specification purposes. In the UK the emphasis was placed on the domestic and small business application, whereas in Sweden the large business cordless PABX application was the driving force; it is this difference that is generally accepted as the main reason for the UK specification being FDMA and the Swedish TDMA. Both systems, however, use Time Division Duplex (TDD) to achieve a pseudo-duplex speech path over a single RF channel. TDD gives the operational advantage of a symmetrical transmit and receive propagation path with the ability to get the full benefit of aerial diversity by provision of such diversity at one end of the radio link only. A major benefit in the implementation is that there can be a simplification in the RF frequency synthesiser, particularly in zero IF designs, where no transmit/receive switching is required.

There is further simplification and relaxation of specification possible in the frequency synthesiser for a TDMA design since there are fewer but wider RF channels than in an FDMA design. The wider bandwidth of the TDMA channels clearly placed different demands on the filter technology but generally this presents no real problem and the front end aerial filter is no different than for FDMA. Relaxation of the RF channel frequency tolerance in a TDMA design is offset by the need for a very accurate control of the channel time slots in the base stations in order to avoid fast slot slip in relation to unsynchronised neighbours. Although the clocks controlling these time slots operate at frequencies where technology is well understood and characterised, the accuracy demanded must not be underestimated and great care must be taken in the implementation of this function. For an FDMA design with more and narrower bandwidth RF channels, the RF frequency stability requirements are demanding, with 900 MHz being a reasonable upper limit for the technology of this generation of handsets. Dynamic channel assignment and call set-up timings do require a capability of fast switching between channels from the frequency synthesiser, which certainly means designing at the technology limits.

It is worth noting at this point, the significant difference in base station architecture between TDMA and FDMA designs. In a multi-channel TDMA base station only one radio transmitter and receiver is required, compared with one per channel in the FDMA approach. It is this feature which makes TDMA more attractive to the business, multi-channel application. However, a simple domestic single channel base station has to carry the complication of the synchronised time slot capability. This is an issue more of basic architecture than implementation technology, although there is a strong link between architecture complication and the affordability and justifiability of the implementation technology.

Having considered the basic differences between TDMA and FDMA of the Swedish and UK designs, they do have a large area of commonality in the digital signalling and digital speech coding, at least in respect of the implementation technology. The requirements of the digital signalling functions are well served by the semiconductor processes in CMOS integrated circuits and the ever-increasing processing powers of microprocessors. Even in a business application the demands on the signalling channel are a small part of the total communication channel, which is dominated by the speech path. There are two exceptions to this however: firstly during the radio link establishment and call set-up phases, which are short periods of intense signalling, and secondly in a cordless data terminal application. This latter case will not be pursued in this section since it is really only a different use of the speech channel for carrying standard data formats with or without additional error control and management.

In considering a cordless telephone system design it is important to get the distribution of intelligence correct between base station and portable transceiver. Even though technology enables very low power digital processing, it is dangerously easy to impose a heavy burden of system management onto the portable unit, resulting in a significant power consumption problem. This can become more user-apparent in domestic applications where the ratio of active to standby use is very low and the background processing power consumption dominates.

The UK CT2 standards allowed realisation of the portable transceiver signalling in commercially widely sourced 4 bit microprocessors – a situation which was preserved when the UK Industry Group companies cooperated in producing the Common Air Interface (CAI) standard. Design partitioning between hardware and software realisation of the signalling functions is an important issue involving the generally conflicting aspects of unit cost, development cost, development time and product size. Most initial products may be expected, however, to have a similar compromise in this area, employing a low-power CMOS microcontroller and a mixture of custom and catalogue logic parts. The level of integration can be expected to increase in future products, though. Two recent developments may have a bearing on this.

Firstly, over the last few years semiconductor manufacturers have begun to target microcontrollers towards specific market segments. Thus, in addition to devices containing the standard assortment of RAM, ROM and general purpose I/O ports, products are now available with most specialised peripherals (e.g. a DTMF generator for the telecommunications market).

Some manufacturers also offer a "microcontroller customisation" facility whereby users may configure their own microcontroller from a core processor plus a selection of peripherals.

Secondly, as the complexity of application specific integrated circuits has increased, some semiconductor manufacturers have started to introduce popular microprocessors such as the 8085 to their cell libraries. Thus it is now theoretically possible for cordless telephone equipment manufacturers to design their own semi-custom integrated circuits containing a microprocessor, RAM, ROM and custom high-speed signalling logic, although it may be some time before the technology permits the entire digital subsystem to be integrated on one chip!

An indication of the signalling and processing requirements for a UK CT2 handset is shown in Fig. 9.7, where the B channel is for communication (normally speech), SYN channel is for system synchronisation and the D channel is for control signalling. Details of the CAI standard signalling are given in Appendix 2.

Digital speech encoding is the most fundamental difference between digital cordless telephones and earlier generations. As previously mentioned, digital speech techniques had become well established in the telecommunication system industry at that time with the CCITT G.721 ADPCM algorithm a widely accepted standard. Being developed primarily for network applications, the G.721 algorithm includes companded 64 kbit/network interfaces, which may be omitted to the benefit of complexity and speech performance in the cordless telephone application. Companies therefore embarked on developments to implement variations of the algorithm more appropriate to low-power transceivers. This included component manufacturers as well as equipment suppliers in some cases undertaking joint activities, giving some indication of the resources in both skill and funding necessary to successfully achieve the objective (see e.g. [6]).

It is very easy to get carried along on the tide of "everything is possible in digital processing" and this aspect must not be underestimated. There is a great deal of complex calculation and signal processing necessary to achieve the reduction from the initial 64 kbit/s signal to the transmitted data

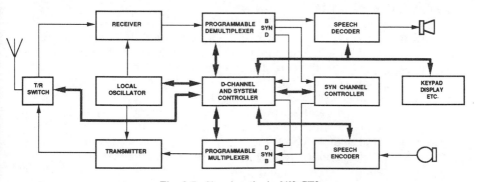

Fig. 9.7. Signal paths in UK CT2.

rate of 32 kbit/s. Even with the use of small geometry CMOS semiconductor processes, this can require significant power consumption of around 70 mW. Producing a new speech encoding algorithm is an extremely expensive and lengthy operation complicated by the fact that the algorithm is a dynamic and adaptive operation not lending itself to simple objective test measurements. Agreement on subjective testing is in itself a major task, let alone designing something to pass the test! The use of a standard algorithm (G.721) provides the potential to obtain type approval by proving that the algorithm has been implemented rather than having to submit to the uncertainty of the subjective test. It is therefore not surprising that the first products to be manufactured to the UK CT2 standard fell into two categories: those using a variant of the G.721 algorithm and those using simpler speech encoding. The attraction of the Continuously Variable Slope Delta (CVSD) modulation method of speech encoding is clearly indicated by the power consumption requirement of about one tenth of that of the G.721 realisation. It is really only the transcoding requirement for direct interfacing with the digital network which prevented the wider adoption of CVSD for the CT2 application.

Reverting to the implementation of the radio section of the portable transceiver, the UK CT2 products classically demonstrate the implementation technology options and trade-offs. There cannot possibly be any definitive judgement on which is the "right choice" since manufacturers' objectives and business ambitions are different and each will have a different definition of success, but the products illustrate the different approaches. A key input into the UK CT2 specification definition was to anticipate the near-future technology and to recognise the more distant developments, making them applicable but not necessarily essential. A technology intercept of under 5 years from start of work on the specification to product launch was envisaged. This has been borne out by the launch of the first products during 1989 and predictably these first products are applications of proven technology to the new requirement. The basic radio architectures are essentially traditional with little, but significant, new features in their realisation of key functions such as the frequency synthesiser. Manufacturing technology is also well proven although in the quest for increased customer appeal through a smaller product, the standard and tolerancing is to a noticeably tighter level than in earlier products.

Other product releases following these first launches benefit from improved technology, having undergone an extended gestation period. The improvements are not confined to larger scale integration of circuit functions but include changes to the core design concept, with the first signs of digital signal processing coming into the traditional analogue radio design. The potential advantages of such an approach to radio design were recognised some years ago now (see e.g. [7]), but it is only recently that such concepts have begun to be commercialised for consumer products. It is the lure of increased digital signal processing that for some manufacturers is a prime driving force behind adoption of a zero IF or direct conversion design, since the task of integration and digital processing is directly related to the signal frequency. However, the attractions of a zero IF architecture detailed earlier were sufficient for other companies. Thus, products were developed using mathematically derived modulator, demodulator, AFC and AGC functions requiring no adjustment or alignment in the manufacturing process.

This was the case for the design produced by STC under a development contract for British Telecom where these functions are just a part of a custom designed digital CMOS integrated circuit. Here, by digital conversion of the receiver baseband signals the demodulation process is reduced to a look-up table and some simple logic processing followed by digital filtering and slicing to produce the digital output signal. This is subsequently demultiplexed into the control (D) channel and the communication (B) channel for handling in the control microprocessor and the ADPCM codec circuitry. The modulation process is much easier, with the transmitter I and Q baseband signals being digitally constructed before filtering and mixing with the local oscillator followed by RF amplification to produce the required output. An important benefit of this approach is that the modulation index is very accurately controlled, allowing the use of a higher value than would be safe for simple modulation in the local oscillator or frequency synthesiser. These products required heavier development costs and extended timescales in order to achieve performance consistency and manufacturability.

Active filters were an established technique at the time of CT2 but their penetration into products in general, rather than cordless telephones specifically, can best be described as erratic. Taking the term "active filter" to include switched capacitors, gyrators and other types, they do have fundamental problems which limit their applicability to high performance equipment. Operating dynamic range and noise performance are chief among their limitations for receiver functions, particularly when viewed against progress in other technologies such as ceramic resonators. Having made this point, they should not be written off and their use will certainly increase, even if somewhat disappointingly slowly for the technocrat.

Having considered the UK CT2 position in some detail, we now consider the Swedish second generation cordless developments. These centred on one major company, Ericsson, and were aimed mainly at the business application as mentioned earlier. Ericsson's approach was somewhat more ambitious in respect of the implementation technology demands. A good example of this is the echo control function at the audio line interface. As explained in Chapter 4, echo control at the audio line interface is necessary when the two-way loop delay round the transmit-receive path in a cordless telephone base station and portable configuration exceeds ~5 ms. The burst structure of a TDMA system gives a typical delay of at least 10 ms and, at that time in equipment design, echo cancellers were relatively expensive by virtue of being low-volume products. This was clearly not a deterrent, especially with confident forecasts of low-cost, high-performance integrated designs on the horizon. At that time there was also no existing system working on a TDMA format, but the opportunities were evident from the system design concept and again there was a confidence that technology could deliver the goods when required. It was recognition of the opportunities of TDMA with a matching against the emerging technology which was largely behind the European decision for its adoption as the basis of the Digital European Cordless Telecommunications (DECT) standard.

9.4 Technology for DECT

Once again, the scarcity of radio spectrum availability was a key feature in the definition of the DECT standard, and from the outset it was clear that operation above 1.6 GHz would be required.

For low-power, low-cost portable transceivers, RF frequency stability is a major problem and operation much above 900 MHz is approaching the limit of practical realisations of narrowband systems. This was a lesson well learnt from the CEPT CT1 experience. The UK CT2 benefited from the wider 100 kHz channel but further widening for 1.6 GHz operation could not really be justified on the user density against spectrum allocation issue.

The wider channel spacing of 1728 kHz in the DECT system allows the use of SAW filters in the receiver and a general easing of the IF design compared with narrow band superheterodyne designs. For zero IF designs, the IF filtering and bandwidth is less of an issue but a single conversion from 1.6 GHz to baseband is more questionable. It is more probable that an additional intermediate frequency conversion, such as discussed in Section 9.1, will be beneficial.

Another significant difference in a TDMA design is the need for a much higher transmitted data rate than in narrow band systems. For DECT this is 1152 kbit/s bringing special demands on technology for a successful design. At the time of product introduction, however, this should present no insurmountable difficulties provided that care is taken in the design.

One aspect of the high transmitted data rate is that the propagation time delay becomes an important issue, with some degree of equalisation necessary for extended operating ranges. Early thoughts were that operation without equalisation would be limited to distances where the root-mean-square (RMS) delay spread is less than 10%–20% of the symbol length which, in the case of DECT with 1152 kbit/s, would be a path length spread of about 50 m, giving an estimated operating range of around 200 m. Work on the GSM cellular radio standard with its 270 kbit/s transmitted data rate had shown the complexity of a four symbol equaliser to be a major challenege and even a reduction to two symbol equalisation did not present an attractive proposition for a cheap cordless telephone application.

Some companies involved in DECT (e.g. Ericsson) are encouraged by the published results of work such as that by Chuang [8] on the topic, which shows that time dispersion errors are very bursty and occur in conjunction with fading dips. By the use of aerial diversity at the base station end only, as previously mentioned, and considering quasi-stationary operation, there is the hope that the DECT 200 m range figure may be increased up to 500 m and possibly beyond, without the need for any equalisation. It must be added, however, that although there is unanimous hope for this, some companies remain sceptical and are awaiting early demonstration.

More recent work on DECT is showing more opportunities for reducing the demand on the implementation technology by product architecture changes. An example of this is a multi-carrier TDMA/TDD system where a base station with a single radio transceiver can change carrier frequency between time slots, thereby reducing the system capacity limitations due to adjacent channel attenuation and intermodulation performance. Another opportunity is for a reduction in the local oscillator stability requirements of the portable transceiver. This can be achieved because a DECT base station can be always active on at least one channel, allowing the portable transceiver to lock onto the base station transmission before transmitting any signals itself.

One thing is certain though: DECT will benefit from the slightly later product entry by being able to take advantage of a later technology intercept with improved performance semiconductor processes. This is particularly important in DECT which has a fairly complex digital signal processing requirement tailored to even further expansion by concatenation of time slots, for example,

Based on the experience of the evolution of product designs in other applications such as radio paging, the DECT product range will make use of the improving technology largely in respect of enhanced user features and facilities. This is obviously the case for some of the more sophisticated terminals which will undoubtedly make up the DECT product range.

9.5 Future Trends

Silicon technology will continue to be developed, stretching the power/frequency performance and enabling portable products to operate above 2 GHz. The power consumption requirement of gallium arsenide is likely to be eased, but possibly not quickly enough for significant early application in cordless telephones. It should be noted, however, that some companies are adopting a much more bullish approach to this technology.

In the general area of improving semiconductor processes, the pressure from the designers is for lower operating voltage and power, together with higher speed/frequency performance. It is worth noting that the majority of analogue circuits are current-operated, with only specific areas such as the receiver front end requiring the voltage headroom to meet blocking performance. With combined analogue and digital processes, the so-called BIMOS or merged processes, already firmly established for reasonable performance, it is possibly in this area that advances will become most evident. At present, the performance of a combined process cannot match that of separately realised, highly specialised single processes.

As previously mentioned, timescales for active filter realisations are uncertain and filter technology needs to concentrate on the front end filters, which remain a difficult problem area. SAW devices are at last improving beyond their frustrating "almost there" position for most applications.

Changes in product technology are more likely to be seen in design architecture, where the first move seen in CT2 designs will continue towards a more digital implementation. It is already possible to realise a transceiver in which it is only the front end and mixer that are analogue designs and the remainder digital, but the extensive use of powerful digital signal microprocessors such as the Texas Instruments TMS320 series makes the power consumption out of the range which can be considered for a hand portable product. This can only be a temporary position, however, with semiconductor processes and microcomputers ever improving.

A highly digital implementation will include programmable filtering and operating mode to give a dynamically configurable design capability if required. This could well prove significant for using a common portable unit for a number of different systems with different standards – the truly "flexible terminal" [9].

Low power consumption is of vital importance for portable units and a continuing concentration on circuit techniques and process technology will be essential. This, together with the application of any new battery technology, will greatly enhance customer appeal by making more complex terminals truly pocketable rather than just portable.

Pressure of success is continuing to push the operating spectrum higher, as witnessed by the advent of Personal Communications Networks (PCNs), and these products may be an important step in the convergence of cordless telephones and cellular radio within the next few years. This is also supported by the RACE activity [9] which is working towards the single communicator goal.

There is also likely to be a spin-off benefit to cordless telephones from PCN in the short term, as companies involved in PCN are certainly involved also in cordless telephones and advanced development is so precious that cross-fertilisation is desirable.

9.6 Summary

It is hoped that this chapter will have given the reader an insight into the parallel paths of theoretical design, component and process technology and product requirement specifications for cordless telephone products.

From the earliest single channel simple analogue products working on low band VHF, we have moved quite rapidly into an era when digital based designs offer products far beyond a basic telephone at prices which will ensure large market success. Design architectures are unlikely to undergo any major upheaval apart possibly from the totally digital transceiver, which is currently limited only by power consumption and size. The role of the administration approval specifications must not be dismissed; it is vital that people involved in their production have direct product experience to ensure a sensible match.

Acknowledgements The assistance of colleagues in producing this chapter is greatly appreciated and particular thanks are due to Peter Hulbert of Roke Manor Research, Heinz Ochsner of Ascom and Dag Åkerberg of Ericsson.

References

1. W Gosling (ed), "Radio receivers", Peter Peregrinus (IEE), London, 1986
2. FM Gardner, "Phaselock techniques", Wiley-Interscience, New York, 1979
3. V Manassewitsch, "Frequency synthesisers: theory and design", Wiley-Interscience, New York, 1980
4. MC Wilson et al., "A 10.7 GHz frequency divider using a double layer silicon bipolar process technology", Electronic Letters, vol 24, pp 920ff, 1988
5. RA Meyers and PH Waters, "Synthesiser review for pan-European digital cellular radio", IEE Colloquium on VLSI Implementations for Second Generation Cordless and Mobile Communications Systems, London, March 1990
6. P Dent, R Bharya, R Gunawardana and JM Baker, "Algorithm specific speech coder architecture for second generation cordless telephones", IEE Colloquium on Digitised Speech Communication via Mobile Radio, London, December 1988
7. AP Cheer, "Architectures for digitally implemented radios" (and other papers), IEE Colloquium on Digitally Implemented Radios, London, October 1985
8. JCI Chuang, "The effects of time delay spread on portable radio communication channels with digital modulation", IEEE Selected Areas in Communications, vol SAC-5, no. 5, pp 879ff, June 1987
9. J Gardiner, "The flexible terminal – personal communications during the evolution of RACE", Workshop on Digital Mobile Communications, Lund University, Sweden, April 1987

THE FUTURE

10 The Future of Personal Communications

John Gardiner and Wally Tuttlebee

The 1980s saw the widespread acceptance in Europe of the concept of limited mobility in the provision of telecommunication services. Markets for both analogue cellular radio and first generation (analogue) cordless telephones saw huge growth. Accompanying this was a similar growth in the availability, use and services offered by wide area paging systems. The decade also saw major progress in the development of common pan-European standards for digital cordless telephony, digital cellular radio telephony and radio paging. These factors together formed the seedcorn for the emergent concept of "personal communications".

The term "personal communications" has varied widely in meaning across European industry, depending upon the background and perspective of the user of the term. Recent developments have been such that what began as a rather vague concept in the mid 1980s is now taking on an increasingly well-defined form. On one thing many agree, namely that personal communications will be one of the major European growth industries of the 1990s [1].

In this chapter we trace something of the emergence and evolution of the concepts of personal communications. We review recent initiatives in Europe, notably the RACE Mobile Telecommunications Project and Personal Communications Networks (PCNs). The global implications of personal communications require that a description of the valuable work undertaken by the CCIR Study Group 8 on the topic of Future Public Land Mobile Telecommunications Systems (FPLMTS) be included, as well as the recent development within the CCITT of the Personal Telecommunications concept. Finally, on the basis of this survey of today's situation, we speculate upon the products and systems of tomorrow.

10.1 The RACE Mobile Telecommunications Project

The Mobile Telecommunications project of the European Community (EC) RACE programme has without a doubt been a significant stimulus in developing European thinking about personal communications on both a technical and commercial level, albeit perhaps more subtly in this latter respect. What were the origins of this project and its goals? This section addresses these questions and considers where the project may lead.

The RACE programme itself, like ETSI, had its foundations in the recognition by the EC of the key importance of telecommunications to the future of the European economy, subsequently detailed in the Green Paper [2]. Thus the *R*esearch and development of *A*dvanced *C*ommunication technologies in *E*urope, RACE, initiative was born. The RACE programme is geared, as part of its rationale, towards engendering a climate of cooperation between telecommunication administrations and industry across Europe that will facilitate a liberalisation of the market. The more tangible goal of the programme is the consensus development of specific telecommunications technology and infrastructure, notably an Integrated Broadband Communications Network (IBCN) across Europe. The RACE programme comprises many interrelated projects, 50% funded by the EC and 50% by industry. As part of this programme, the Mobile Telecommunications project is specifically addressing the evolution of personal communications within Europe over the next decade, with a view to defining a convergent, possibly flexible, air interface for cordless and cellular access.

A one-year definition phase project, involving just six partners, was completed in 1986. It was from this programme that the potential convergence of cordless telephone and cellular radio systems began to be mooted in the public fora [3]. At this time such a concept was generally greeted with scepticism rather than enthusiasm! From the technical viewpoint, in the mid 1980s, the relevance of mobile communications to the overall RACE programme seemed a little dubious. Cordless telephones were restricted to analogue systems and their potential market was widely unappreciated by the wider telecommunications community. Cellular radio had only recently been introduced on a widespread scale and, with hindsight, growth projections at that time were rather conservative. However, the clear conclusion of the definition phase programme was that by the early twenty-first century a large proportion, perhaps as much as 50%, of the traffic carried on the public telephone network would involve mobile users. This would obviously have architectural implications for the IBCN if the latter were indeed to be an integrated network, supporting both fixed and mobile users. The definition phase identified the key areas where substantial further work would be needed if a Universal Mobile Telecommunication System (UMTS) definition was to emerge.

In the summer of 1987 some twenty-five organisations, including key players in the European mobile communications industry, came together to form a single consortium to define the main phase activity for the RACE Mobile Communications project. The CEC recognised that if the growth projections for mobile communications were even partly correct the impact upon the telecommunications infrastructure would indeed be profound, and so it was that the main phase RACE Mobile programme was endorsed, with work beginning in early 1988.

The programme proposed originally covered a five-year period although, in common with many RACE projects, the initial contract let by the EC was for just three years. The first two years of the project have seen wide ranging research undertaken which has laid the foundation for the detailed system definition which is now under way. This work has included the evolution of new concepts for the fixed network infrastructure, propagation research around 2 GHz, diversity techniques, multiple cellular architectures and more.

The aims of the project have been to explore the ways in which cordless and cellular telecommunication systems may converge over the next decade, with the view to defining a common interface standard, a UMTS capable of supporting cordless and cellular type operation from a single handset. One view of this potential convergence is illustrated in Fig. 10.1. The other key goal of identifying the impact of the UMTS upon the design of the fixed telecommunications network has already been mentioned.

The concept of the UMTS as it is currently emerging is of an environment sufficiently standardised that a single pocket communicator will be viable in the home, the office, and outdoors in both rural and urban environments [4] – i.e. widespread geographical coverage will be achievable with a truly pocketable telephone. The system could support simple voice terminals, more advanced terminals supporting basic UMTS data services and perhaps a third class of terminal supporting advanced, higher rate (up to 1–2 Mbit/s) limited-coverage data services as IBCN service extensions. The system would be not simply one public network but would consist of public and private network elements combined to allow a customer to be located, tracked during a call and charged correctly. It is envisaged that the UMTS system will evolve from the service viewpoint from the GSM cellular and the DECT cordless systems, but will include new services beyond those provided by these networks.

In addition to the UMTS the project is also considering the extension of the broadband service, of 2 Mbit/s and above, which may be provided by the IBCN to the mobile environment, by means of a Mobile Broadband System (MBS) [5]. This would use radio transmission at millimetric wave frequencies of 30–60 GHz. Work to date has focussed on propagation, channel equalisation and network architecture.

The introduction of a UMTS system is expected to be in the late 1990s or around the turn of the century, although much will depend upon the form of the UMTS system definition and upon how existing mobile networks develop, both conceptually and in practice in the interim. Another potentially

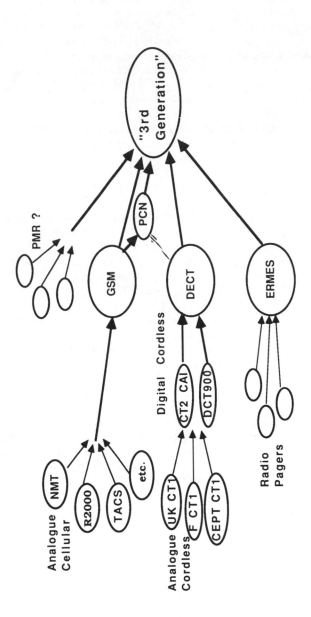

Fig. 10.1. A possible convergence scenario for mobile and personal communications.

important factor is the establishment of an ETSI ad hoc UMTS Technical Committee, which met for the first time in August 1990.

10.2 Personal Communications Networks, PCNs

PCNs have been described as "generation two-and-a-half" – a system for more imminent introduction initially within the UK, and in due course Europe, based upon existing technology.[1]

10.2.1 Background

On 26 January 1989, the then Secretary of State for Trade and Industry, Lord Young, whilst announcing the award of the UK Telepoint licences also introduced a discussion document "Phones on the Move – Personal Communications in the 1990s" [6] announcing the UK Government's intention to licence two or three new mobile telecommunications operators who would be encouraged to develop networks operating in the frequency range 1.7–2.3 GHz. As with the introduction of the Telepoint service, bids were to be invited from consortia of would-be licensees and successful applicants selected on the advice of the Director General of Telecommunications of OFTEL, Professor Sir Bryan Carsberg. The concept of PCNs was outlined only briefly at this stage, it being clear that the new networks would differ from the existing cellular networks in that they would be "based on digital personal communicators so linking and developing both the cellular and Telepoint concepts".

The reasoning behind the PCN concept and the timing of its announcement were based on a number of technical and strategic considerations. The stimulation of competition in service provision had been a cornerstone of UK Government policy for telecommunications and two aspects of this undoubtedly played a part. First, with regard to the existing analogue cellular (TACS) systems operated by Racal Vodafone and Cellnet, the enormous demand which the cellular services had generated had produced capacity difficulties and in some areas the resulting grade of service was falling below public expectations. Introducing a further element of competition would allay suspicions of complacency on the parts of both Government and cellular network operators. Second, and more significantly, there had been a long-standing imbalance in the nature of competition in the fixed networks of British Telecom (BT) and Mercury.

On privatisation in 1984, BT had taken over the huge national infrastructure

---

[1] The term Personal Communications Network is also now in use in the USA, referring to the provision of a personal communications service, but probably based on different technology. The US PCN concepts are not described in this chapter.

of buried copper connecting individual subscribers and Mercury had from the outset complained about their difficulties in competing in the "local loop" arena. A radio solution catering for anticipated massive growth in the use of enhanced cordless telephony, would restore competitive balance.

As a result of these considerations it was decided to exclude BT and Racal from the community of bidders – a decision which was received by these organisations with considerable indignation. However, both BT and Racal have been given to understand that they will not be debarred from applying for licences in the next (third) generation of networks which will develop during the later life of the PCNs. In any case, both are now confident that they can develop and provide services very similar to those of PCNs and have been told they can do so, within their existing 900 MHz frequency allocations.

As regards the technical issues, several factors were significant. The cellular user population in the UK had grown far faster than expected and it was anticipated that saturation in the TACS networks would be noticeable in areas of peak demand (London particularly) by the time the GSM digital system is introduced in 1991. Because of the need to support TACS for a substantial period after the introduction of GSM, it will not be possible to realise the full capacity advantages of the digital system (probably twice to two and a half times that of TACS) until TACS is finally phased out. A capacity problem in the mid-to-late 1990s therefore remained which, with the possible exception of the Paris region of France, was unique to the UK. (In early 1990 the UK had only 17% of the European Community population but 56% of the cellular mobile radio activity.)

Turning to spectrum issues, it was soon evident that there was no realistic possibility of accommodating further network operators in the 900 MHz band, but a significant aspect of experience with the 900 MHz system was drawn upon, namely the capacity potential of the new Telepoint services.

Clearly what was needed in the PCNs was a combination of features which would provide the capacity characteristics of short-range, low-power cordless telephony coupled with the service capability of cellular systems proper. In order to encourage the latter, an extra degree of freedom was to be allowed to PCN operators, namely the opportunity, if they wished, to interconnect cell sites by radio links rather than relying entirely on the fixed network provided by BT or Mercury. The remaining technical factor was related to the availability of much of the 1.7–1.9 GHz band for mobile use and to the maturity of 2 GHz radio technology, which was judged to have reached a stage at which terminals of moderate cost could be realised.

Overall, the combination of elements, together perceived as PCNs, offered an exciting prospect in promoting competition, tackling the future needs of the user population and promoting innovative technology.

10.2.2 PCN Technology

Within the above broad framework identified at the beginning of 1989, further constraints emerged as the major contenders for licences began service planning. Briefly these constraints were as outlined below.

Timescale

From the above rationale for PCNs it was evident that the target timescale for implementation should be the early 1990s rather than later in the decade. This was a significant factor because it clearly set a tight deadline for any developments in air interface design if these were to stand any chance of acceptance as European standards. With the 1.7–1.9 GHz band generally under consideration for Europe-wide system implementation, it was essential that air interface parameters chosen for PCNs should have the agreement of the rest of Europe.

Choice of Air Interface

Bearing the foregoing in mind, an obvious way forward was to consider one of the air interfaces which had already achieved acceptance through the procedures of ETSI or were in the process of being accepted. This reduced the choice essentially to GSM and DECT and, after a three-month consultation period following the January 1989 PCN announcement, the DTI issued guidelines to potential licence bidders confirming that GSM and DECT air interfaces should be the basis of proposals. Minor changes might be permissible but the need to benefit from economies of scale in mass production of GSM and DECT components inevitably imposed constraints on the extent of divergence. Additionally it would clearly be desirable to maintain backwards compatibility between any new PCN standard and GSM and DECT systems proper in order to maintain maximum flexibility of use in accessing services in regions where PCNs were nct implemented.

Radio Intersite Links

The possibility referred to above of deploying radio intersite links in PCNs had some bearing on interests in the Radio Communications Agency of the DTI in the use of the radio spectrum at frequencies above 30 GHz. A Green Paper of September 1988 [7] had sought responses from potential users, spectrum regulators and equipment manufacturers regarding exploitation of the millimetre wave radio spectrum and there had been much enthusiasm expressed in these responses for fixed, short-haul point-to-point link applications. The technology was considered adequately mature and the opportunity to deploy large numbers of such links Europe-wide would provide the market pull necessary to stimulate volume manufacture of millimetre wave products.

The Network and Personal Mobility

If PCNs are to use existing air interfaces, then what will distinguish them from the GSM and DECT networks already in planning? The answers to this question relate closely to the more general issue of what will constitute "third generation" personal communications. The obvious distinction between first generation analogue cellular and second generation digital systems tended some time ago to encourage emphasis on further new air interfaces as the essential basic feature of a new generation of network, but this is an oversimplification. In PCNs and subsequently in third generation systems, the greatest scope for innovation will lie in the areas of services and mobility management in the fixed elements of the networks. In particular, the general trend towards contacting an individual rather than simply calling a number at a fixed location, the principal requirement of truly personal communications – and additionally the requirement to provide users with a range of different services supported in a common system architecture – will be the major targets for development efforts by the new PCN operators.

10.2.3 Applicants and Licence Awards in the UK

Following "Phones on the Move" and a period of consultation, the UK Government invited bids for operating licences, these to be submitted by mid September 1989. Recalling earlier comments regarding the rationale for PCN introduction and the competitive position of Mercury in relation to BT, it was announced that, subject to satisfactory proposals being forthcoming, Mercury would be one of the licensees. Ultimately a total of eight applications were received, involving all the major players in mobile communications in the UK (excluding BT and Racal as indicated previously). Principal contending consortia had been instructed to meet several strategic objectives. The financial investment implicit in establishing a PCN dictated that smaller engineering specialists had to involve banking or business investment companies in their consortia. The potential for PCN exploitation throughout Europe and in North America encouraged the involvement of organisations in France, Germany and Spain and also USA telecommunications operators.

Much debate surrounded the issue of how many licences should be awarded, since it was decided that the available spectrum would have to be partitioned among the PCN operators and there was concern about the likely future demands on the 1.7–1.9 GHz band by services such as the Terrestrial Flight Telephone System (TFTS) and by possible expansion of the 1.88–1.9 GHz slot currently proposed for DECT down to 1.85 GHz. Moreover, if GSM were to be used for the air interface then, since this is a two-frequency duplex system, further spectrum would be lost due to the need to provide a guard band between transmit and receive allocations. (Judicious combination of GSM and DECT in the later stages of PCN development, when pressure on spectrum builds up, was mooted as permitting exploitation of the band with higher efficiency.)

Ultimately it was judged feasible to award three licences, the successful consortia being as follows:

Mercury Personal Communications Networks Ltd: Cable and Wireless, Motorola and Telefonica

Unitel Ltd: STC, Thorn EMI, US West and Deutsche Bundespost

Microtel Ltd: British Aerospace (Space Communications), Matra Communication, Millicom UK, Sony and Pacific Telesis

At time of writing, relatively little detail had been made available about the intentions of the various licensees from a technical standpoint, other than that the new networks would be largely based upon the GSM cellular radio standard rather than DECT. There were early suggestions that a two-layer cellular structure might be required, with the upper layer providing macrocells for low-capacity area coverage and the lower layer supporting microcells to cater for high-capacity demand in localised areas. The macrocell, or "overlay" infrastructure could largely be that established for GSM, providing direct access for mobile (i.e. vehicle-mounted) terminals and possibly support for the network of microcell base stations which could handle the quasi-static or slow-moving personal terminals. The potential could exist, in due course, to support both GSM and DECT air interfaces within the microcell environment, although whether such an evolution will occur is a matter of speculation.[2]

The principal remaining strategic issue was that of introducing PCN standards into the European environment via ETSI. The ETSI Strategic Review Committee recommended that since initial implementation would be based on GSM, it would be appropriate for a technical committee, or sub-committee, within the current GSM framework to take on board any variations in standards required by PCNs. To some extent this view has derived from the general thrust of thinking which favoured strongly the standardisation of a GSM system in the 1.8 GHz band to enable administrations to meet capacity demands. This approach clearly makes considerable demands in terms of effort and expertise if PCN standards work is not to hinder consolidation of GSM in the 900 MHz bands and its development at 1.8 GHz. However, the timescale for introduction of GSM 900 has necessitated stabilisation of phase 1 standards by the end of March 1990 – an essential step to enable equipment manufacturers to prepare designs for production – and this will release some, at least, of the GSM resources for other tasks. In any event it would appear that PCN standards

---

[2] Such concepts may not be incorporated within early PCNs because of the time scale constraints in establishing the GSM-based standard.

will be defined within ETSI GSM and this must draw on the expertise the UK licensed PCN operators. At the time of writing, the timescale and workplan for this activity, now known as DCS1800, are yet to be determined, but this will need to begin in mid-1990 if standards making is to be completed and equipment developed in time for the projected inauguration of service in 1992.

10.3 The Role of CCIR-FPLMTS

10.3.1 Interim Working Party 8/13: Origins and Terms of Reference

Thus far, the view of the future presented in this chapter has concentrated on the European position, but parallel activities in Study Group 8 of CCIR have addressed the wider issue of progress towards global conformity to standards associated with Future Public Land Mobile Telecommunications Systems (FPLMTS). Interim Working Party (IWP) 8/13 was set up to tackle this issue following expressions of concern at Study Group 8 meetings at Geneva in 1984 and 1985 relating to short-term developments in systems deploying small, inexpensive hand-portable telephones. Previously, when mobile communications had been dominated by vehicle-mounted mobiles, intercontinental roaming had not been considered of great significance as a general requirement. The change of heart was prompted by the anticipated demands of international travellers for the convenience of being able to use a single personal communicator anywhere in the world.

By the time IWP 8/13 had met for a second time in Melbourne in April 1987, progress had been made in defining the desired features and architecture of FPLMTS in general terms. To a large extent this had been derived by investigating and comparing the requirements and implementation methods of emerging digital cellular radio systems such as GSM and progress in cordless systems such as Telepoint, and by looking for commonality in trends and implementation techniques. (It is of interest to note that the UMTS concept emerging from RACE was presented to the IWP 8/13 at its Melbourne meeting.)

Four scenarios were identified.

Scenario 1 envisaged the future personal system being accommodated as a subset of the mobile infrastructure so that the personal station, while of pocket-size dimensions, would be capable of working both inside and outside buildings.

Scenario 2 envisaged the future personal system using a new infrastructure separate from the mobile one. The personal station would work to a personal base station, either inside or outside buildings, or vehicles, where such base stations would be connected to the PSTN either directly or via the mobile network.

Scenario 3 envisaged the future personal system being accommodated by radio distribution from neighbourhood PSTN distribution points. The personal terminal would work to this outside personal base station and would offer an alternative to the wired telephone.

Scenario 4 envisaged the future personal system being an extension of the public network termination point. The personal station would work to a personal base station (usually inside) which would allow multiplex capability, much like the current wire-less PABX concepts.

At that time, it was anticipated that IWP 8/13 would complete its work in time for the final meeting in late 1989, but some uncertainty about this was inevitable since the outcome of the impending 1987 Mobile WARC, in terms of its allocation of spectrum to mobile services, was still unknown. IWP 8/13, however, made projections on requirements for spectrum and reviewed possible candidate bands for worldwide harmonisation from 800 MHz to 64 GHz! On the question of required bandwidth, estimates were based on extrapolation of targets for GSM and second generation cordless systems. With traffic per subscriber of 0.025 erlang for cordless and 0.1 erlang approximately for cellular, an estimate was set at 0.05 erlang per subscriber to reflect the overall mix of usage in rural cellular and dense urban cordless environments. Again in estimating the numbers of subscribers requiring service, figures were arrived at on the basis of GSM expectations of 1000–2000 subscribers/km^2 and cordless estimates of up to 20 000 subscribers/km^2. IWP 8/13 decided to set a target of 10 000 subscribers/km^2 for general urban business areas with local peaks of 100 000 subscribers/km^2 (or 1 subscriber/10m^2). This resulted in an estimated capacity requirement of 500–5000 erlang/km^2. Translated into bandwidth requirements, assuming 25 kHz voice channels (or the equivalent in TDMA or CDMA) and a 2% grade of service, 5000 erlang/km^2 would require 350 MHz of bandwidth using 7 cells per cluster and a cell diameter of 677 m. On the other hand, if cell diameters could be reduced to 200 m, then 35 MHz of bandwidth would suffice. Clearly much needed to be done to refine estimates of how technology might progress towards a late 1990s implementation target.

10.3.2 Technical Concepts

The decision at the 1987 Mobile WARC to allocate spectrum in the 1.5–1.6 GHz band to satellite mobile services added a further dimension to IWP 8/13 studies, culminating in the evolution of a fully unified system. This has many features in common with those emerging for RACE UMTS and, more immediately, the PCNs, but in other respects significant differences are discernible as a result of the wider global brief of the CCIR activities.

In particular the very different requirements of dense urban areas in Europe and the sparsely populated regions of countries in the developing world can only be accommodated by defining a hierarchy of air interfaces from the low-power, high-density personal communications system at the one extreme to satellite mobile systems at the other. The complete family of radio interfaces is illustrated in the Draft New Recommendation of FPLMTS to CCIR which describes these interfaces as follows:

R1: The radio interface between a mobile station (MS) and a base station (BS)

R2: The radio interface between a personal station (PS) and a personal base station (CS)

R3: The radio interface between a satellite and a mobile earth station (MES). FPLMTS may also allow for the automatic routing of traffic between terrestrial and mobile satellite systems

R4: An additional radio interface used for alerting (e.g. paging) in the case of a call terminated at an FPLMTS terminal

The needs of developing countries are also catered for by proposals to allow FPLMTS to be used as a temporary, or permanent, substitute for fixed networks where provision of rural line networks would be uneconomic due either to the long distances involved or to difficult terrain.

10.3.3 Current Status

It is of interest to note a difference in emphasis in the IWP 8/13 relative to that of the RACE community. The latter, in evolving their vision of the UMTS from the basis of the broadband fixed network looking out into the mobile periphery, have perceived the UMTS as, in effect, a third generation European system embodying the combined attributes of digital cellular systems and cordless telephony, as in PCNs, but achieving greater flexibility in service provision by employing a new air interface. In IWP 8/13 the approach has been more general, focussing on the radio-connected user community and its needs and working back towards the PSTN/ISDN as the fixed backbone of the FPLMTS. It has also emphasised flexibility in system structure to facilitate matching of network investment to revenue growth, adaptation to environmental factors and new developments without restricting innovation.

By the end of 1989 the overall form of FPLMTS had taken shape and been embodied in the draft recommendation referred to earlier. In "General" and "Technical Objectives" there is much in common with GSM and PCNs, supplemented by the requirement to use FPLMTS as a means for serving fixed users, and with emphasis on a structure with modular form allowing for growth in size and complexity in response to demand. Additionally FPLMTS will aim to support the communications requirement of road traffic management and control systems. Signalling interface standards will conform to the OSI model, high information rate services may be provided under favourable circumstances and integration of terrestrial and satellite mobile networks will be implemented. It is intended that FPLMTS will support bearer services equivalent to ISDN B&D channels with both carrier and circuit mode and packet mode bearer services supported in accordance with CCITT recommendations. In addition to telephony and paging, text, videotext, facsimile, data, short messages and point-to-multipoint operation will be offered.

In the interval between the 1987 Melbourne meeting and the Geneva meeting of Study Group 8 in November 1989, the spectrum requirement issue had been further addressed and the following four points had been concluded:

- FPLMTS should be allocated to spectrum below 3 GHz
- Voice services will require between 110 and 160 MHz of spectrum according to the progress of possible technical solutions
- Non-voice services will require an additional 65 MHz of spectrum
- Where 50 MHz of spectrum is already allocated below 1 GHz for cellular services, the traffic carried by these could be subtracted from the FPLMTS estimates resulting in a saving which gives a final requirement in the range 130–180 MHz, depending on technology progress

On system architecture, IWP 8/13 recognises that increasing commonality is evident between the fixed network elements of FPLMTS and the PSTN/ISDN, and FPLMTS will be integrated into the PSTN/ISDN to whatever degree is appropriate to achieving the level of service required at minimum cost to the end user. Therefore the Mobile Services Switching Centres (MSCs) may be separate from or completely integrated into the PSTN/ISDN. With regard to radio transmission considerations, the emphasis again is on flexibility in the multiple access scheme to accommodate the wide range of traffic densities and services offered – from fixed services in developing countries through to dense urban requirements in Europe, North America and Japan.

10.3.4 Continuing Activities

Developments in the recent past, relating to DECT and PCNs particularly have made it extremely difficult to encapsulate the output of IWP 8/13 in its original target time frame in a form which can be regarded as complete. The November 1989 Geneva meeting of Study Group 8 confirmed the requirement for continued efforts by IWP 8/13 in the preparations for the 1992 WARC at which the spectrum for 1.5–3 GHz will be comprehensively re-assessed. The issue of worldwide harmonisation of an appropriate spectrum segment is clearly crucial to development of the global standards which by allowing economies of scale in product manufacture will force down prices to end users and provide for truly international roaming.

The other major challenge facing IWP 8/13, however, is the relationship between FPLMTS and the emerging PCNs, the European implementation of a GSM type system at 1.8 GHz, and the as yet undefined third generation of European system together with the relationship which this might have with RACE UMTS and recent North American developments. Realistically, IWP 8/13 recommendations, although available for the CCIR interim meeting scheduled to follow closely after the 1992 WARC, are unlikely to make their way into official CCIR documentation until the 1994 Plenary Assembly. The challenge for IWP 8/13 is to chart a way forward to implementation of its deliberations in the late 1990s without seeing its best endeavours overtaken by events in the rapidly changing European and North American arenas.

10.4 The Role of CCITT – Personal Telecommunications

In addition to the work on mobility performed within CCIR, which reflects the radio-based nature of CCIR, the CCITT has begun to study the concept of "Personal Telecommunications" (PT), which will offer the potential for limited mobility to users of the fixed network as well as users of mobile networks.

The provisional definition of PT is as follows[8]:

Personal Telecommunication (PT) service is a telecommunication service which will enable users that have subscribed to this service and to related basic telecommunication services, to establish and receive any type of calls on the basis of a network independent unique Personal Telecommunication Number, PTN, across multiple networks at any user-network access, fixed, movable or mobile, irrespective of the geographical area, limited only by terminal and network capabilities.

In providing network-independent mobility, PT service will add a new dimension of mobility to the fixed network, whilst also being used within future mobile networks. PT is related to the emerging Intelligent Network (IN) technology [9] and the personal numbering concept. The concept of PT has already, from an early stage, been proposed as an important part of the RACE UMTS.

The interaction between the PT concept and radio-based mobility is clearly important and it has been recently suggested within ETSI that steps be taken to develop PT, with a view to defining a European PT service by the end of 1993. Such a step will also be aimed at coordinating European input into SG XI, the relevant CCITT Study Group developing PT.

Historically the mobile telecommunications industry has its roots in two separate camps: telecommunications and radio. This is reflected, for example, in the structuring of the UK DTI into a TP (Telecommunications and Posts) division and RD (Radiocommunications) division.[3] The evolution of the work on PT within CCITT and the work on FPLMTS in CCIR similarly reflect such origins. Thus we are seeing the need for increasing cooperation

---

[3] Since April 1990, The Radiocommunications Agency.

across traditional boundaries of responsibility as the telecommunications infrastructure of the twenty-first century emerges, implicitly incorporating radio technology as an integral component.

10.5 Towards the Personal Communicator?

In the immediate future we would expect to see the continuing rapid growth of cordless and cellular radio markets, with the arrival of CT2 digital cordless telephones and the forthcoming GSM, DECT and PCN systems. Looking beyond this, will we see the emergence of a truly personal communicator?

10.5.1 CAI and DECT

The short-term prospect for cordless telephones would appear to be bright, although it must be said that, in offering totally new services in Telepoint and wireless PABXs, these products carry with them the risks associated with the launch of any new product concept.

The take-up for CT2 CAI in the short term will be interesting to view. Already several European countries have signed the relevant Memorandum of Understanding, indicating an intention to install CAI Telepoint systems, as discussed in Chapter 4. The decision that CAI should become an Interim European Telecommunications Standard for Telepoint systems will no doubt accelerate this take-up. The progress of the forthcoming Telepoint trials in many European countries will be keenly observed by many. Likewise, with wireless PABX products to be launched in the near future it will be of interest to chart the growth of the market and of customer preferences.

Once CAI Telepoint networks are fully established it is possible that some users will want to use the service for data. Provided a suitable regulatory framework can be established, it is possible that cordless data could perhaps see its introduction prior to DECT with CAI, although for higher data rate ISDN terminals it would seem that the market is likely to evolve towards the DECT standard. The demand for both public access data and private in-building data services will determine the take-up of these types of service.

Thus, how CAI and DECT will compete with or complement each other for different applications in the broad European marketplace is still unclear and will be influenced by many different factors, a major one of which will be the demands of the consumer! The success or otherwise of DECT in achieving its target timescales will also be an important factor influencing the market development.

10.5.2 PCN

At the time of writing ETSI has undertaken, within the framework of GSM, to develop the PCN standard, to be known as DCS1800. Initial PCN products are likely to find their way to the UK market by 1992/93, based on a modified GSM standard at around 2 GHz. Future extension to support DECT may also occur but is uncertain. The availability and functionality of PCN equipment is thus likely to be closely tied to the success and timeliness of the development of GSM, and possibly DECT, equipment.

What form will subsequent products and systems actually take?

10.5.3 The Personal Communicator

With the recognition of the possible convergence of cellular and cordless services that came from the RACE Mobile Telecommunications project was born the concept of the "Personal Communicator" – the idea of a mass market, pocket-sized, radio-based telephone product capable of providing "universal" geographical access. (By analogy with the device used in Star Trek by Captain Kirk the concept has become known affectionately in the industry by the term "Beam me up Scottie"!)

The product concept was fuelled by early market growth projections and by the rapid progress in radio-based telephone products, both cellular and cordless. It was also fuelled by media coverage at the end of the 1980s associated with Telepoint and latterly with the PCN initiative.

As described earlier, the issue of geographical coverage is more related to infrastructure than to the terminal itself. In this respect, the implementation of GSM, PCN, ISDN and Intelligent Networks will all have a part to play. The Open Access Network concepts elucidated in Chapter 5 may have far-reaching implications if an appropriate and acceptable regulatory framework can be developed. Given the significant interest and role of the Commission of the European Communities (CEC) in the field of mobile telecommunications, it is not inconceivable that such a common framework could evolve.

In considering handset equipment, we may postulate what kind of cordless telephone product is likely to emerge for third generation systems. As alluded to earlier, the differences between second and third generation systems will relate more to network and service issues than simply to the radio interface. What will be required, however, given the likely prior investment in infrastructure by the time third generation systems are introduced, will be some means of backwards compatibility to accommodate the system transition. Thus it is possible that such a Personal Communicator would need to support more than one radio interface within the same telephone. This requirement may not be as difficult as perhaps it sounds today, given the rate of technology development. Already we are seeing the introduction of Digital Signal Processing (DSP) into radio telephones to perform modulation/demodulation, coding and equalisation functions, etc., which only a few years ago would have been impossible in hand-portable equipment. The limiting factor with today's DSP is its power consumption. Over the next few years, however, the standard operating voltage for silicon integrated circuits is expected to fall from 5 V to 3.3 V and feature size is likewise expected to be reduced. Together these should lead to a significant reduction in the power consumption of DSP, such that software reconfigurable terminals may be envisaged which could implement the programmable modulation/demodulation and other features necessary for a flexible air interface. The other key areas of terminal technology development necessary over the next few years relate to batteries and packaging.

In practice, it is likely that the growth of the personal communications industry over the next decade will, rather than simply giving rise to a single product concept, in actuality spawn a plethora of different competing products. The emergence of common standards, as outlined in Chapter 3, should encourage new entrants to the marketplace, with small firms competing with niche products against the larger industry players. The development of new products and systems will depend upon many different drivers, beyond those outlined within this chapter. It will not be new technology alone, nor manufacturers' research and development initiatives, nor standardisation programmes; rather, it will be a blend of these various activities, together with market forces – what the consumer wants and how the manufacturers together "educate" the market. In this sense, "personal communications" may prove to be a very apt term for the services which emerge – i.e. rather than a bland product, personal communications may instead offer the consumer a communications service package tailored to the needs of the individual, synthesised from a broad range of facilities supported by the emerging technical standards. Already there are basic examples of this; in the UK, for example, Mercury Callpoint are offering a combined paging/Telepoint package.

The industry is in the process of moving from being technology driven to market driven and future technical developments will be increasingly influenced by the emerging market structures. These themselves will be shaped by the growing liberalisation of the telecommunications market within the EC. The emergence of a significant potential market in Eastern Europe may also be expected to have an impact upon the direction and pace of industrial strategy with respect to mobile communications in Europe.

10.5.4 A Future World Standard?

The theme of this book has been cordless communications in Europe. At the start of the 1990s Europe is at the forefront of implementing advanced cordless telecommunications technology and systems. Europe has begun to get its act together in terms of common standards.

Cooperation within the European industry has not been without its problems but it has indeed facilitated much in terms of the pace of standards, systems and technology development in recent years. It is to be hoped that this cooperation will continue to grow and perhaps be emulated increasingly on the world stage as we look towards the emergence of world standards for future integrated cordless and cellular systems. This may be an optimistic hope given the very diverse and disparate national views and interests, but there remains much to be gained from a cooperative approach – both in terms of common standards and systems, with their implications for economies of scale and user benefits, and in terms of the efficient use of limited engineering resources. The CCIR IWP 8/13 offers a forum for such a standard to emerge, including as it does representation not only from Europe, reflecting some of the systems and technologies described within this book, but also from North America, the Far East and elsewhere.[4]

Cordless telecommunications represent the beginnings of the personal communications revolution. Universally available communications will change our individual lifestyles and our business practices. In the same way that the advent of universally available power gave rise to the industrial revolution with major social consequences, so we are in the midst of a global communications revolution which is already having major social implications. Personal communications are but a small part of this, but a part which will actually touch many of us individually over the next decade.

References

1. M Ross (AD Little, Inc), "The growth of mobile cellular communications in Europe", paper presented at the Financial Times conference, London, 7–8 November 1988
2. CEC, "Towards a dynamic European Economy – Green Paper on the development of the Common Market for telecommunications services and equipments", COM(87) 290, Brussels, 1987
3. RW Gibson, RJG MacNamee and SK Vadgama, "Universal mobile telecommunication system – a concept", paper presented at the European Seminar on Mobile Radio Communications, Brussels, April 1987
4. T Parrott, "What comes next: RACE-Mobile?", paper presented at the Digital Cordless Telephones and PCN Conference, organised by Blenheim Online, London, May 1990
5. C Shepherd, "Mobile broadband system air interface and system aspects", paper presented at the RACE Mobile Telecommunications Project Annual Review, Cambridge, UK, January 1990
6. "Phones on the Move – personal communications in the 1990s", Discussion Document, UK Department of Trade and Industry, Telecommunications and Posts Division, January 1989
7. "The use of the radio frequency spectrum above 30 GHz", Consultative Document, Radiocommunications Division of the UK Department of Trade and Industry, September 1988
8. M. Meier, "The role of the fixed infrastructure in UMTS RACE project 1043", paper presented at the RACE Mobile Telecommunications Project Annual Review, Cambridge, UK, January 1990.
9. WD Ambrosch, A Maher and B Sasscer, "The intelligent network", Springer-Verlag, Berlin Heidelberg, New York, 1989

[4] Whilst this book has focussed geographically upon developments in Europe the reader should not underestimate these other potential contributions, as recent North American developments in particular – D-AMPS, CDMA trials etc. – have demonstrated.

TECHNICAL APPENDIXES

This appendix details the technical operation of the DCT900 system which was presented in overview in Chapter 2. Familiarity with the concepts covered in the latter half of this book will help the reader in understanding this appendix. Conversely, the descriptions provided here serve to illustrate and perhaps clarify the interrelationships between some of the issues covered in earlier chapters.

Further analysis and description of traffic simulations, operation of adjacent non-synchronised systems and echo control requirements and solutions are presented in [1].

A1.1 System Architecture

Prior to detailing system operation we briefly recap on the overall system architecture, defining terms (see also Fig. 2.2).

The cordless radio subsystem (CSS) can be interconnected with a PABX or PSTN and consists of four building blocks:

- Radio Exchange or Common Control Fixed Part (CCFP)
- Satellite (SAT)
- Base station, Radio Fixed Part (RFP)
- Handset or Cordless Portable Part (CPP)

Every CSS contains one CCFP and a number of satellites, each of which may serve a number of base stations. Every base station covers one cell in the micro-cellular system. Base stations may also be directly connected to the CCFP.

Digital transmission is used between base station and handset with speech coding performed in the CCFP and the handset, using 32 kbit/s ADPCM. Multiple-Carrier (MC) TDMA/TDD is employed for the radio interface. Decentralised Dynamic Channel Assignment (DCA) optimises the distribution of available channels per cell according to changing traffic requirements. These aspects are explained below, together with descriptions of the handover techniques, capacity and interface issues.

A1.2 System Concepts

A1.2.1 TDMA/TDD Format

Every radio carrier in the DCT900 system supports eight TDD channels. These consist of eight pairs of timeslots (channels) per 16 ms TDMA time frame, as shown in Fig. A1.1. The TDMA frame is divided into two equal parts: the first half for transmission from base station to handset, the second half for transmission in the opposite direction. Each part consists of eight timeslots of 963 μs with a guard space of 37 μs between the timeslots to allow for transmitter ramp-up, ramp-down, cable delays, etc. The data rate is 640 kbit/s which results in a radio channel bandwidth of 1 MHz. This corresponds to a capacity of 616 data bits per timeslot, the guard time of 37 μs corresponding to 24 bits. Of these 616 bits, 32 bits are used for bit- and burst-synchronisation which takes place every timeslot, i.e. every 1 ms.

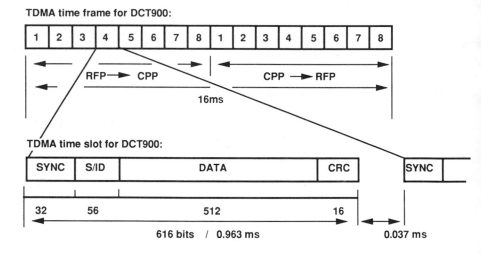

SYNC : sync word for bit - and burst - synchronisation
S / ID : signalling and identification
DATA : speech data
CRC : CRC check bits
GS : 0.037 ms guard space (equiv. to 24 bits)

Fig. A1.1. TDMA frame and slot structure for DCT900.

In every timeslot 56 bits are available for signalling and identification. Of these, 32 bits are used for identification and control of the radio channel leaving 24 bits available for high-level signalling. These 24 bits per slot result in a signalling channel capacity of 1.6 kbit/s. The capacity of the speech channel is 32 kbit/s (512 bits/slot). Every timeslot is terminated with a 16 bit CRC check list that is used for quality control.

A1.2.2 Multi-Carrier Operation

The system is designed for a maximum of eight carriers, needing a total bandwidth of 8 MHz (1 MHz per carrier). This means that, with eight TDMA duplex slots per carrier, a total of 64 system channels are available. The number of channels that are active per cell in a high-capacity multi-cell system is limited. For this reason, it was decided to use only one receiver and one transmitter for every DCT900 base station. This means that each base station can handle a maximum of eight simultaneous calls. However, the transceiver is so agile that adjacent timeslots can handle calls on different frequencies. This base station concept uses the TDMA properties to greatly decrease the risk of interference due to intermodulation or poor adjacent channel attenuation, since calls connected to the same base station always use different timeslots.

In the example shown in Table A1.1 the base station is active on timeslot 2, carrier 3 and timeslot 3, carrier 1. Both transmitter and receiver of the base station can switch between these carriers within the guard time available. Timeslot 2 on carriers 1, 2 and 4 cannot be used, nor timeslot 3 on carriers 2, 3 and 4. This means that of the 30 channels (32−2) that in principle are free when two channels are active, only 24 channels (32−8) are actually available. Simulations have shown that this results in only a marginal decrease in capacity. Having only one transceiver per base station in an n-carrier system also means that all non-active channels only can be scanned every n^{th} time frame. Therefore multi-framing is used. This means that, for example, in a four-carrier system every four frames form a multi-frame. The beginning of a multi-frame is indicated by a special bit in the signalling part of every timeslot that is transmitted by the base stations. On the non-active channels the base station then listens to carrier 1 during

Table A1.1. Example channel occupancy for four carrier frequencies, eight timeslots

Carrier frequency	Timeslot							
	1	2	3	4	5	6	7	8
1	O	X	A	O	O	O	O	O
2	O	X	X	O	O	O	O	O
3	O	A	X	O	O	O	O	O
4	O	X	X	O	O	O	O	O

A, active channel; O, free channel; X, unusable channel.

the second frame, etc. The handset takes this scheme into account when starting a call set-up.

A1.2.3 Dynamic Channel Assignment, DCA

In common with other digital cordless systems the DCA principle is employed, allowing all possible channels to be used in every cell. This is different from systems that use a fixed channel allocation where only subsets of the available channels are allowed in every cell in order to avoid adjacent cells using the same channel. Fixed channel allocation needs careful system planning based on analysis of the capacity needed in every cell. In the DCT900 system it is basically possible to use the same channel (same timeslot, same carrier) for different calls in adjacent cells. Since the system is interference limited, it is sufficient that the interference caused by the call in the adjacent cell is low enough to give a carrier over interference ratio (C/I) that is above a certain minimum level. The DCA principle used automatically adapts the channel distribution in the system to the actual capacity needed. The flexibility and speed of the DCA arise from the fact that the one radio in the handset can be used to obtain continuous information on all the channels available. Decisions on DCA are decentralised and handled by the handset and the base station control logic. This is discussed in more detail when call set-up and handovers are described below.

A1.3 Call Protocols

A1.3.1 Idle State

Each base station in the system is always active on at least one timeslot. This can be a traffic slot that is used for an ongoing call between a base station and a handset, or a so-called dummy slot. Both traffic slots and dummy slots contain system and base station identification. In idle state, a handset scans on a regular basis the available timeslots and locks on to the base station that has the strongest field strength, and which belongs to its own system. Whenever another valid base station gives a higher field strength the handset will lock on to the new base station, although some hysteresis is built in to stabilise the system.

A1.3.2 Call Set-up

If there is an incoming call for a specific handset, a paging message containing the handset identification will be sent on the signalling channel of all the active timeslots (traffic and dummy slots) in the system. This message will be read by the handset. If the handset is locked on to a traffic channel it will take the best timeslot available (with the lowest measured field strength) in the first half of the frame and then send a call request in the corresponding timeslot in the second half, addressing the base station it was locked on to in the idle state. After the handset and base station control logic have agreed on the timeslot to be used, the CCFP will switch the incoming call to the appropriate base station and timeslot. If an outgoing call is initiated from the handset, a call request is sent in the same way as described for the incoming call. After the handset and the base station have agreed on the timeslot to be used, the CCFP will allocate a speech channel to the call and send out the dialling information to the PABX.

A1.3.3 Handover

The principle of handover will be discussed using a simplified model of a single carrier system with two cells (RFP1 and RFP2) and two handsets (CPP1 and CPP2). Assume the following situation, depicted in Fig. A1.2a. CPP1 is in conversation with RFP1 using timeslot TS2, a traffic channel. CPP2 is in idle state and is locked on to RFP2 using timeslot TS5, a dummy channel. The dummy channel on TS5 is also monitored by CPP1 which is geographically somewhere between RFP1 and RFP2. Apart from the timeslots they are locked on to, CPP1 and CPP2 will scan all the other seven available timeslots on a regular basis and will store information in memory on the status of these alternative timeslots (relative field strength, signal strength and base station/handset identity information).

When CPP1 now moves from RFP1 towards RFP2, the field strength measured on TS5 will increase and at a certain moment will become higher than the decreasing field strength measured on TS2. If the difference exceeds a certain value, say 8 dB, handset CPP1 will decide to initiate a handover. For this, CPP1 transmits a connection request on the next possible occasion in TS5 on the second half of the time frame. This connection request includes the identification of CPP1 and of RFP2, the base station that is

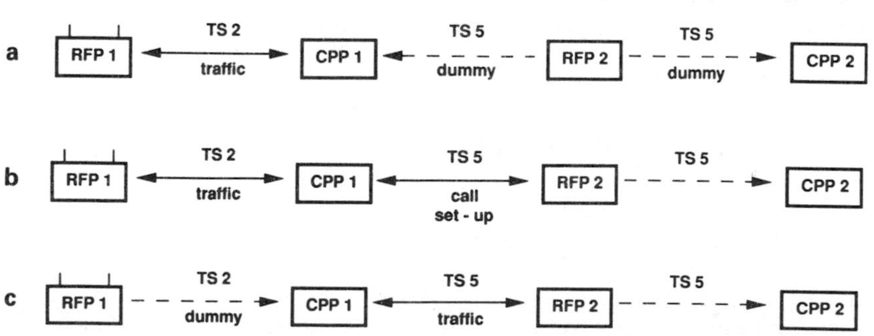

Fig. A1.2. Performance of handover.

addressed. RFP2 will answer in the corresponding timeslots TS5 in the first half of (one of) the following frame(s). After some specific signalling CPP1 and the base station control logic of RFP2 will agree on the timeslot to be used, which in this case will be TS5. (Note that if TS5 had been a traffic channel instead of a dummy channel, the connection request from CPP1 to RFP2 would have been transmitted on the timeslot where the lowest field strength had been measured by CPP1, being the best channel). During the time needed to set up a new channel to RFP2, CPP1 maintains in parallel the existing channel with the ongoing call on TS2 to RFP1 (see Fig. A1.2b).

When the new channel to RFP2 has been set up, the CCFP will be informed that a handover will be made and the CCFP will then switch the ongoing call to the appropriate base station and timeslot. This switching can be done without the user of CPP1 noticing it, since the old and new channels overlap for a short time. After handover the channel to RFP1 will be released (see Fig. A1.2c).

The handover just described is called an inter-cell handover and is the most common type. It makes sure that the system is always in a stable mode with all the handsets locked on to their 'nearest' (i.e. strongest signal) base station. No deterioration of the existing call quality will be detected before the handover occurs.

It can arise that a handset is locked on to its nearest base station but that suddenly interference occurs on the timeslot in use. Such interference can be from another handset in the system or from outside the system. This situation causes a so-called forced handover to occur. The handset will first try to initiate a handover to another channel on the same base station, an in-cell hand-over. This can be very fast since it is handled entirely by the handset and the base station control logic, the CCFP being informed afterwards. The procedure followed is basically the same as for the standard handover. If no in-cell handover is appropriate then an inter-cell handover will be initiated, following the same procedure as described above. Since it is not possible in this case to maintain the conversation on the old channel, some speech data bits will be lost. However, the fact that the handset has instantaneous information available in its memory on the status of all available channels means that the call disruption is limited to a relatively low number of frames. Muting of the speech output under these conditions will make this situation almost unnoticeable to the user.

A1.4 System Capacity and Interfaces

A1.4.1 Capacity

In order to cover high-density traffic situations very small cells are required. In a three-dimensional environment each cell is surrounded by other cells. The available channels will be shared and dynamically allocated to all surrounding cells. In order to assess the capacity of the air interface, simulations have been performed for high-density office systems using a practical propagation model that takes into account attenuation by walls and floors. The model assumes 32 kbit/s speech coding and a Carrier-to-Interference (C/I) limit of 21 dB [1]. These simulations have shown that in such an environment each base station can serve:

- 0.6 erlang, 4 handsets, if 16 channels are available (2 MHz)
- 1.5 erlang, 10 handsets, if 24 channels are available (3 MHz), or
- 2.4 erlang, 16 handsets, if 32 channels are available (4 MHz)

These figures assume traffic levels of 150 milli-erlangs per handset (business environment) and a grade of service (GOS) of 0.1–0.5%. In the latter case, a capacity of up to one handset per 20 m² per floor is offered with 25 m base station separations, assuming a maximum of half of the ground area is building.

These simulations also show that in such a three-dimensional environment, on average, only a limited number of channels per cell is active. It can be concluded that for a flexible DCA in high user density systems a minimum number of channels (say 32) has to be available in every cell, but that on average only a limited number of these channels will be in use within a cell at the same time (two or three in the simulations referred to above). This property makes it possible to simplify the base station design. In public environments the capacity issue will be different. The traffic generated per phone will be lower, for example 20–50 milli-erlangs, and the density of phones per area on average will be lower, allowing for larger cell sizes in many situations.

The capacity of the standard CCFP is 64 simultaneous calls. This means a traffic handling capacity of more than 48 erlangs for a GOS of 0.5%. The number of base stations that can be connected to one CCFP is, in principle, limited only by the traffic capacity required per cell. In a three-dimensional environment where a high user density is anticipated, small cells will be required with, for example, a traffic of 2–3 erlangs per cell. In such a case about 25 cells can be connected to one system. In cases where lower capacity per cell is needed, more than 100 cells can be connected. An extended version of the CCFP (consisting of four cabinets) can handle over 200 calls at the same time, resulting in a traffic handling capacity of more than 200 erlangs.

If the average traffic generated to and by a handset in the service area of the system is assumed to be 150 milli-erlangs in offices, then one system can support approximately 320 handsets. In public Telepoint applications the traffic per subscriber is expected to be considerably lower. Thus, for example, 50 milli-erlangs would correspond to 1000 users and 15 milli-erlangs to 3200 users within the service area.

A1.4.2. Interfaces

For the interface between CCFP and PABX two possibilities exist. The interface may be based on standard analogue two-wire subscriber lines, in which case one dedicated analogue line per handset is needed. A wired phone can be connected to the same line (in cascade). The interface may also be based on a primary rate digital trunk interface, according to CCITT G.732 (optional 30 channels, 2.048 Mbit/s, or 23 channels, 1.544 Mbit/s, T1, with ISDN protocol).

The interface between the CCFP and SAT is also based on a 2.048 Mbit/s digital trunk (CCITT G.732) with proprietary protocol. The maximum number of base stations that can be connected to one SAT is determined by the fact that the interface between the CCFP and SAT can handle a maximum of 30 (23 with T1 trunk) duplex calls simultaneously.

The 2.048 Mbit/s trunks can be carried by twisted pair or coaxial lines, optical fibres, microwave links, etc. The standard version of the interface boards will be for twisted pair and coaxial links. If needed, repeaters can be added to handle large distances. Optional alternative links will be available.

Reference

1. D Åkerberg, "Properties of a TDMA picocellur office communications system", paper presented at the 39th IEEE Vehicular Technology Conference Proceedings pp 186–191, San Francisco, USA, May 1989.

Appendix 2 The Common Air Interface MPT 1375

Richard Steedman

The Common Air Interface Specification [1] is designed to ensure interoperability between second generation digital cordless (CT2) handsets and base stations from different manufacturers. It was agreed at the ETSI RES meeting in March 1990 that it should be prepared for submission as an Interim European Telecommunications Standard (I-ETS). This appendix briefly describes some of the technical details of the standard.

A2.1 Aims of MPT 1375

The Common Air Interface Working Group in the UK set itself the following aims in preparing the standard:

1. To produce a standard which would ensure interoperability between different manufacturers' products and comply with the existing UK CT2 coexistence specifications MPT 1334 and BS 6833 [2,3]
2. To permit manufacturers to produce cost effective equipment across a range of product specifications, i.e. to prejudice neither simple nor complex products
3. To cater for all possible modes of operation envisaged at the time and not to restrict future enhancements
4. If necessary, to sacrifice base station simplicity if doing so would decrease handset complexity

The third aim was perhaps the most challenging but was clearly necessary. Although an individual manufacturer using a proprietary signalling scheme would have been able to change it completely to cater for a new model with extra features, this obviously would not have been possible with MPT 1375. It was necessary to provide clear paths for enhancement, for example, by reserving signalling messages for future use, etc.

A2.2 Structure of MPT 1375

MPT 1375 is divided into four parts as follows:

Part 1 defines the radio interface by specifying details such as timing and the exact modulation method to be employed. Data is exchanged between handset and base station (referred to as CPP and CFP in the specification) in binary form using the same radio channel for both directions. This is done by a method known as Time Division Duplex (TDD). Each end of the radio link transmits data at 72 kbit/s for 1 ms, then receives data for 1 ms, then transmits, and so on. After allowing for "guard time" (when the transceivers switch from receiving to transmitting and vice versa), this system provides two-way communication at up to 34 kbit/s. (The bandwidth of each channel is 100 kHz.)

Part 2 specifies the manner in which the available bandwidth is partitioned into speech, signalling and synchronisation data channels and also defines the bottom two layers of a three-layer protocol for the signalling channel. The bottom layer (layer 1) covers link initialisation while layer 2 deals with handshaking, error correction and data re-transmission so that error-free data is passed to layer 3. Layer 2 is based on two existing data transmission standards: MPT 1317 and CCITT I.441 [4,5].

Part 3 defines the top layer of the signalling protocol, which consists of a set of message definitions covering, for example, user dialling, handset ringing, Telepoint authorisation, etc. The message set is adapted from the ISDN 'Digital Access Signalling System' [6] used by many modern digital telephone exchanges.

Part 4 defines the contents of the speech channel, together with associated acoustic/audio specifications. As with the other parts of MPT 1375, frequent reference is made to existing standards.

Each of these parts is described in more detail in the following four sections.

At the time of writing, three annexes to MPT 1375 have also been published, covering the testing of equipment to ensure compliance with the standard, the allocation of certain signalling codes for CAI use within the UK, and a uniform method of programming handsets with details of new Telepoint accounts, respectively. These annexes are not discussed further in this appendix.

A2.3 Part 1: The Radio Interface

The Radio Interface specifies the conditions pertaining to the transmission of digital data across the RF link. Most of the specifications within it concern the transmitter. In fact, the only conditions placed on the receiver are that it must have a sensitivity of at least 45 dB relative to 1 μV/m (in order to guarantee a BER of less than 1 in 10^3) and must meet the blocking and intermodulation requirements of BS 6833.

As mentioned previously, the radio interface employs TDD transmission at 72 kbit/s. The signal must be transmitted using two-level FSK with a modulation index between 0.4 and 0.7, i.e. the peak deviation from the centre frequency under all possible patterns of "ones" and "zeros" must lie between 14.4 kHz and 25.2 kHz. The FSK signal must be filtered using an approximately Gaussian filter to avoid interference to adjacent channels. (The permitted interference levels are specified in MPT 1334.)

The transmitter centre frequency must be within ± 10 kHz of the published channel centre frequency. This ± 10 kHz frequency accuracy means that it is possible for the two ends of a link to be transmitting at frequencies up to 20 kHz apart. Since the FSK deviation may be as low as 14.4 kHz, this means that it is possible for a transmission never to cross over the centre frequency of the receiver. Receivers must therefore employ some form of AC-coupled data demodulation or AFC to receive data. If AFC is used, then it is permitted for this to be linked to the handset transmitter, to bring its transmitted centre frequency closer to that of the base station. (Clearly, transmitter AFC cannot be permitted at both handset and base station, otherwise both ends could "pull" each other off frequency!)

In order to increase user density and also so that a handset close to a multiple-transceiver base station does not desensitise the base station receivers, thereby "drowning out" other calls, a means of transmitter power control is provided. All handsets must be capable of transmitting at two power levels, the normal power level being between 1 and 10 mW and the low power level being between 12 and 20 dB lower than the normal level. Low power transmission is only used if the handset receives a command (defined in layer 2 of the signalling protocol) from the base station. It is not mandatory for the base station to issue such commands, but it may only do so if the received signal strength exceeds 90 dB relative to 1 μV/m.

The TDD signalling scheme is illustrated in Fig. A2.1 and works as follows: Each end transmits bursts of either 66 or 68 bits every 2 ms at a rate of 72 kbit/s. The use of 68 bit bursts is optional – both ends of the link use 66 bits at the start of communication and switch to 68 bits only if one requests it and the other end indicates that it is capable of supporting the option. Whereas the use of 68 bit bursts obviously increases the signalling bandwidth, 66 bits permits simpler transceiver design or, alternatively, the possibility of accommodating propagation delays of greater than 1 bit.

Each transmitted burst is surrounded by "ramp-up" and "ramp-down" periods, in other words the transmitter power rises and falls gradually at the start and end of a burst. This is done to avoid AM splash, that is, modulation products outside the frequency bands caused by rapid switching of transmitter power level. In addition, a mandatory "suffix" of half a bit period must be transmitted at the end of each burst to overcome any dispersion which may occur in receiver channel filters.

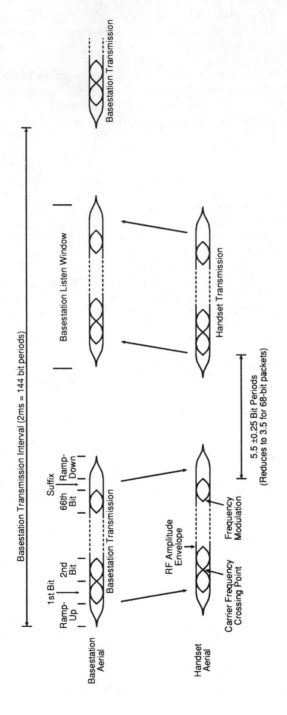

Fig. A2.1. CAI time division duplex (66 bit packets).

In order to synchronise the two ends of the link, so that one transmits while the other receives and vice versa, the base station is deemed to be a "master" and the handset a "slave". The base station is permitted to start transmitting its first burst at any time, thereafter sending bursts at 2 ms intervals. The handset must then "lock on" to these transmissions and arrange for its transmissions to coincide with the base station's receive period. Put more precisely, the start of the first data bit of a 66 bit handset burst must be transmitted (at the aerial) 5.5 ± 0.25 bit periods after the end of the 66th bit of the base station burst has been received (again at the aerial). For 68 bit bursts, this "turnaround time" is reduced to 3.5 ± 0.25 bit periods.

The reason for making the base station the master is that, in applications such as Telepoint where a base station contains more than one transceiver, the transceivers must all transmit and receive at the same time to avoid mutual inteference. It is therefore often not possible for a base station to alter its receive window to align with a handset's transmission. This leads to a problem in that, with the approach thus far described, all communication sessions must be initiated by the base station. Put another way, the handset is unable to initiate communication with any guarantee that its initial transmission will be received by the base station. One solution to this would be for base stations to transmit bursts continually, purely for synchronisation purposes. A much better solution however, in terms of both power efficiency and channel re-use, is for the handset to transmit a special burst of longer duration than normal when it wishes to initiate communication. Such a scheme is adopted in the CAI. The handset transmits for 10 ms, then listens for 4 ms, before transmitting again. No matter where the base station's listen window is, it is bound to receive part of this "long" burst.

Finally, the rate of data transmission must be maintained to an accuracy of ± 50 ppm by the base station and ± 100 ppm by the handset. The handset must also, of course, maintain long-term synchronisation with the base station burst rate due to the master–slave relationship explained above. The reason for specifying ± 50 ppm at the base station is to ensure that any handset using the CCITT G.711 standard for PCM coding of speech [7] will not violate the ± 50 ppm tolerance specified therein as a result of slaving to a base station.

A2.4 Part 2: Signalling Layers 1 & 2

Part 2 of MPT 1375 defines the bottom two layers of the data signalling protocol together with the bandwidth allocations for the various channels at different stages of a call. Three channels are defined, viz:

1. The B channel, primarily intended for speech, although data may be transmitted over this channel using a modem

2. The D channel, used for in-band signalling
3. The SYN channel, used to allow both ends of a call to obtain bit and
    burst synchronisation

These channels are then allocated various bandwidths in four different
allocations or "multiplexes" as follows:

1. MUX1.2 is defined as a 66 bit burst containing 64 B channel bits and
2 D channel bits. It is used after a call has been set up and therefore there
is no SYN channel. (Each end of the link must rely on edge detection to
maintain synchronisation in this multiplex.) Since these bursts are transmitted
every 2 ms, the resulting data rates are 32 kbit/s for the B channel and 1
kbit/s for the D channel.

2. MUX1.4 is similar to MUX1.2 except that the burst is 68 bits long
and there are 4 D channel bits. Consequently the D channel data rate is
doubled (2 kbit/s). This multiplex is only used if both ends of the link
indicate during call set-up that they are capable of supporting 68 bit bursts.

3. MUX2 is a 66 bit burst consisting of 32 D channel bits and 34 SYN
channel bits. It is used at the start of a call to allow both ends of the link
to synchronise and to transfer data at a high rate (16 kbit/s) prior to a
change to one of the MUX1 variants and connection of the B channel.
(There is provision within MPT 1375 for communications to revert from
MUX1 back to MUX2 for high-speed data applications, but this would not
normally happen in the course of an ordinary telephone call.) The SYN
channel consists of 10 bits of preamble (101010... pattern) followed by one
of three different 24 bit synchronisation patterns, referred to as CHMF,
SYNCP and SYNCF. (A fourth pattern, CHMP, is also defined and is used
in MUX3: see below.) These patterns are specially chosen to have low
correlation with each other and other commonly occurring bit patterns in
order to reduce the probability of false detection. The use of a particular
pattern out of the three depends on whether it is being transmitted by a
base station or a handset and whether or not that end is trying to initialise
the link.

4. MUX3 is the "long" 10 ms burst transmitted by the handset when it
is trying to establish a link with a base station. In this multiplex, the 10 ms
transmission is divided into five 2 ms "frames", each of which is divided
into four identical "sub-frames", i.e. data is repeated four times within each
frame. The first four frames contain 20 bits of D channel and 16 bits of
preamble in each sub-frame, while the fifth frame contains only SYN channel
(12 bits of preamble and the 24 bit synchronisation word CHMP in each
sub-frame). The fourfold repetition of data ensures that no matter where
the base station's listen window is positioned relative to the start of the
handset's burst, the base station will be able to see one of the sub-frames
of each of the five frames and thus lock on to the CHMP pattern and
receive 80 bits of D channel data. The reason that preamble is transmitted
in the first four frames is to ensure that the D channel data does not
accidentally mimic CHMP and thus cause incorrect synchronisation.

Layer 1 of the signalling protocol deals with link initialisation, handshaking and link re-establishment following loss of data. Layer 2 defines the contents of the D channel and also the provision of services such as error detection, data re-transmission and link maintenance.

Link initialisation operates in two different ways depending on whether the handset or the base station wishes to set up the link. In the case of link initialisation by a handset (for example, if a user wishes to make an outgoing call), the handset starts by repeatedly transmitting a MUX3 burst, receiving for 4 ms between each 10 ms transmission. The base station scans all 40 RF channels periodically for the CHMP pattern and when it detects one, decodes the following 80 D channel bits. These will contain a layer 2 message called LINK_REQUEST. If the base station "recognises" the handset (depending on the contents of various fields in the LINK_REQUEST message), it replies in MUX2 with a message called LINK_GRANT. The handset then slaves to the MUX2 bursts, transmitting in MUX2 aligned to the base station's receive window. After a period of data exchange in MUX2, the base station sends a layer 3 message ("Channel Control") to the handset telling it to switch to MUX1. When the base station receives a reply in MUX1 it switches to MUX1 itself.

Link initialisation by the base station (for example, when incoming call ringing is detected by the base station) is slightly different in that the base station may "broadcast" messages to up to 32 different handsets. This provides a "group call" facility. Only one handset may request the link, however. (This would occur when a user decided to answer a call. At that point, the other handsets would "drop out" and stop ringing.) It is important to realise that the case of a base station calling a single handset is in fact a special case of "group call".

When a base station wishes to call one or more handsets, it starts transmitting MUX2 bursts using the CHMF pattern in the SYN channel. The contents of the D channel are a sequence of messages every other one of which is a "poll" message to indicate which handset(s) is/are being called. For example, if three handsets are being called, then three different poll messages are transmitted in a cyclic fashion, one message addressing each handset. (The other intervening messages are broadcast to all the handsets being polled and might include commands to switch the ringer on and off, to flash an icon or to display a message. These intervening messages may, however, be omitted and the equivalent amount of "idle" pattern (see below) be transmitted instead.) A handset scans all 40 channels periodically and if it detects a CHMF, decodes the following D channel data. If it is being called, it replies with a poll response message in three MUX2 bursts. (When more than one handset is being called, their responses are interleaved.) When all the polled handsets have replied, the base station switches to using the SYNCF pattern in the SYN channel, to avoid waking up other handsets. When one of the polled handsets wishes to establish the link, it replaces its poll response with a LINK_REQUEST message. The base station then replies with LINK_GRANT and the set-up proceeds in the same manner as for the handset-to-base process described above.

Throughout link establishment, a series of timeouts ensures that neither end repeats transmission of a message "for ever". Safeguards are also built in to resolve "deadly embrace" (i.e. both ends trying to establish a link simultaneously) and response collision situations.

Once a link is set up, both ends transmit handshake messages in the D channel at a rate of between once every 400 ms and once every second. The lower rate is chosen to ensure that losses of link can be detected reasonably quickly, while the upper rate ensures that handshakes are not "forced through" a poor-quality link by rapid re-transmission.

If either the handset or the base station detects that the link quality is poor (e.g. through loss of handshake messages), it may request that the link be "re-established" (on the same RF channel). Re-establishment is similar to link set-up by a handset in that the handset starts transmitting in MUX3, the base station replies in MUX2, and so on. It is not permitted to occur more than once every 600 ms when using MUX1.2 or once every 300 ms when using MUX1.4. The handset may also attempt to re-establish the link on a different RF channel, but this may only be done after handshake messages have been lost for at least 3 s.

Layer 2 of the signalling protocol is responsible for link maintenance, i.e.

- Providing error-free communications between the handset and base station layer 3 processes
- Acknowledgement and re-transmission, if necessary, of messages. (Unacknowledged transmission is also provided and is used, for example, for broadcast messages from a single base station to multiple handsets)
- Validation of handset and/or base station identities during link set-up
- Monitoring of link quality and re-establishment if necessary

It is based on the existing data signalling protocol MPT 1317 [4]. "Packets", consisting of between one and six "code words", are transmitted in the D channel, each preceded by a 16 bit synchronisation word (called SYNCD). Each code word consists of 48 data bits and 16 check bits. The first code word in a packet is called an Address Code Word (ACW) and subsequent code words are called Data Code Words (DCWs). If there are no packets to send, an idle pattern (IDLE_D) is transmitted.

Layer 2 packets are divided into two types: fixed length and variable length. Fixed length packets consist of a single ACW and are used during link set-up and also for handshaking. (The messages LINK_REQUEST and LINK_GRANT mentioned above are examples of this type of packet.) Note that a fixed length packet occupies 80 D channel bits (16 bit SYNCD + 64 bit ACW) and therefore fits into one MUX3 burst or three MUX2 bursts.

Variable length packets consist of an ACW and optional DCWs and are further subdivided into two types called "information" and "supervisory". Information type packets contain layer 3 messages while supervisory types contain messages concerned with link maintenance. (Examples of the latter include the command from the base station to the handset to switch the latter's transmitter power between the normal and low settings and the message from either end requesting link re-establishment.) Both types of variable length packet may be sent unacknowledged or acknowledged. In the case of acknowledged transmission, packets are alternately numbered 0 and 1 and a packet is transmitted repeatedly until an acknowledgement is received. The acknowledgement takes the form of a 1 bit number indicating which packet is next expected (i.e. the inverse of the packet last successfully received) and is contained in one of the fields of a packet being transmitted in the opposite direction (a technique known as "piggybacking"). Such an acknowledgement/re-transmission scheme is known as a "1 bit sliding window protocol" [8].

A2.5 Part 3: Signalling Layer 3

Layer 3 of the signalling protocol defines the meaning of the messages which are passed between handset and base station by layers 1 and 2. As mentioned previously, it is based on the ISDN DASS, although only a subset of the messages has been used. (This has also been re-coded and a number of new messages added.)

The signalling system used in layer 3 is known as Stimulus Mode Signalling. In this type of signalling, the information contained in messages is of a fairly low-level nature. Thus, instead of the handset sending a command message to the base station such as "Attempt to connect to telephone number 0123 456789", the messages contain information such as "The user has pressed the 0 key", or commands such as "Switch the ringer on".

It is not mandatory for either the handset or the base station to generate or respond to the entire message set. For example, handsets without a display may ignore commands to display numerals and/or icons. A minimum subset of messages must, however, be supported by equipment claiming to be compatible with Telepoint use.

The message set may be divided into the following broad areas. (It is not intended to discuss individual messages in detail. Readers are referred to [1] for further details.)

- Transmission of dialled digits from handset to base and display information vice versa
- Generation of tonecaller alerting signals (incoming ringing, error, etc.)
- Outgoing call selection, including ordinary domestic, Telepoint, PABX intercom, emergency, etc., together with other exchange features such as recall, follow-on, hold, etc.
- Call progress indication (This might be used, for example, to control icons on a handset display)

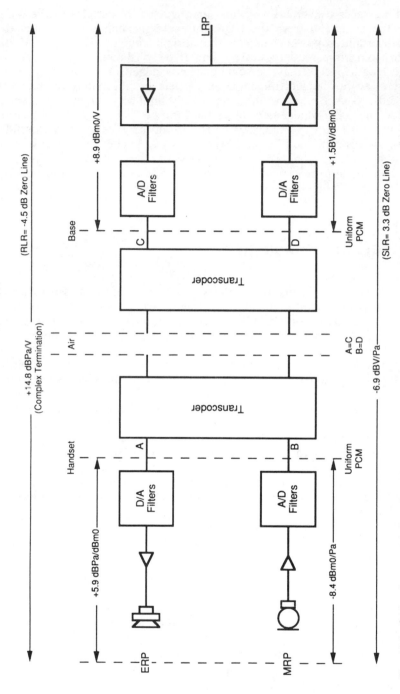

Fig. A2.2. CAI voice transmission plan. Note that: (1) line interface gains are for zero line lengths; (2) any companding/CODEC functions are contained within the A-D/filter function blocks. (© Crown Copyright. Reproduced from MPT specifications 1375, published by UK Department of Trade and Industry, Radiocommunications Division 1989.)

- Connection and disconnection of the audio channel together with side tone control
- Registration of handsets to base stations "over the air" (Base stations do not recognise handsets until they have been programmed to do so)
- Telepoint Call Authentication (Whereas a domestic base station only recognises handsets which are registered on to it, Telepoint base stations initially recognise all handsets and then proceed to determine whether or not the user has a valid account with the service provided)
- Indication of handset and base station capabilities (For example, a handset may indicate to a base that its display can only indicate numerals
- Storing and retrieval of "parameters" (information particular to an individual handset or base station). For example, a base station may programme handsets with different "classes of service" (ability to make international calls, etc.)
- Selection of alternative message sets for future enhancements.

A2.6 Part 4: Speech Coding and Transmission Plan

Part 4 of MPT 1375 contains the specifications for coding and decoding of analogue information transmitted in the B channel. These are subdivided into two categories:

- The specifications relating to the conversion of the analogue signals to digital form and their subsequent compression
- The specifications for the remaining analogue parts from the Mouth Reference Point (MRP) to the telephone line and back to the Ear Reference Point (ERP) – the "Transmission Plan"

The analogue-to-digital conversion specification is straightforward, viz. that the preferred content of the B channel is that produced by the ADPCM algorithm defined in CCITT recommendation G.721(1988) [9]. (Unfortunately, this algorithm differs sufficiently from the one published in the previous CCITT recommendations (1984) to make inter-working between the two impossible.)

Two concessions are permitted from the full G.721 algorithm in certain instances. Firstly, if a base station is connected to an analogue line interface (as opposed to, say, an ISDN interface) it need not implement features such as PCM format conversion. Secondly, a handset may use an algorithm of reduced specification provided that, when used with a base station employing the full algorithm, the speech quality tests contained in BS 6833 are met.

The transmission plan specifies parameters such as frequency response, loudness, noise and distortion for the various analogue processes. (A high-level block diagram of the plan, with nominal values for some of these parameters at 1 kHz, is shown in Fig. A2.2.) It also specifies a maximum handset "loop" delay, i.e. the time taken for a signal to travel from the handset MRP to the base station and back to the ERP. This has been specified as 4 ms (when tested with a special base station which loops back the ADPCM signal without converting it to PCM or analogue) and has been chosen to maximise the permissible processing time for the ADPCM algorithm whilst avoiding the need for echo cancellation.

The transmission plan has been devised to comply with BS 6833 Part 2 (which only covers connection to analogue line interfaces) and NET 33, the emerging standard for connection to digital exchanges [10]. One important consequence of making the CAI compatible with digital interfaces is that handsets must be capable of generating side tone locally. (With an analogue connection, side tone is generated by the hybrid circuit in the base station.)

References

1. UK Department of Trade and Industry, "Common air interface specification" MPT 1375, London, May 1989 (amended November 1989, February 1990)
2. UK Department of Trade and Industry, "Performance specification for radio equipment for use at fixed and portable stations in the cordless telephone service operating in the band 864 to 868 MHz", MPT 1334, London, 1987
3. UK British Standards Institution, "British Standard: apparatus using cordless attachments (excluding cellular radio apparatus) for connection to analogue interfaces of public switched telephone networks", BS 6833: 1987, London 1987
4. UK Department of Trade and Industry, "Transmission of digital information over land mobile radio systems" MPT 1317, London, 1981
5. CCITT, "Integrated services digital network (ISDN)" Red Book, vol. III, fascicle III.5, recommendation I.441, 1984
6. CCITT, "Digital access signalling system" Red Book, vol. VI, fascicle VI.9, recommendation Q.931, 1984
7. CCITT, "Pulse code modulation (PCM) of voice frequencies" Red Book, vol. III, fascicle III.3, recommendation G.711, 1984
8. A.S. Tanenbaum, "Computer networks", Prentice Hall, Englewood Cliffs, 1981
9. CCITT, "32 kbit/s adaptive differential pulse code modulation (ADPCM)", Blue Book, recommendation G.721, 1988
10. CEPT, "Approval requirements for telephony characteristics of terminal equipment for ISDN", NET33 Draft T/TE 04-15, recommendation T/TE 04-153

Appendix 3 **The Digital European Cordless Telecommunications Specification, DECT**

Heinz Ochsner

*DECT makes so much sense !
I salute to the creators !*

The DECT specification being developed by ETSI RES3 will provide an air interface specification to support a wide variety of services. It will be a common interface specification (see Chapter 3). A subset of it, however, may be used as a coexistence specification. The DECT standardisation process is still under way. It is, however, expected that the standard will be commercially available by 1992.

A3.1 The DECT Services

The main objective of the DECT standard is to provide a specification which will support many applications such as residential cordless telephones, business systems, public access networks (Telepoint), and evolutionary applications such as radio local area networks (radio LAN).

The main service principles adopted were to provide a system specification for both voice and non-voice applications. DECT equipment should function as an equivalent replacement for a wired telephone connected directly or indirectly, i.e. via a PABX, to a public wired network such as a PSTN or an ISDN.

In the following sections the four areas of application are described in more detail.

A3.1.1 Standard (Residential) Cordless Telephony

This is the ordinary cordless telephone, known from existing products. In its simplest form it consists of a cordless handset and a base station which also acts as a charging unit for the handset's batteries. Evolutionary applications of the residential cordless telephone may include several handsets with an intercom facility and more than one PSTN line.

A3.1.2 Cordless Business Communications Systems

Cordless business communications systems will basically provide the same functions as today's business telephone networks, e.g. key telephone systems or private automatic branch exchange (PABX) systems. To provide the user's premises with enough capacity while using the spectrum efficiently, the use of cellular coverage is envisaged. As illustrated in Fig. A3.1, a cordless business communications system would consist of a wired switching system with wired extensions to cordless base stations. The extensions will route calls to base stations in one or several cells via which cordless handsets or portable radio data terminals can communicate with the network. Portable-to-portable traffic would always go via the network, even though the radio conditions could allow direct communication. Of course the cordless extension in this case would need to provide mobility functions known from cellular systems, in particular handover or, in the case of very large systems, location registration. Many terminals of the system may still remain wired, for example high comfort telephones, work stations, or access lines to mainframe computers.

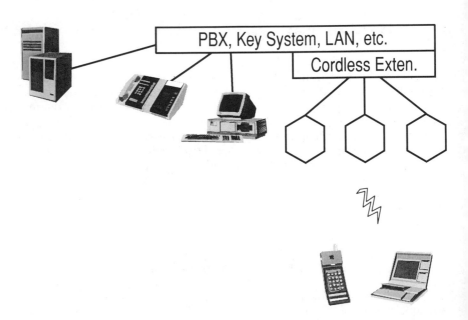

Fig. A3.1. DECT cordless business communications systems.

A3.1.3 Public Access – Telepoint

The Telepoint service provides cordless access to the public telephone network via public base stations. As such they can be seen as "cordless coinboxes". A handset, which can also be used at home and in the office, can access the telephone network and the owner will be billed to his home address. An authentication and billing centre is needed (Fig. A3.2). Telepoint base stations are not intended to provide nationwide coverage but will be installed at locations where high call traffic is to be expected, such as railway stations, airports, shopping centres, restaurants – everywhere where coinboxes are available today. The main difference between a Telepoint service and a cellular mobile telephony service is that Telepoint makes use of the existing telephone network while cellular systems require dedicated intelligent networks including mobile switching centres, location registration centres, and so on. It is these differences which allow Telepoint to be a cheaper service, as well as requiring cheaper equipment compared with cellular systems. In return, the limited capabilities of today's telephone network do not yet allow outgoing calls from the network to the handset. This drawback, however, may be overcome with the evolution of the wired network into ISDN (offering supplementary services such as "follow me") or by using complementary services such as wide area paging.

A3.1.4 Evolutionary Applications

DECT will integrate voice and non-voice services into one radio transmission scheme. In particular, cordless data applications such as the radio LAN are foreseen. Powerful dynamic allocation of radio spectrum will allow efficient use of the available capacity and as such provide high data rates. Throughput

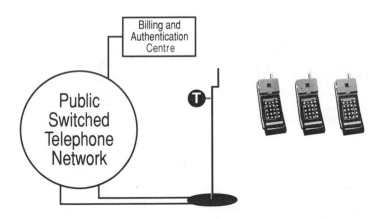

Fig. A3.2 DECT Telepoint.

rates as high as 250 kbit/s are envisaged. Efficient use of radio spectrum in the case of bursty or variable throughput data transmission is guaranteed by appropriate radio access techniques.

A3.2 Structure of the Specification

The specification of DECT will contain several sections. Part 0 gives an introduction to the layered structure of the DECT standard and an overview of the protocol architecture. Parts 1 to 4 describe the functions of the four layers in detail. Each of parts 1 to 4 has five sections describing the services provided by the individual layers, as well as the messages and procedures. The four communication layers are controlled by the Management Entity, which is described in part 5. Finally, parts 6 and 7 specify the requirements for voice and data transmission, respectively. Parts 1 to 4 and 6 will be described here. The other parts are not yet sufficiently advanced at the time of writing (March 1990) to be described in any detail.

A3.3 Part 0: The Introduction

The introduction to the DECT specification, besides containing editorial information such as scope of the document, list of references, etc., introduces the basic concepts of the DECT radio communication. It is noted that the DECT standard only specifies the radio communication link between a DECT terminal and the network (which may contain many base stations, common control modules, possibly even location registers). Although the standard is based on certain assumptions about the network architecture, it does not deal with the functions within the network.

Fig. A3.3 shows the layered structure employed for the communication protocols. Two layers are common to both user data and signalling data: the Physical Layer (PHL), which transmits the data over the radio link, and the Medium Access Control Layer (MAC), which is responsible for effective allocation of radio resources and for multiplexing user and signalling data onto one bit stream. PHL and MAC layers together provide the radio transmission. The communication peers are, therefore, the portable handsets and the base stations in the cells.

The upper layers are separate for user data and signalling. The Data Link Control layer (DLC) maintains a secure data link for signalling even when the cell has to be changed during a call, i.e. when a handover is executed. The Network Layer (NWL) is responsible for routing the calls from a portable wishing to make a call to the fixed network and vice versa. In contrast to PHL and MAC, the DLC and NWL layers' tasks are to "hide"

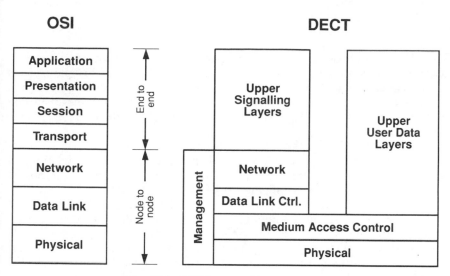

Fig. A3.3. DECT protocol layers.

the presence of non-ideal and possibly changing radio transmission links from the upper communication layers. Their procedures thus involve the DECT network control and the portables, but not the base stations.

Not directly involved in the peer to peer communication is the Management Entity (MGE) which controls the four lower layers and takes the necessary decisions. A typical decision might arise if the quality of the radio connection were no longer adequate, in which case the MGE would decide to initiate a handover.

For reference, Fig. A3.3 also shows the standard OSI layered structure. Two points need to be mentioned here. Firstly, in the OSI model anything above the Network Layer concerns end-to-end communication, while the lower three layers belong to the communication between nodes. The same applies to DECT. As a consequence, the fact that there is a radio link, and functions to deal with a difficult communication channel, is known only up to the Network Layer. Secondly, the DECT structure uses four layers for the node-to-node communication, i.e. DECT terminal to DECT network, while OSI would use only three. The OSI model, however, does not adequately consider multiple access to one transmission medium. Most specifications dealing with multiple access systems do in fact have the MAC Layer, or an equivalent of it. In the CAI, as specified in MPT 1375, the Radio Interface specification is equivalent to the DECT Physical Layer, the CAI Signalling Layer 1 corresponds to the DECT Medium Access Control, while CAI's Signalling Layers 2 and 3 have, with a few exceptions, their counterpart in the DECT Data Link Control and Network Layers.

A3.4 Part 1: The Physical Layer, PHL

The PHL is responsible for segmenting the radio transmission medium into physical channels. This is done using a Time Division Multiple Access (TDMA) scheme on multiple carriers. Ten carriers are envisaged in the frequency band between 1880 MHz and 1900 MHz (although the extension of the band down to 1850 MHz, to support future demand, has been suggested).

Each carrier contains the TDMA structure. A time frame of 10 ms is formed and each frame is divided into 24 timeslots (Fig. A3.4), resulting in timeslots of approximately 416.7 μs. During these timeslots, data can be sent in packets. As seen from Fig. A3.4, the burst contains two fields, a synchronisation field of 32 bits, and a data field of 388 bits. The synchronisation data allows the receiver to demodulate a single packet immediately. This is necessary to enable very fast call set-up and unnoticeable handovers to be performed. The data field is received from the MAC Layer.

The total 420 bits are modulated onto the carrier using a two-level FSK modulation with Gaussian prefiltering at a relative bandwidth (BT product) of 0.5. If the modulation were coherent it would be GMSK; coherence is, however, not necessary. The chosen modulation scheme permits the use of a simple receiver with non-coherent demodulation, bit-by-bit decision, easily implementable IF filters, and so on. The modulated data rate is 1152 kbit/s.

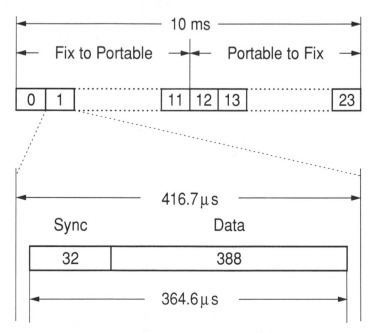

Fig. A3.4. DECT Physical Layer, PHL.

The complete packet therefore has a length of 420 bit/1152 kbit/s, i.e. 364.6 μs.   *60 bits*

When these [packets are transmitted within a timeslot, there remains a guard space of *52* μs. This guard space is needed to allow for propagation delays, smooth ramp-up and ramp-down of the transmitter, and synthesiser switching between packets.

A physical channel is created by transmitting one packet every frame during a particular timeslot on a particular carrier. The throughput of a physical channel available to the MAC Layer is therefore 388 bit/10 ms, i.e. 38.8 kbit/s. The average transmitted power per physical channel is 10 mW.

The Physical Layer does not decide on which timeslot and carrier it is to transmit but is instructed by the MAC layer.

As indicated in Fig. A3.4, the first 12 slots are normally used for transmission to the portable and the second 12 slots for transmission in the opposite direction. The Physical Layer, however, does not know that there is a Time Division Duplex (TDD) transmission mode, but is simply told by the MAC to transmit on timeslot 5 and to receive on timeslot 17, for example. *Obviously, it's possible to make the link asymmetric w/ incremental unit being one slot.*

A3.5 Part 2: The Medium Access Control Layer, MAC

The MAC Layer performs three main functions. Firstly, it allocates and releases physical resources according to the requests of the upper layers. Secondly, it multiplexes the logical channels from both the upper layers of signalling and user information onto the physical channels offered by the PHL. Finally, it guarantees the secure transmission of both the signalling and user information by appropriate error control.

A3.5.1 Allocation and Release of Physical Resources

Three special features make up the DECT radio resource management: the Dynamic Channel Selection (DCS), the use of a so-called beacon at each base station, and the possibility of allocating multiple physical channels to a connection.

By using a DCS algorithm, the full capacity offered by DECT is available to all DECT users, no matter whether they belong to one installation or to different ones. Whoever wants to activate a physical channel (this is usually the portable) looks for a channel which is free locally and then may use it. There are no pre-assigned channels or frequencies for a particular cell site, as is the case in a cellular radio network. In this way the algorithm may adapt to changing, or unknown, propagation and traffic conditions. DCS is a prime requirement for effective use of radio spectrum in cordless applications. It is, therefore, not surprising that DCS has already been applied in CEPT CT1, in CAI, and in the Swedish DCT.   *one timeslot*

Another special feature of DECT is the use of a so-called beacon at each base station. Every base station transmits on at least one channel. The portable then scans the channels until it finds the transmissions of a close base station and locks onto this channel. Call set-up requests (so-called paging calls) from the network are then transmitted using this channel. The portable receives these requests and may immediately respond to the request. This procedure has the main advantage that the portable does not need to scan all the channels continuously but may stay on an appropriate one. By doing so, very fast channel set-up times can be realised (which is important particularly for non-voice services) and the portable's power consumption is considerably reduced since there is no need for continuous scanning.

Of course it would not be wise to dedicate a particular channel only for the purpose of calling portables. If a dedicated channel is subject to interference, the base station could then no longer be used. Furthermore, the relatively moderate load of paging calls does not justify one complete channel to be used at each base site. The concept chosen for DECT rather allows any base-to-portable down-link, which is in use for a specific terminal, to act simultaneously as a beacon. If there are, say, six conversations going on at one base site, this site would be equipped, momentarily, with six beacons! Only in the case when there is no conversation going on at all is one idle channel (usually the last one that was in use) kept active as the beacon.

When the portable is in idle mode, i.e. not currently involved in a conversation, it will scan the environment for the beacon signals of a nearby base station. Once found, its receiver will stay locked onto this signal. Should the radio environment change, or should the locked-on channel disappear, the portable would look for a new beacon.

It is noted that the type of call set-up described in this section is suitable for circuit-oriented connections as necessary for telephony. Other mechanisms for packet orientated transmissions similar to those described in Chapter 8 are provided by DECT as well.

A3.5.2 Multiplexing of Logical Channels

The second task of the MAC Layer is in multiplexing the information coming from the upper layers onto one physical channel. The multiplex scheme is illustrated in Fig. A3.5. Information coming from the upper layers is grouped in logical channels, I, C, P, Q and N.

Information from the upper layers is provided as a continuous bit stream, as is the case for speech transmission, or in complete data frames, as the Data Link Control Layer would provide them, in the case of signalling information. In both cases, the MAC has first to create short data segments that fit into the packets of 388 bits that the Physical Layer can transport.

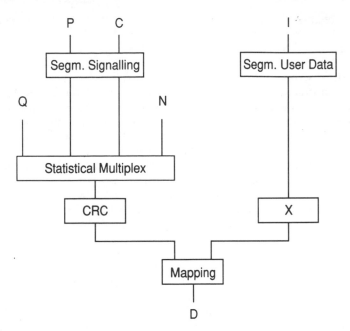

Fig. A3.5. DECT U-Multiplex.

The information channel I bears the user information. As Fig. A3.6 shows, 320 bits are available in each packet, hence the I channel throughput is 32 kbit/s. In the case of telephony this would be a bit stream of ADPCM coded speech. An I channel exists in both fixed-to-portable and portable-to-fixed directions.

The control channel C is used for the actual signalling data. "Signalling" embraces everything that is needed to set up, maintain and release a call with a particular terminal. Again a C channel exists in both fixed-to-portable and portable-to-fixed directions.

As explained in Section A3.5.1, network originated call set-up is carried out by paging the portable which then, in return, builds up the link. Any active channel can be used to page a portable. The paging information is carried by the P channel and is therefore broadcast to all portables locked

Then the portable need to read all slots in a radio channel

PHL Packet	32	388		
	Sync	MAC Data		
MAC Packet	48	16	320	4
	C/P/Q/N	CRC	I	X

Fig. A3.6. DECT Medium Access Control Layer, MAC.

C – signalling, call set up   X – Interference Detection
P – Paging channel, down link only
Q – system IDs, down link only
N – Portable & Base station IDs

on to the channel, whilst the signalling data carried by the C channel is intended only for the one receiver in conversation. Obviously a P channel exists in the fixed-to-portable direction only.

On the N channel, identities of the portable and the base station are exchanged at regular intervals (hand-shake).

Before a portable can lock on to a base station, it has to verify that the base station belongs to a system which it wants to communicate with. The system identification, together with some other important parameters, are broadcast in the Q channel. The Q channel again exists in the down-link direction only and is a logical channel within the MAC Layer only.

The C, P, Q and N channels are multiplexed onto 48 bits of each burst. Together they may occupy a signalling rate of 4.8 kbit/s. The allocation to the individual channels is, however, dynamic and depends on the actual needs. The algorithm of this statistical multiplexing scheme is such that for each logical channel a minimum throughput is guaranteed.

$$4.8 \times 12 = 57.6 \text{ K b/s} \quad \text{each way}$$

A3.5.3 Error Control

The multiplexed C, P, Q and N channels are protected by a Cyclic Redundancy Check (CRC) with 16 bits. The CRC allows recognition of transmission errors. In the case of the C, an Automatic Repeat Request (ARQ) protocol is used to recover from transmission errors. The data of the other channels is not retransmitted. The CRC only allows verification of the correctness of the received data.

As Fig. A3.6 illustrates, the I field is followed by 4 further bits denoted X. These are calculated from the bits in the I field. They are not used to protect the information data; a 4 bit parity check never can reasonably protect 320 bits of data. The X bits are rather used to recognise interference which only affects a part of the burst. This is the case, for example, if the interferer is a signal from an unsynchronised system drifting slowly into the wanted signal. Recognising the interference by constantly observing the X bits allows counter-action to be taken, e.g. by handing the connection over to another channel.

The multiplex scheme outlined in Figs. A3.5 and A3.6 is called the U-Multiplex, U indicating that the multiplex contains user data. In DECT there exists also an E-Multiplex which does not have an I channel but has increased capacity for an extended C channel. This multiplex is used in particular during the channel set-up phase.

A3.6 Part 3: The Data Link Control Layer, DLC

As mentioned earlier, the radio link becomes less and less visible at higher layers. This is mainly due to the DLC Layer, the main task of which is to guarantee error-free transmission to the Network Layer. Once a data link is set up by the DLC Layer it has the task of maintaining this link even if physical resources have to be changed during the conversation. This is the case where, for example, a handover must be executed, or when the data throughput needs are changed during a call and the allocated resources need to be adapted accordingly.

Another consequence of the invisibility of the radio communication to the higher layer is that more and more existing protocols may be used. These may be adapted to fit the particular needs of DECT but they do not need to be completely newly designed, Thus, the DLC protocol of DECT belongs to the class of HDLC protocols.

A3.7 Part 4: The Network Layer, NWL

The highest protocol layer covered within the DECT specification is the Network Layer (NWL). As for the DLC Layer, there is no need to define a completely new protocol, as an existing specification can be used. In the case of a DECT circuit oriented transmission, a network protocol similar to the ISDN I.451 protocol is used.

One task of the NWL which is unique to a cellular network application such as DECT is that it has to route calls to a handset the exact location of which is not *a priori* known. Therefore, the protocol needs to be expanded to include such mobility management procedures.

A second unique task is the provision of security-related functions, in particular authentication.

A3.8 Part 5: The Management Entity, MGE

At the time of writing this part of the specification was not sufficiently advanced for a description of it to be included.

A3.9 Part 6: Audio Transmission

The problems arising from delay in cordless telephony systems have already been discussed extensively in Chapter 6. In DECT a system-inherent one-way delay of 10 ms is introduced, arising from the TDMA framing. Other delay sources, e.g. digital signal processing, may add further delay to total no more than 15 ms. Part 6 of the DECT specification defines all the necessary steps to be taken to guarantee high-quality telephone conversations with DECT systems. These include the complete end-to-end transmission planning with all the echo control requirements, necessary loudness ratings, etc.

Part 6 also defines the digital speech coding to be used in DECT. The requirement is that the resulting speech quality perceived by the user must be equal to the quality of a fixed digital telephone. Therefore, the quantisation distortion of the speech coding should be acceptable even in normal fixed telephony networks. The Adaptive Differential Pulse Code Modulation (ADPCM) coding algorithm defined in CCITT Rec. G.721 fulfils this requirement with a data throughput need of 32 kbit/s. Since no codec with lower bit rate but fulfilling the quality requirement currently exists, the G.721 algorithm has been chosen for the DECT standard. Nevertheless, the standard is open to allow other speech coding algorithms should they become available in the future.

A3.10 Part 7: Data Transmission

At the time of writing this part of the specification was not sufficiently advanced for a description of it to be included.

Appendix 4 **Glossary of Terms**

This glossary provides short definitions of a range of abbreviations in use within the cordless telecommunications field. Some of the terms are defined in greater detail elsewhere in the book.

ACK	Acknowledgement
ACW	Address Code Word (part of CAI)
ADM	Adaptive Delta Modulation
ADPCM	Adaptive Differential Pulse Code Modulation
AFC	Automatic Frequency Control
AGC	Automatic Gain Control
ARQ	Automatic Repeat Request
AWGN	Additive White Gaussian Noise
B	Echo Balance Return Loss
B channel	User information channel (64 kbit/s in ISDN)
BABT	British Approvals Board for Telecommunications
Base Station	The fixed radio component of a cordless link. This may be single-channel (for domestic) or multi-channel (for Telepoint and business)
BCT	Business Cordless Telephone
BER	Bit Error Rate (or Ratio)
BS 6833	A UK standard for digital cordless telephones allowing for proprietary air interfaces, (mainly specifying telephony related aspects)
BT	British Telecom
	or
	Bandwidth-Time product for GMSK modulation
BTR	Bit Timing Recovery (used to permit synchronisation across a radio link)
CAD/CAM	Computed Aided Design/Computer Aided Manufacture
CAI	Common Air Interface Standard (for CT2/Telepoint)

CBCS	Cordless Business Communication System, supporting wireless PABX and data applications, for example, in the business environment.
CCFP	Common Control Fixed Part
CCH	CEPT Committee for Harmonisation
CCIR	Comité Consultatif International de Radio, part of the ITU
CCITT	Comité Consultatif International des Télégraphes et Téléphones, part of the ITU
CDC	Cordless Data Controller
CDMA	Code Division Multiple Access
CEC	Commission of the European Communities
CEN	Comité Européen de Normalisation
CENELEC	Comité Européen de Normalisation Electrotechnique
CEPT	Conference of European Posts and Telecommunications Administrations
CFP	Cordless Fixed Part, e.g. a cordless telephone base station
CHMF	Synchronisation pattern used in CAI
CHMP	Synchronisation pattern used in CAI
CI	Common Interface, type of specification *or* Channel Identity sequence, used for over the air identification of a radio transmission
CISPR	Comité International Spécial Perturbations Radio
CIT	Computer Integrated Telephony, a means of controlling PABX functions by a separate computer
CLR	Connection Loudness Rating
CNET	Centre National d'Etudes Télécommunications
COST	European Cooperation in the Field of Scientific and Technical Research
CPFSK	Continuous Phase Frequency Shift Keying
CPP	Cordless Portable Part, the cordless telephone handset carried by the user
CR	Comité de Coordinations des Radiocommunications, Committee of the CEPT charged with administering frequency allocations, also sometimes abbreviated to CEPT RC *or* Carrier Recovery
CRC	Cyclic Redundancy Check
CRE	Corrected Reference Equivalents (related to OELR)
CSMA	Carrier Sense Multiple Access
CSMA/CA	Carrier Sense Multiple Access with Collision Avoidance
CSS	Cordless Subsystem
CT1	Cordless Telephone Generation One. In UK, factored

	and modified analogue VHF/LF units. In Europe 900 MHz analogue FM-CEPT CT1
CT2	Second Generation Cordless Telephone – Digital
CVSDM	Continously Variable Slope Delta Modulation
CVSDM-SC	CVSDM with Syllabic Companding
CX	Coexistence, type of specification
D Channel	Control and information data channel (16 kbit/s in ISDN)
DASS	Digital Access Signalling System
DCA	Dynamic Channel Assignment (or Allocation)
DCS	Dynamic Channel Selection, same as DCA
DCT	Digital Cordless Telephone
DCW	Data Code Word (part of CAI)
DECT	Digital European Cordless Telecommunications
DLC	Data Link Control layer, protocol layer in DECT
DM	Delta Modulation
Downlink	The transmission link from the fixed part to the portable part
DPCM	Differential Pulse Code Modulation
DPNSS	Digital Private Network Signalling System
DRIVE	Dedicated Road Infrastructure for Vehicle Safety in Europe
DRT	Diagnostic Rhyme Test, used in speech quality measurements
DSP	Digital Signal Processing
DSRR	Digital Short Range Radio
DTI	UK Department of Trade and Industry
DTMF	Dual Tone Multiple Frequency (audio tone signalling system)
Duplex	Simultaneous two-way communication
DVSDM	Digitally Variable Slope Delta Modulation
EC	European Community
ECTEL	European Association of the Telecommunications Industry
ERMES	European Radio Messaging System, pan-European standard being specified within ETSI
ERP	Effective Radiated Power
	or
	Earpiece Reference Point
ESPA	European Selective Paging Association
ESPRIT	European Strategic Programme for Research and Development in Information Technology
ETS	European Telecommunications Standard
ETSI	European Telecommunications Standards Institute
Euromessage	A paging system, which began operation in 1989,

intended to provide transnational paging between
certain European countries, prior to ERMES

FCS	Free Channel Search
	or
	Frame Check Sequence
FDD	Frequency Division Duplex
FDMA	Frequency Division Multiple Access
FEC	Forward Error Correction
FPLMTS	Future Public Land Mobile Telecommunications Systems, being studied by CCIR IWP 8/13
FSK	Frequency Shift Keying
GA	General Assembly (of ETSI)
GMSK	Gaussian Filtered Minimum Shift Keying
GSM	Group Spéciale Mobile, committee now within ETSI (previously within CEPT) responsible for specifying the pan-European digital cellular radio system. The system itself is often referred to simply as "GSM"
Handoff	The procedure whereby communications between a cordless terminal and a base station are automatically routed via an alternative base station (or possibly via an alternative channel to the same base station) when this is necessary and appropriate to maintain or improve communications
Handover	Another term for Handoff
HDLC	High level Data Link Control, a type of protocol
HLR	Home Location Register, used in cellular systems and which might be used in future enhanced Telepoint or PCN systems
IBCN	Integrated Broadband Communications Network
IEC	International Electrotechnical Commission
IF	Intermediate Frequency
IFRB	International Frequency Registration Board
IN	Intelligent Network
IPRC	Intellectual Property Rights Committee (of ETSI)
ISM	ISDN Standards Management Committee (of ETSI)
ISDN	Integrated Services Digital Network
ISO	International Standards Organisation
ISPABX	Integrated Services PABX
ITSTC	Information Technology Steering Committee
ITU	International Telecommunications Union
IWP 8/13	Interim Working Party 8/13 of Study Group 8 of the CCIR

JLR	Junction Loudness Rating
LAN	Local Area Network
LCD	Liquid Crystal Display
LDM	Linear Delta Modulation
LPC	Linear Predictive Coding
LPC-10	A particular implementation of the LPC algorithm with 10 coefficients
LR	Loudness Rating *or* Location Register (as in cellular radio)
MAC	Medium Access Control, protocol layer used in DECT
MAP	Mobile Application Part of SS7, developed for GSM
MBS	Mobile Broadband System, possible future broadband mobile services being explored under the RACE Mobile Telecommunications research programme
MC	Multi Carrier
MDT	Mobile Data Terminal
MEG	Mobile Experts Group, set up to advise the Strategic Review Committee of ETSI on future ETSI work relating to mobile telecommunications
MES	Mobile (satellite) Earth Station
MGE	Management Entity, controls the four protocol layers in DECT
Microdiversity	Diversity between antennas with relatively small spacing (of the order of a quarter wavelength) to counter multipath fading effects
MOS	Mean Opinion Score, used in speech quality measurements
MoU	Memorandum of Understanding
MPT 1317	UK standard for data signalling over a radio path
MPT 1334	UK standard for digital cordless telephones allowing for proprietary air interfaces (mainly specifying radio related aspects)
MPT 1375	UK Standard for Common Air Interface (CAI) digital cordless telephones
MRP	Mouthpiece Reference Point
MSC	Mobile Services Switching Centre (as in cellular radio)
MSK	Minimum Shift Keying
MUX1.2	The multiplex within the CAI standard containing 64 B channel bits and 2 D channel bits
MUX1.4	The multiplex within the CAI standard containing 64 B channel bits and 4 D channel bits
MUX2	The multiplex within the CAI standard containing 32 D channel bits and 32 SYN channel bits

MUX3	The "long" 10 ms burst transmitted by a CAI handset when trying to establish a call
NACK	Not Acknowledge, a form of protocol where action is taken if no acknowledgement is received
NET	Norme Européene de Télécommunications, a type of standard
NET 33	The NET defining the connection of digital telephones to the ISDN
NMT	Nordic Mobile Telephone, cellular radio telephone system used in Scandinavia
NWL	Network Layer, protocol layer in DECT
OELR	Overall Echo Loudness Rating
OFTEL	The UK Office of Telecommunications
OLR	Overall Loudness Rating
OSI	Open Systems Interconnection, the ISO standard for communications, a seven-layer reference model for protocol specification
PABX	Private Automatic Branch Exchange
PARS	Personal Advanced Radio Service (also known as DSRR, Digital Short Range Radio)
PCM	Pulse Code Modulation
PCN	Personal Communications Network
PHL	Physical Layer, lowest protocol layer in DECT
Picocells	Very small cells used within an interference-limited high-density cordless environment, of typical radius ~ 10 m
PIN	Personal Identity Number
PLL	Phase Lock Loop
PMR	Private Mobile Radio
Pointel	The French Telepoint System
PSK	Phase Shift Keying
PSTN	Public Switched Telephone Network
PT	Personal Telecommunications
PTN	Personal Telephone Number
PTO	Public Telecommunications Operator
PTT	Term used to refer to a national telecommunication administration
QDU	Quantisation Distortion Unit
Quantisation	The process of representing samples of an analogue waveform by the nearest whole number of pre-defined voltage steps
R1–R4	Radio interfaces defined within FPLMTS
RACE	Research and development in Advanced

	Communication technologies in Europe, research initiative instigated by the CEC
RARF	CEPT committee charged with adminstering frequency allocation prior to CEPT CR
RC	Alternative designation of the CEPT CR Committee
RD	Radiocommunications Division of the UK DTI; now, since April 1990, the Radiocommunications Agency
RES 3	Technical Sub-committee, Radio Equipment and Systems 3, of ETSI, responsible for the specification of DECT
RFP	Radio Fixed Part, same as Cordless Fixed Part
RLR	Receiving Loudness Rating
RPE-LTP	Regular Pulse Excitation – Long Term Predictor, the type of voice coding employed in the GSM system for full rate speech coding
RRCSMA	Reservation Request CSMA
RSSI	Received Signal Strength Indication
SAW	Surface Acoustic Wave
SCI	Synchronisation, Control and Information
SDLC	Synchronous Data Link Control
SF	Services and Facilities committee of the CEPT "T" Commission
SF2	Services and Facilities working group of ECTEL TCS
SG	Study Group (within CCIR or CCITT)
Sidetone	An attenuated component of the speakers voice signal fed back to his own earpiece to provide confidence that the equipment is functional
Simplex	One-way communication
SLR	Sending Loudness Rating
SMT	Surface Mount Technology
SNR	Signal-to-Noise Ratio
SQER	Signal-to-Quantising-Error Ratio
SRC	Strategic Review Committee (of ETSI)
SS7	CCITT Signalling System No. 7
STMR	Side Tone Masking Rating
SYN	The channel used in CAI to allow synchronisation to be established
SYNCD	Synchronisation pattern used in CAI
SYNCF	Synchronisation pattern used in CAI
SYNCP	Synchronisation pattern used in CAI
TA	Technical Assembly (of ETSI)
TACS	Total Access Communication System, the UK analogue cellular system, based upon AMPS, the US system
TAL	Telephone Acoustic Loss
TC	Technical Committee (of ETSI)

TCS	The cordless telephone subgroup of ECTEL
TDD	Time Division Duplex
TDM	Time Division Multiplex
TDMA	Time Division Multiple Access
TELR	Talker Echo Loudness Rating (nearly the same as OELR!)
TFTS	Terrestrial Flight Telephone System, in-flight telephone system currently being specified within ETSI
TIM	Telephone Identity Module
TP	Telecommunications and Posts Division of the UK DTI
TRAC	Technical Recommendations Applications Committee (of CEPT)
UMC	Universal Mobile Communicator
UMTS	Universal Mobile Telecommunication System, being explored by the RACE Mobile Telecommunications project
Uplink	The transmission link from the portable part to the fixed part
UW	Unique Word, used for synchronisation and/or identification across a radio link
VCO	Voltage Controlled Oscillator
VDU	Video Display Unit
WARC	World Administrative Radio Conference, part of the ITU activity
WPABX	Wireless Private Automatic Branch Exchange
ZAP	Function used within some Telepoint systems to disable unauthorised handsets.

Contributors' Biographical Details

Editor

Dr. Wally H.W. Tuttlebee
Roke Manor Research, Romsey, UK

Wally Tuttlebee, CEng, graduated from the University of Southampton with a BSc (Hons) in Electronics in 1974. Following PhD studies and postdoctoral research he joined Roke Manor in 1979, initially developing frequency agile radio systems. Since that time he has contributed to and led studies and development teams relating to several successful radio communication systems.

In recent years, as Chief Engineer within the Radio Communications Division, Wally has been responsible for a wide range of R&D, with particular interests in the field of personal communications. He has presented several invited papers at conferences on this theme. Recent programmes undertaken by his division have related to CT2 and DECT cordless telephony, the GSM pan-European Cellular Radio system, and the pan-European paging system, ERMES, with involvement with the relevant technical standards committees of these systems. Wally has also been responsible for the division's work on the RACE Mobile Telecommunications project and contributed to one of the UK PCN licence applications. He is a Senior Member of the IEEE (SMIEEE), as well as a Member of the IEE (MIEE)

Wally's management responsibilities include development of the future work of the Radio Communications activity at Roke Manor. Reflecting his management interests, he is undertaking an MBA degree (Masters in Business Administration) with the Cranfield School of Management, Bedford, UK.

Contributors

Dr. Dag Åkerberg
Ericsson Radio Systems AB, Stockholm, Sweden
Dag Åkerberg is manager in the area of Cordless Telephones and Paging Systems at the central Radio Research department of Ericsson Radio Systems, Stockholm. He joined Ericsson in 1971, after obtaining his Dr Sc (Tekn Lic) from the Royal Institute of Technology in Stockholm and, until 1984, was technical manager of the Paging Systems department. Since that time his main activities have been studies, specifications and international standardisation work related to wire-less office communications. Since September 1989 he has been seconded as project leader of the ETSI Project Team 10 (PT10) supporting the specification of the Digital European Cordless Telecommunications (DECT) system.

Brian Bidwell
STC Technology Ltd., Harlow, UK
Since joining STC in 1952 Brian Bidwell, CEng, MIEE, has been active in many areas of mobile and, more recently, personal communications. He was project manager for the successful STC Radio Pager, which won a Design Council Award in 1982, and transferred to STC Technology Ltd. in 1986 where he took over the project management of the feasibility phase of the CT2 development contract for British Telecom. With the award of the full development contract, he was appointed to the position of CT2 System Design Authority.

External activities have included representing TEMA on the BSI committee which produced the UK BS 6833 specification and, since July 1988, he has been Chairman of the EEA Mobile Radio Committee Cordless Telephone Working Group. Brian has also been heavily involved in the UK Industry Group which produced the CT2 Common Air Interface Standard MPT 1375, as Chairman of the Technical Working Group.

Andrew Bud
Olivetti Systems and Networks, Ivrea, Italy
Andrew Bud is Manager of Telecommunications Research for Olivetti Systems and Networks in Ivrea, Italy, where he is responsible for all activities in the area of Personal Communications. He joined Olivetti in 1988 from PA Technology in Cambridge, England, where he had been centrally involved in the invention and development of the Ferranti Zonephone CT2 system. A Member of the IEE, he has a first class honours degree in Engineering from the University of Cambridge. He holds a number of patents in the area of cordless telephones.

Andrew has been involved with the standardisation of Digital European Cordless Telecommunications (DECT) by ETSI Committee RES 3 since its beginning and is currently Chairman of the ETSI Working Group on DECT Network Architecture and Compatability (RES 3N). He is also a member of the Italian delegation to ETSI RES 3 and a member of the Italian Joint Committee on Cordless Systems.

Ed R. Candy
BYPS, Cambridge, UK
Ed Candy is currently the Technical and Operations Director of BYPS, a consortium company of Barclays, Philips and Shell which was awarded one of the four UK Telepoint operator licences.

In his previous role as Corporate Technology Manager for Philips Radio Communication Systems, he was responsible for radio system development and whilst in that position established the EEC collaborative venture for RACE Mobile to set standards for the personal communicator to be implemented in conjunction with the Integrated Broadband Communications Network in Europe.

Prior to coming to England in 1987, Ed was State Manager for Philips Communications Systems in New South Wales, Australia, and responsible for radio, computer and telecommunication systems.

Dominic Clancy
GEC-Plessey Telecommunications, Nottingham, UK
Dominic Clancy is Manager for Product Strategy in GPT Mobile Systems and Terminals Group. Previously he was Project Director for the BIS Mackintosh Mobile Communications Information Services, which provided detailed critical market analysis of the whole mobile communications marketplace in Europe and North America. He has been studying the market for digital cordless telephones since 1986, including the cross elasticity of cordless telephones with other mobile communications services. He has an MBA from Bradford University and a BA in Philosophy from the University of Liverpool. He is also responsible for working with the CEC and ETSI for GPT's mobile communications activities.

Prof. John Gardiner
University of Bradford, UK
John Gardiner obtained BSc (Hons) and PhD degrees from Birmingham University and worked for several of the Racal companies prior to joining Bradford University in 1968 as a lecturer. He is currently Professor of Electronic Engineering and head of the postgraduate division of the department. In addition to his academic responsibilities John also acts as consultant in radio communications to both the UK Department of Trade and Industry and to DGXIII of the European Commission. He is coordinator for the Personal Communications Programme of the UK LINK initiative, a member of CCIR Study Group 1 and of several UK government committees, including the CEPT Consultative Committee.

A. Peter Hulbert
Roke Manor Research, Romsey, UK
Peter Hulbert, CEng, MIEE, received his BSc in Electronic Engineering in

1974 and joined Roke Manor Research (at that time part of the Plessey Company) in 1975. Currently a Consultant within the Radio Communications division, he has contributed over a very wide technical base to numerous research and development programmes. Specifically, he was responsible for the cordless telephone research at Roke Manor during the period 1982 to 1988. He has published several technical papers and was Honorary Editor of the IEE Proceedings F, "Communications, Radar and Signal Processing", between 1984 and 1987. He is also the holder of several patents in the radio communications field.

Dr. Heinz Ochsner
Ascom Autophon, Solothurn, Switzerland
Heinz Ochsner received his Dr Sc Techn (Doctor of Technical Science) degree from the Swiss Federal Institute of Technology in 1987. His thesis covered aspects of the use of spread spectrum techniques in mobile radio. Since 1987 he has been with Ascom Autophon AG in Solothurn where he was responsible for system studies for mobile radio and cordless telecommunication systems. In this capacity he was the Swiss representative in the CEPT/GSM Permanent Nucleus during 1987 and 1988. Since 1989 he has also been Chairman of the ETSI RES 3R Working Group which is responsible for defining the radio interface of the Digital European Cordless Telecommunications system (DECT). He is currently R and D manager of Assom's Cordless Terminals and Systems product division.

Frank Owen
Philips Research Laboratories, Redhill, UK
Frank Owen, AMIEE, received his BSc (Eng) in 1986 from Queen Mary College, University of London. After a period of involvement in cordless local area network design with Philips, Frank has, since 1988, headed the cordless telephony programme within Philips Research, principally targeted towards the Digital European Cordless Telecommunications (DECT) system. He was also responsible in the autumn of 1988 for organising the technical input for the successful Telepoint licence application of the Barclays, Philips, Shell consortium, BYPS. A member of the ESPA cordless telephony committee and of the ETSI RES 3R Working Group, he is also the Philips representative on the ETSI RES 3 Technical Subcommittee.

Norbert Soulié
Matra Communication, France and Spain
Norbert Soulié graduated from the ESCP business school. After four years with Alcatel, he joined the Matra group working on automation products. He was Product Manager at the Radio Division for cordless products and Chairman of the ECTEL cordless expert group (TCS) prior to his recent nomination as Deputy Manager of Matra de Communicaçiõnes (Spain).

Richard A. J. Steedman
Roke Manor Research, Romsey, UK
Richard Steedman received a BSc (Hons) degree in Computer Science and Electronics from Edinburgh University in 1985. After graduating, he joined the VLSI design group at Roke Manor and has since designed a number of semi-custom ICs for both military and civil applications, as well as carrying out associated studies and feasibility demonstrations. Richard has contributed to the development of a CAI compatible CT2 product and, as part of that activity, sat on the Technical Working Group which produced the CT2 CAI standard, MPT 1375.

Peter Striebel
Deutsche Bundespost TELEKOM, Bonn, Germany
Peter Striebel studied Electronics and Telecommunications at the Technical University of Munich, receiving the degree Diplom-Ingenieur in 1970. He has worked for the Deutsche Bundespost since 1971 with the Regional Directorate in Munich, the Telecommunications Engineering Centre in Darmstadt, the Telecommunications Office in Frankfurt and the Ministry of Posts and Telecommunications in Bonn. Since January 1990 he has been based at Headquarters, Deutsche Bundespost TELEKOM. He has held responsibility, since 1988, for mobile communications, specialised to Telepoint (including cordless telephones) and public trunked networks.

Bob Swain
British Telecom Research Laboratories, Martlesham, UK
Bob Swain, CEng, MIEE, is Head of the Personal Radio Systems Section of British Telecom's Martlesham Research Station, with responsibility for analogue and digital cordless communications systems research and development since 1980. This work involved extensive propagation and system studies and contributed significantly to the digital CT2 Common Air Interface standard.

Internationally, Bob Swain has close involvement with the personal mobile communications work of the European Telecommunications Standards Institute (ETSI), the Conference of European Posts and Telecommunications (CEPT) and the European Conference of Telecommunication Manufacturers' Associations (ECTEL). Currently he is Chairman of the ETSI RES 3S, Services Definition and Authentication, Working Group for the Digital European Cordless Telecommunications standard (DECT).

Julian R. Trinder
Roke Manor Research, Romsey, UK
Julian Trinder, MA, CEng, MIEE, MIOA, received an honours degree in Physics from Oxford in 1971. This was followed by a six year period of voice communications research with Plessey. He then worked for the UK Medical Research Council Institute of Hearing Research in the field of speech signal processing, followed by a change to radio communications research with Multitone Electronics. During this latter period Julian worked

with the ESPA cordless telephone Working Groups, towards TDMA digital cordless telephony. He also developed a CDMA cordless telephone demonstrator as part of a joint venture with Mitel. Since joining Roke Manor as a consultant in 1987 Julian has been involved in the CT2 CAI Working Groups dealing with radio and speech aspects as well as related theoretical and hardware studies. Julian is the author of numerous papers and holds several patents, including ones relating to cordless telephony.

Subject Index